Frederick Marchmont, William Thomas Lowndes

A Concise Handbook of Ancient and Modern Literature

Frederick Marchmont, William Thomas Lowndes

A Concise Handbook of Ancient and Modern Literature

ISBN/EAN: 9783337295998

Printed in Europe, USA, Canada, Australia, Japan

Cover: Foto ©Thomas Meinert / pixelio.de

More available books at **www.hansebooks.com**

Handbook of
Anonymous and Pseudonymous
Literature.

Faithfully Yrs
Fredk Marchmont

A

CONCISE HANDBOOK

OF

Ancient and Modern Literature,

ISSUED EITHER
ANONYMOUSLY, UNDER PSEUDONYMS, OR INITIALS

COMPILED BY
FREDERICK MARCHMONT.

SIX SHILLINGS NETT.

London:
(FOR THE AUTHOR),
300, SOUTH LAMBETH ROAD, S.W.
1896.

Preface.

THIS little work is offered to the Trade, Librarians, and the Public for use as a supplementary volume to LOWNDES'S "*Bibliographer's Manual.*" Having had fifteen years' LONDON experience as a *Professional Cataloguer*, to such firms as Messrs. J. & M. L. TREGASKIS, *of the "Caxton Head"* ; Mr. E. MENKEN ; Messrs. A. I. MYERS & CO.; Mr. ALFRED COOPER; Messrs. J. BAMBER & CO., etc., I have, during that time, had opportunities of handling some of the best stocks on the London Market, and have, naturally, met with many curious anonymous and pseudonymous works needing elucidation, to say nothing of hundreds of interesting items to which the author's name is appended, but of which no notice can be found either in Lowndes or Allibone. My original intention, when I began this work some twelve years ago, was to form a *fresh* Manual for Bibliographers, brought up to date, most of the matter given in Lowndes having long been obsolete, whilst, of course, no mention of Books published within the last twenty-five years can be found there at all. To that effect, particulars of every work which came under my notice whilst cataloguing, to which no reference could be found in above Bibliographical works, were carefully noted, also *all* anonymous and pseudonymous Literature. Nor must the London Sale Rooms be omitted. Having attended most of the principal London auctions at Messrs. SOTHEBY'S, CHRISTIE'S, and PUTTICK'S for many years, a fair picking has resulted from these quarters. Of the existence of Messrs. Halkett & Laing's work on Anonymous Literature, etc., I am quite aware, and shall always regard it as the *standard* work on the subject, and not likely to be superseded. The amount of labour involved in its compilation I can somewhat gauge from the time spent in the construction of this small volume. But alas! it has one inevitable fault, if one may be allowed to use such a word in connection with so splendid a work—its *price* precludes many persons from adding it to their collections; particularly the Bookseller, who, as a business man, cannot afford to let so much capital lie idle for " Works of Reference." That much, if not all, of the matter contained in this small book may be found in the four thick volumes of the above is highly probable, but I cannot express an opinion on the subject, not having had the good fortune to be able to afford myself a copy, though it is a work I should dearly like to possess, and my advice to all who can afford it is *get it* by all means. In compiling this volume I have had to rely *mainly* on works which have come under my own observation, either as a Cataloguer or in the Sale Room. There is an admirable list in the older edition of Clegg's " Directory of Booksellers," and I have been able to reduce the *bulk* of the present work a great deal by excluding *much* matter which, though it has actually passed through my hands, may readily be found by referring to that useful little volume which is, doubtless, in the possession of *most* Booksellers to-day. My chief aim has been, not *competition* with anything at present on the market (indeed as far as Halkett and Laing's work is concerned, in my opinion this would not be possible), but rather to supply, as far as in my power, information not readily to be found in Lowndes, Allibone, or Brunet; and in attempting the same, to study accuracy in detail. To *ensure* this I have spared neither time nor trouble. As may be supposed some errors have, doubtless, crept in, and with regard to these I shall be glad to receive notices and corrections from the reader, with a view to possible amendment in any future edition. The compilation of the work has been to me more of a pleasure than labour, and was not *primarily* executed as a means of making money. Should the little volume meet any present trade requirements, I shall consider myself *more* than repaid for my labour; and in putting it on the Market I do so with a hope that Booksellers, Librarians, and even Private Collectors, into whose hands the work may come, will find in its pages *some* information with which they were previously unacquainted.

PREFACE.

The arrangement adopted has been alphabetical, under author's real name (the usual brackets used being excluded), with references in the Text to Pseudonymns and Initials, besides full and complete Index of Titles to anonymous works noticed. Immediate reference to any desired book is thus rendered most simple. I may mention, with regard to the PRIVATELY PRINTED items noticed, that whilst the majority are anonymous, still a few are *not*. However, I have allowed them to remain, the number being very small. Respecting the prices affixed, they are only approximate, and in most instances where no price is mentioned the value is under 5s., though this is not *always* the case.

Should this small volume meet with sufficient encouragement, and my business engagements permit, I may be tempted to issue *another* volume containing similar accounts of works which, though not anonymous or pseudonymous, cannot be found either in Lowndes, Brunet, or Allibone.

FREDERICK MARCHMONT.

South Lambeth, S.W.
   1896.

Handbook of Anonymous & Pseudonymous Literature

A.—*See* Arnold (Matthew).

A. (Major)—*See* Coles (B. Coles).

Acheta Domestica.—*See* Bugden (Miss L. M.).

Adams (W. D.) The Eastern Archipelago, the Scenery, People, etc., map and 60 illustrations, thk. sm. 8vo, 1880.

Addison (J.) Remarks on several parts of Italy, &c., in 1701-3, 8vo, 1705. First edition, 7s. 6d.

Adolphus (J. L.) Letters to Richard Heber on the Series of Novels beginning with "Waverley," and an attempt to ascertain their author, post 8vo, 1822. The Waverley Novels were either Anonymous or Pseudonymous, and their authorship excited much controversy, many celebrated Writers (including Byron) having been suspected. The *real* Author at the time denied their paternity.

A. F. F.—*See* Arbuthnot (F. F.).

A. H.—*See* Anderson (H.).

Aikens (J.) Manual of Chemistry, its Operations, Products, etc., 12mo, 1786.

Ainslie (Philip) Reminiscences of a Scottish Gentleman, commencing in 1787, by Philo Scotus, cr. 8vo, 1861.

A. K. H. B.—*See* Boyd (A. K. H.).

A. L. O. E (A Lady of England).—*See* Tucker (Miss C. M.).

Albania, a Poem, addressed to the Genius of Scotland, dedicated to Gen. Wade, 24 pp. folio, 1737. Only one copy of this has ever come under my notice, about ten years ago, and the Bookseller, in whose possession it then was, priced it at £5 5s. He was of opinion that it was probably the only copy in existence.

Albere (Ernest) L'Alcoran des Cordeliers ; c'est à dire Recueil de plus notables Bourdes et Blasphemes de ceux qui ont osé comparer Sainct Francois à Jesus Christ, 21 beautiful plates by Bernard Picart, 2 vols., thk. post 8vo, 1734. Rare, 10s.

Allen (Jos.) Memoir of the Life and Services of Admiral Sir W. Hargood, portrait, roy. 8vo, 1841. Privately Printed.

Allen (W.) Mystery of the Temple and City in Ezekiel, 12mo, 1677. This author was Vicar of Bridgewater.

Allen (William) Discourse of Divine Assistance and the method thereof, fcp. 8vo, 1693. Praised by Bishops Williams and Kidder.

Alt (George) The Nuremberg Chronicle, by Hartman Schedel, German Text. nearly 2500 woodcuts by Wolgemut (Master of Albert Durer) and Pleydenwurff, folio, *Nurem. Ant. Koberger*, 1493. Rare and valuable. A good and perfect copy is worth £10 to £12.

Amateur (An).—*See* Egan (Pierce).

Amateur (An).—*See* Winston (C.).

Amateur of Fashion (An).—*See* Roby (J.).

Amherst (Nicholas) Terræ Filius, or Secret History of Oxford University, etc., frontispiece by Hogarth. post 8vo, 1726. Further particulars may be gleaned from the *Gent's Mag*., 1837, p. 373, and the third vol. of Hallam's Constitutional History. Present market value about 10s. 6d.

Amours and Gallantry, History of Noble and Polite Persons at Home and Abroad, with Curious Observations, trans. from the French, 2 vols., 1728. The author of these Scandalous Memoirs *still* remains anonymous. Their style reminds one forcibly of Mrs. Manley's "Atlantis." A good copy is now worth a guinea.

Amyot (Jacques) Longus. Amours de Daphnis et Chloé, with reproductions of the figures of the Regent Phillippe (without Letters), including "Les Petits Pieds," fcp. 8vo, *Londres*, 1779. A rare edition. Sells readily at 21s.

Anandria, ou Confession de Mademoiselle Sapho, avec la clef, 12mo, 1778—1866. Contains 4 plates. The Key gives the names of Mme. De Fleury, The Duchess of Villeroy, The Marchionesses of Villeroy, Senecterre, and De Luchet. About 15s.

Anburey (T.) Travels through the Interior Parts of America, by An Officer, map and plates, 2 vols., 8vo, *London*, 1789.

Anderson (H.) The Court Convert (Poetry), sm. 12mo., *For the Author s.d.*

Anderson (J.) Sketches of Edinburgh Clergy, 6 ports., 8vo, 1832. About 5s.

Anderson (J. L.) Life of Bp. Ken, by a Layman, 8vo, pubd. by Pickering, 1851. There is also another edn. in 2 vols., pubd. by Murray, 1854. Neither is worth more than 5s.

Anderton (John, *a Lancashire Priest*) The Protestant Apologie for the Roman Church, by J. Brereley, fcp. 8vo, 1608. Very rare, £1.

Angler (An).—*See* Davy (Sir H.).

Annual Anthology, Two Series, 2 vols., fcp. 8vo, *Bristol*, 1799—1800. Contains some of the very earliest pieces by Chas. Lamb, and his Friend Charles Lloyd, S. T. Coleridge, etc., etc.

Anser Pen Drag-on.—*See* Ireland (W. H.).

Anthologia Hibernica, plates, 4 vols., 8vo, *Dublin*, 1793-4. Contains the earliest Literary effort of the Celebrated Tom Moore.

Anti-Gallican (The), or Standard of British Loyalty, etc., folding and other caricature plates (Gillray's style), 8vo, 1804. 7s. 6d. An amusing "Buonaparte" item. The plates are sometimes coloured.

Antiquary (Au).—*See* Thomson (Richard).

Antony (Real).—*See* Michel (Fernand).

Apperley (J. C.) Horse and Hound; *with plates and woodcuts*, cr. 8vo, 1842, first edition. Most of the plates are by Henry Alken. Sells at about 10s. 6d.—Nimrod's Memoirs of the Life of John Mytton, Esq., 18 coloured plates by H. Alken and T. J. Rawlins, roy. 8vo, 1837, £6 or more. The second edition, issued the same year, is really the best, contains 6 plates not in the first; a good copy, £10. The third edition, with all the 18 plates, roy. 8vo, 1851, is also rare.—The Chase, The Turf, and The Road, by "Nimrod," first edn., 8vo, *Murray*, 1837, portrait by Maclise, and illusts by H. Alken, about £2 —Sporting, edited by "Nimrod," 38 beautiful plates by Landseer, Gainsborough, Cooper, etc., folio, *Baily*, 1838, first edn., 30s.—The Chase, by "Nimrod," fcap. 8vo, sewed, illustrated, 1852.—Nimrod's Remarks on the Conditions of Hunters, etc., 8vo, *Pitmann*, 1834, 7s. 6d. Another edn., 8vo, 1837.—Nimrod's Hunting Tours, with Letters on Riding to Hounds, 8vo, 1835, first edn., 15s.

Appleyard (E. G.) Principles of Protestantism considered with a View to Unity, post 8vo, 1849. The Greek Church, a Sketch, 1851.

Arbuthnot (F. F.) and **Burton** (R. F.) The Kama Sutra of Vatsyayna; Ananga Ranga, or Hindu Art of Love; and Perfumed Garden of the Sheik Nefzaoui, 3 vols, sm. 8vo. All printed for Private Circulation only by the Kama Shastra Soc., 1883-6. These 3 vols, all highly *erotic*, are worth together £6.

Armstrong (Dr.) The Œconomy of Love, a Poetical Essay, 8vo, 1749, 7s. 6d. Rare.

Arnold (Matthew) The Strayed Reveller, and other Poems by "A," sm. post 8vo, *Fellowes*, 1849. Of great rarity in the original cloth and uncut. Only 100 copies were printed, and it was withdrawn from publication by the author. £5 to £6. Has sold at auction within the last few years for £10. The companion volume, "Empedocles on Etna," same size and publisher, 1852, was suppressed before 50 copies were sold. It is of similar value.

Artemus Ward.—*See* Browne (C. F.).

Ashbee (H. S.) FRAXI. A complete set of his work comprises: Vol. I., Index Librorum, etc., 1877. Vol. II., Centuria Librorum, etc., 1879. Vol. III., Catena Librorum, etc., 1885. All thk. impl. 8vo. The three together are worth £18; and if there is any choice, the first volume is slightly more valuable than the others.

Ashe (T.) The Spirit of "The Book," or Memoirs of Caroline, Princess of Hapsburgh (a Political and Amatory Romance), 3 vols., post 8vo, 1811. Ten or twelve shillings.

Ashmore (J.) Certain Selected Odes of Horace Englished, with Lat. and Eug. Epigrammes, etc., 4to. *R. Moore*, 1621. Griffith prices this at £4 4s. There is also a notice in *Censura Literaria*.

Asserino (L.) Almerinde, sm. 8vo, 1646. Has large woodcut device by Augustin Courbe on title.

Astruc (Jean) Conjectures sur les Mémoires Originaux dont il paroit que Moyse s'est servi pour composer le Livre de la Genèse, 8vo, *Bruxelles*, 1753.

Atkinson (A.) Roll of a Tennis Ball through the World, by a Solitary Traveller, 8vo, *Dublin*, 1812. Contains curious Articles on Chastity, Mrs. Woolstonecraft's Rights of Woman, and Account of the Mennonists.

Avonmore (Viscountess).—*See* Yelverton (Therese).

A. W.—*See* Allen (William).

Aytoun (W. E.) and **Martin** (Sir T.) Bon Gaultier's Book of Ballads, illust. by Alf. Crowquill, 12mo, *Orr & Co.*, 1845. This, the first, issue is very rare, and worth to-day at least 30s.

Aytoun (Prof.) Firmillien, the Student of Badajoz, by T. Percy Jones, *i.e.*, Prof. Aytoun, post 8vo, 1855.

Bacon (J.) Festorum Metropolis: The Metropolitan Feast on the Birth Day of Our Saviour Jesus Christ, annually to be kept Holy, 77 pp., 4to, 1652. Contains an exceedingly curious old Christmas Carol at pp. 23-6. Attributed to J. Bacon, of Sheirborne, Gloucester.

Baddeley (R.) The Boy of Bilson: the pretended expulsion of the Devil out of a young Boy in the County of Stafford, sm. 4to, 1622. Curious and rare.

Badeslade (T.) Hist. of the Ancient and Present State of the Port of King's Lynn, Cambridge, etc., engravings, plans, etc. (some coloured), folio, 1766. About 15s.

Bailey (S., *of Sheffield*) Essays on the Formation, etc., of Opinions, 8vo, 1826. Rationale of Political Sentiments, 8vo, 1826. The latter item is scarce.

Bainbridge (William) Alpine Lyrics, thk. 12mo, 1854.

Baker (David Erskine) The Companion to the Play-House, an Historical Account of all Dramatic Writers of the U. K. alphabetically arranged, 2 vols, sm. post 8vo, 1764, 10s.

Balcarres (Earl of) An Account of the Affairs of Scotland, relating to the Revolution in 1688, 8vo, 1714. Park, in his edition of Walpole's "Royal and Noble Authors," says he never saw a copy.

Baldwin (E.).—*See* Godwin (William).

Balfour (Sir J.) History of the Picts, with Catalogue of their Kings and a Clavis (Key), p. 8vo, 1706. Often attributed to Henry Maule, of Melgum.

Ballantyne (J.) The Gaberlunzie's Wallet, with etchings and woodcuts. The original edition (of which a good clean unbound copy is worth £2 2s) appeared in 13 parts. *Edinb.*, 1842.

Ballantyne (J., *Canon of Ross*) Works of (containing the well known translation of Hector Boece's Hist. and Chronicles of Scotland, etc.), woodcut facsims., 3 vols., 4to, *Edinb.*, 1821-2. Edited by Sir W. Scott. About £4.

Banks (Mrs. G. Linnæus).—*See* Varley (Isabella).

Bankes (John) History of the Life and Reign of William III., Prince of Orange, etc., 12mo, 1714.

Bankes (W.) Observations on the Temporal Conduct and Actions of Our Saviour, sm. 8vo, *Wigan*, 1800. An anonymous private issue. Not published.

Bard (A.).—*See* Crane (John).

Barham (Rev. R. H.) The Ingoldsby Legends, or Mirth and Marvel, by T. Ingoldsby, with etchings by G. Cruikshank, 3 series in three vols., med. 8vo, first editions, *Bentley*, 1840-42-47 respectively. About £6.—The Ingoldsby Lyrics, by Thos. Ingoldsby, edited by his Son, cr. 8vo, 1881, with portrait, first edition.

Barham.—My Cousin Nicholas, with frontis. by J. Leech, cr. 8vo, 1846, first edition, scarce, 7s. 6d.

Barker (M. H.) Jem Bunt, with 23 illusts. by R. Cruikshank, 8vo. N.D. About 12s. if unfoxed, which it seldom is, and slightly more in parts.—Land and Sea Tales by "The Old Sailor," cr. 8vo, 2 illusts by G. Cruikshank. *E. Wilson*, 1836. About 10s., clean in cloth.—Tough Yarns, by "The Old Sailor," of similar value.—The Old Sailor's Jolly-Boat, etchings by R. Cruikshank, 8vo, 1844, first edition, 12s. to 15s.—Nights at Sea, by "The Old Sailor," illustrated by G. Cruikshank. This originally appeared in Bentley's Miscellany.

Barkham (J., *of Bocking* .—Guillim (J.) A Display of Heraldry, etc., folio, 1638-40. Best edition, with additions by R. St. John Clarenceux, the subsequent editions were spoilt by R. Blome and other ignorant editors.

Barrett (E. S.) The Rising Sun, 3 vols., and the Setting Sun, 3 vols., both by Cervantes Hogg. These facetious works, issued early this Century, should have folding satirical frontispieces, in colours (Rowlandson's style), to each volume. Rarely found perfect market value when so, 10s. each set.—The Tarantula, or Dance of Fools, a Satirical Work, by Cervantes Hogg, 2 extraordinary folding frontispieces, 2 vols., post 8vo, 1809. Rare, 10s.

Barrister (A.) —*See* Clark (Chas.).

Barrow (Isaac) Discourse against Transubstantiation, 1684. Discourse against Purgatory, 1685. Both 4to size.

Basire (Dr. Isaac) History of the English and Scottish Presbytery; wherein is discovered their Designs and Practices for Subversion of Government in Church and State, frontispiece, 12mo, *Villa Franca*, 1659. Contains the XXXIX. Articles in **black letter**, etc., Declaration of K Charles in Latin, English, and French, prepared by J. Howel.—Another edn., 1660, both should have frontispieces. There is also a French translation, 1660.

Baxter (Andrew) Enquiry into the Nature of the Human Soul, 2 vols., 8vo, 1737.—Matho, or the Cosmotheria Puerilis, 2 vols., 12mo, 1765. There is an earlier edn. than this, which I have not seen, it is however of no importance.

Baxter (Nathaniel) Sir Philip Sidney's Ourania, *i.e.*, Endimion's Song and Tragedie, containing all Philosophie, by N. B., 4to, *E. Alde, for E. White*, 1606. First edition, and very rare. Four or Five Pounds. Has also been attributed to Nicholas Breton.

Bayley (F. W. N.) Four Years' Residence in the West Indies, with Narrative of Hurricanes and Earthquakes, plates, thk. 8vo, 1833. Pub. at 24s.

Bayly (Lewis, *Bp. of Bangor*) The Practice of Pietie, 24mo (*Delf*), N.D., *circa* 1636.

Beach (J., *of Wrexham*) Eugenio: or Virtuous and Happy Life, a Poem inscribed to Pope (with woodcut view of his grotto), 4to, 1737.

Beauchamp (De) Les Amours d'Ismene et d'Ismenias, vignette, coloured title, and 4 coloured plates. 4to, *Paris*, 1797. Large Paper. No small paper copy has come under my notice. Cohen does not know the work at all.

Beaujeu. Memories du Marquis de B***, temps de Charles IV., Duc de Lorraine, thk. 12mo, *a la sphère, s. l. et a, sed. Cologne?* 16—.

Beaumont (Sir Harry).—*See* Spence (Joseph).

Beaumont (John) Present State of the Universe, an Account of the Rise, Births, Names, Matches, etc., of the Chief Princes, with their Arms, etc., 16 portraits, and 70 coloured engravings, 12mo, 1704. Rare, 10s.

Beau Nash.—*See* Goldsmith (O.).

Becket (Andrew) Lucianus Redivivus: or Dialogues on Men, Manners, and Opinions, 8vo, 1811.

Beckford (W.) Vathek, an Arabian Tale, 8vo, 1786. First edn., and very rare. Exists in 2 states, Large and Small Paper. Ordinary copies worth about 35s., and Large Paper £3 10s.—Vathek, ed. by (Sir) R. Garnett, LL.D., Notes by S. Henley, etchings by Herbert Nye, 8vo, 1893. Only 450 copies for England, 1893. The most beautiful edn. extant.—Memoirs of W. Beckford (by Cyrus Redding), portrait, 2 vols., cr. 8vo, 1859. He also pubd. Biographical Memoirs of Extraordinary Painters, fcp. 8vo, 1834, which is of nominal value.

Beddoes (Thos., *M.D.*, *of Clifton*) Alexander's Expedition down the Hydaspes and the Indus to the Indian Ocean, a Poem, with copious notes, curious woodcuts, 4to, *Madeley, Privately Printed*, 1792. Only a few copies done, and the work was NOT PUBLISHED. It was printed at the expense of W. Reynolds, Esq., and the types were set by *a woman*, whilst the engravings were done by the CLERK OF THE PARISH. For full accounts *see* Bibliotheca Parriana, and Stock's Memoirs of Thos. Beddoes, 1811, p. 68. Worth three guineas.

Bede (Cuthbert).—*See* "Bradley."

Bedford (H.) Hereditary Right of the Crown of England Asserted, History of the Succession since the Conquest cleared, etc., by a Gentleman, folio, 1713, 7s. 6d. H. Bedford, a Clergyman, the assumed Author of this book, was sentenced to a term of imprisonment and a heavy fine for writing the same.

Bee (The).—*See* Budgell (Eustace).

Belcher (W.) Intellectual Electricity, or Novum Organum of Vision, &c., by A Rational Mystic, med. 8vo, N.D., *circa* 1800. 5s. or 6s.

Bell (Acton).—*See* Brontë (Anne).

Bell (Andrew) Men and Things in America, being the Experience of a Year's Residence in the U.S.A., fcp. 8vo, 1838.

Bell (Currer).—*See* Brontë (Charlotte).

Bell (Ellis).—*See* Brontë (Emily J.).

Bell (Thos.) The Survey of Popery, printed by Valentine Sims, 4to, 1596. 𝔅lack 𝔏etter throughout, and very rare.

Bellegarde (J. B. M. de) Reflexions upon Ridicule, 8vo, 1727.

Bellenden.—*See* Ballantyne (J.).

Bennet (Mrs. A. M.) Anna, or Memoirs of a Welsh Heiress, 4 vols., post 8vo, 1786. Rather scarce. Catalogues at 7s. 6d.

Bentley (S.) Excerpta Historica, Illustrations of English History, illustrated, thk. roy. 8vo, 1833, First edn., list of subscribers, 7s. 6d.

Beresford (J.) Bibliosophia, or Book Wisdom, 1810. This gent. also wrote and published, anonymously, "Miseries of Human Life," 2 vols, 12mo, 1826, and "More Miseries."

Berkeley (Bp.) Adventures of Sig. Gaudentio di Lucca, being his Examination before the Fathers of the Inquisition, Bologne, etc., post 8vo, 1774. This curious work is generally attributed to above gentleman, but the authorship is doubtful.

Berridge (Rev. J.) Justification by Faith Alone, 12mo, 1762.

Berthold (E. Von Chiemsee) Tewtsch Rational über das Ambt Leiliger Mess, folio, *München*, 1535, 10s.

Bertola (Le Comte S. de Giorgi) De l'Origine Morale et Religieuse de la Maçonnerie, de sa Mission et de l'Epoque Positive de son Institution Materielle, thin 8vo, *London*, 1841. Not published, and rare, 7s. 6d.

Best (Mr., *of Magdalen Coll., Oxford*) Personal and Literary Memorials, thk. 8vo, 1829. Contains interesting Articles on French Jests. Lincoln Cries, Napoleon, and Nelson. He also wrote "Four Years in France," etc.

Bewick.—The New Robinson Crusoe, with 32 full-page woodcuts (by Bewick), 2 vols., sm. 8vo, 1789. This scarce and little known specimen of Bewick's skill is worth close on 21s.

Bible (The Holy), containing Old and New Testaments, printed in Black Letter, 4to, *Norton and Bill*, 1625. Overlooked by Cotton and Lowndes, who state that no edition appeared in above year.

Bibliotheca Anglo-Poetica.—*See* Griffith (A. F.).

Bird (W. Wilberforce) State of the C. of Good Hope in 1822. Ed. by H. D. Colebrooke, maps, 8vo, 1823. 5s

"B. K."—*See* Keach (Benjamin).

Black (J., *LL.D.*) The Falls of Clyde, a Scottish Dramatic Pastoral, front. and vignette, 8vo, 1806.

Black (John) Palæoromaica, or Historical and Philological Disquisitions, with Supplement and Rejoinder, 8vo, 1823-4. This paradoxical publication created a good deal of controversy. See Horne's Intro. to the Scriptures.

Black (W.) Mr. Pisistratus Brown, M.P., in the Highlands, post 8vo, 1871.

Blackmantle (Bernard).—*See* Westmacott (C.).

Blacksmith (A.).—*See* Kames (Lord).

Blackwell (T.) Enquiry into the Life and Writings of Homer, engravings by Vander-Gucht, etc., 8vo, 1736.

Bliss (Dr.) Oxoniana, Biographical Anecdotes, etc. (ed. by Dr. Bliss), 3 vols., fcp. 8vo, 1810. Scarce, 7s. 6d.

Bloomfield (Bp.).—*See* Cambridge.

Blount (Thos.).—Estienne (H.) Art of Making Devises, transl. into English by T. B., plates, 8vo, 1650. Rare.

Blumstead (G.) Specimen of a Bibliography of Literature illustrative of the Mug, Glass, Bottle, Loving Cup, and Social Pipe, by me G B , cr. 8vo, *Diss.*, 1885. 5s. Only 125 copies issued for Private Distribution.

Bobbin (Tim).—*See* Collier (John).

Bodenham (J.) Politeuphuia, or Wits Common-Wealth, newly corrected and augmented, sm. 8vo, 1669.

Bolingbroke (Lord) Letters on the Spirit of Patriotism; Idea of a Patriot King; and State of Parties at the Accession of George I. (1714), fcp. 8vo, 1750.

Bolton (Ed.) The Elements of Armories, 8vo, 1610.

Bolton (Robt) The Deity's Delay in Punishing the Guilty considered, 1751; On the Employment of Time, 1754; Answer to Where are your Arguments against Lewdness, 1755.

Bon Gaultier.—*See* Aytoun (W. E.) and Martin (Sir T.).

Boos·y (T) Piscatorial Reminiscences, with Bibliography, 12mo, 1835. One of Pickering's charming publications, now scarce and worth 7s. 6d.

Booth (J.) The Battle of Waterloo, by a near Observer, 8vo, 1816. Should have Panoramic Sketch of the Battlefield, other plans, facsim., etc., 7s. 6d

Botfield (B.) A Tour Through the Highlands of Scotland during the Summer of 1829, map, vignette, and frontispiece, post 8vo, *Privately Printed*, 1830.

Boulanger (M. *Ingenieur des Ponts et Chaussés*) Recherches sur l'Origine du Despotisme Oriental, ouvrage posthume de M.B.I D P.E.C., sm. post 8vo, 1763. There exists an English Translation, by John Wilkes, printed at his Private Press at Westminster, bearing imprint "*Amsterdam*," 1764, which is very rare. The work is intended for an Introduction and Key to Montesquieu's Spirit of Laws, and the French ed , though dated from Paris, was probably issued in London.

Boullencourt (Le Jeune de) Descriptions générale de l'Hostel Royal des Invalides, établi par Louis Le Grand daus la Plaise de Grenelle près Paris, plans, profils, etc., folio, *Paris*, 1683. 10s.

Bowles (Caroline) The Cat's Tail, by the Baroness de Katzleben, 3 etchings by Geo. Cruikshank, 12mo, *Blackwood*, 1831. 15s. to 21s.

Boyd (Rev. A. K. H.) Recreations, Graver Thoughts, Autumn Holidays, etc., of a Country Parson. All too well known to need more than mention.

Boyle (Hon. Mrs.) The May Queen, illustrated by E. V. B., 8vo, 1861. Another edition, also illustrated, 1868.—A London Sparrow at the Colinderies, 1886.

Brabazon (Lord) Prosperity or Pauperism ? Physical, Industrial, and Technical Training, by the E. of Meath, 8vo, 1888. Pub. 5s.

Brabourne (Lord), *i.e.* Knatchbull Hugessen (E. H.) River Legends, Father Thames and Father Rhine, illust. by J. Doré, first edition, cr. 8vo, 1875. Other Stories, illust. by Ernest Griset, first edition, cr. 8vo, 1880. The Mountain Sprites Kingdom, illustrated by the same artist, cr. 8vo, 1881. About 5s. each.—Queer Folk, Seven Stories, by E. H. Knatchbull-Hugessen, illust. by S. E. Waller, post 8vo, 1874.—Uncle Joe's Stories, by Hon. E. H. Knatchbull-Hugessen, illustrated by Ernest Griset, first edn., cr. 8vo, 1869.

B

Braddon (Miss M. E.).—*See* Maxwell (Mrs. John).

Bradlaugh (C.) Half-Hours with the Free-Thinkers, edited by "Iconoclast," cr. 8vo, 1858. Now scarce.

Bradley (Rev. E., *better known as Cuthbert Bede*).—His Works consist of: Verdant Green, this should be in three parts, viz., His Adventures, Further Adventures, and Mr Verdant Green Married and Done For; the first edns. were dated 1853-4-7, all post 8vo size. When found together, which they rarely are, they easily realize a guinea. Love's Provocations, extracts from the Diary of Miss Polly C——, engravings, cr. 8vo, the first edn., pub. 1855. Is worth 5s. Nearer and Dearer, illustrated by the Author, 1857. Perhaps the cleverest of his works. Rare, and sells for 15s. or more. Glencreggan, with three maps, eight chromos and cuts, first edn., 2 vols., 1861. About 7s. 6d. Photographic Pleasures, post 8vo, picture bds. Of nominal value. Motley, Prose and Verse, illust. by Author, first edn., cr. 8vo, 1855. Value 5s. Thirty-four Original Etchings, principally of Oxford Life, N.D., *ca.* 1850. Valuable, about £2.—Tales of College Life, 8vo, 1856. Of nominal value.—Happy Hours at Wynford Grange, first edn., 12mo, 1859, with coloured plates by the Author, 7s. 6d. Little Mr. Bouncer and his Friend Verdant Green, illust. by the Author, post 8vo, *Blackwood*, s.d., 7s 6d.— The Curate of Cranston, with other Prose and Verse, by Cuthbert Bede, cr. 8vo, 1862. Very scarce, 12s. 6d.—The White Wife, and other Stories, Supernatural, Romantic, and Legendary, illustrated by the Author, cr. 8vo, 1865, first edition, 7s. 6d.—Fotheringay and Mary Queen of Scots, illustrated, cr. 8vo, 1886.

Bradley (B.) Sunday School Memorials (Bennet St., Manchester), 8vo, *Manchester*, 1831.

Bradshaw.—Staffordshire General and Commercial Directory for 1818, sm. 8vo, *Manchester, J. Leigh*, 1818. Very rare compiled by the originator of the famous "Bradshaw's Railway Guide."

Braithwaite (R.) Drunken Barnaby's Four Journeys to the North of England, in Latin and English, illustrated by J. W. Harding, and advt. relating to the supposed author (Barnaby Harrington), 8vo, 1805, 12s. This edition contains Bessie Bell, in English and Latin verse on parallel pages. Barnabee's Journal, with Author's Life, Bibliography, etc., ed. from the first edition by J. Haslewood (who discovered the authorship), 2 vols., 12mo, 1825. Only 125 copies issued, 30s.

Bramhall.—*See* Bromwell (J.).

Brandon (Isaac) Fragments: in the Manner of Sterne, plates, fcp. 8vo, 1797. The plates are choice. 7s. 6d.

Brassey (Lady) A Cruise in the "Eothen," 1872, illustrated with photos., sq. 8vo, 1873. Privately printed, and rare, selling to-day for 30s. readily.

Brendley (C.) Stable Talk and Table Talk, or Spectacles for Young Sportsmen, 1845. Bipeds and Quadrupeds, 12mo, 1853. The World, How to Square It, 12mo, 1854. The Sportsman's Friend in a Frost, 8vo, 1857. The last item is the scarcest. The Stud, for Practical Purposes, etc., two steel engravings, 1849.

Brereley (John).—*See* Anderton (J.).

Brett (Thos., *LL.D.*) Letter showing Why our English Bibles Differ so much from the Septuagint, though both are transl. from the Hebrew, 8vo, 1743. Second edition, 8vo, 1760.

Brewer (Thomas) Life and Death of the Merry Devil of Edmonton, with pleasant pranks of Smug the Smith, etc., etc., by T. B., 8vo, 1819. A coarse item of Shakespeariana The original of 1631 I have not seen.

B. R. F.—*See* Arbuthnot and Burton.

Bridel (M.) Poésies Helvetiennes, par M. B****, front. by Brandoin, and vignettes, 8vo, *Lausanne*, 1782.

Brinsden and **Collier**.—Political Merriment, or Truths told to some Tune, by a Lover of his Country, fcp. 8vo, 1714. Present selling price about 10s. 6d. This is a translation from the French of above Gents, called the State Oculist and Crooked Attorney.

Brinsley (John) The First Booke of Tullies Offices, transl. grammatically, 8vo, 1631.

Britton's Historical and Antiquarian Account of the Isle of Man, with Historical Particulars, 8vo, 1804.

Bromwell (J., *Archbp. of Derry*) Fair Warning to take heed of Scottish Discipline, etc., 4to, 1649. Curious and rare. Issued the Year of Execution of Charles I. Worth 10s.

Brontë (Anne) is best known by her "Agnes Grey," written under the Pseudonym of Acton Bell.

Brontë (Charlotte) wrote Jane Eyre (under Pseudonym Currer Bell, her most celebrated work). The Professor, the first edn. of which is in 2 vols., post 8vo, 1857. Worth 15s.

Brontë (Emily J.).—This Lady's most celebrated work is "Wuthering Heights," which is most fascinating, albeit somewhat weird in conception. Her Pseudonym was "Ellis Bell."

Brontë (Sisters) Poems by Currer, Ellis, and Acton Bell, 12mo, 1846. Very scarce, 21s.

Brooke (Frances, *née Moore*) Hist. of Lady Julia Mandeville, 2 vols., p. 8vo, 1782.

Brooke (Henry, *of Rantavan*) Historical Memoirs of the Irish Rebellion in 1641, with Appendix of Authentic Papers, etc., 8vo. 1758. Rare, 21s.

Brosses (President, *Count de Tourney*) Du Culte des Dieux Fétiches, on Parallele de l'Ancienne Religion de l'Egypte avec la Religion actuelle de Negritie, p. 8vo, *s. l. (Dijon ?)*, 1760.

Brother of the Birch (A).—*See* Cobbett (W.).

Brougham (Lord) Albert Lunel, or the Chateau of Languedoc, first edn., 3 vols., med. 8vo, 1844. This item (rigidly suppressed) has been catalogued as high as £3 3s., and sold by auction for even more. Its real value is 5s. at the outside.

Brown (Baldwin).—*See* Poems by Three Friends.

Brown (J., D.D., *Vicar of Newcastle*) Letter to the Rev. Dr. Lowth, occasioned by his Letter to the Author of "The Divine Legation of Moses" (Warburton), 8vo, *Newcastle*, 1766.

Brown (Dr. J.) Rab and his Friends, plates, sm. 4to, 1864. Scarce. Marjorie Fleming, a Sketch, by Author of "Rab and his Friends," 4to, *Douglas*, 1884, 7s. 6d. This edn. contains six exquisite sketches and portrait of Marjorie in facsimile of a water-colour drawing.

Brown (Pisistratus).—*See* Black (W.).

Brown (Richard) Memorabilia Curliana Mabenensia, frontispiece, 8vo, *Dumfries*, 1830.

Brown (T. E.) Fo'c'sle Yarns, including Betsy Lee, and other Poems, cr. 8vo, 1881.

Browne (C. F.) Artemus Ward's Lecture, as delivered at the Egyptian Hall, portrait and tinted plates, sq. cr. 8vo, *Hotten*, 1869, first edn. Also Artemus Ward, his Book; Artemus Ward among the Mormons, first English edn., 1865; Artemus Ward in London, comprising Letters to "Punch" and other Humourous Papers, sm. 8vo, *Hotten* (1870); etc.

Browne (Felicia Dorothea Browne, *afterwards Mrs. Hemans*) Poems, with woodcuts, head and tailpieces, 4to, *Liverpool*, 1808, 7s. 6d. Her earliest production, written when she was 12 years of age.

Browne (Jas.) A Critical Examination of Dr. MacCulloch's Work on the Highlands, cr. 8vo, *Edinb.*, 1825.—The Life of the Ettrick Shepherd anatomized in a series of Strictures on the Autobiography of J. Hogg, 8vo, 1832.

Browne (Matthew).—*See* Rands (W. B.).

Browne (Thomas) The Parson's Horn Book, with a large number of etchings, 8vo, 1831. These etchings very much resemble Rowlandson in style.

Browne (Sir Thos.)—*See* Crossley (J.).

Browning (E. B.) The Runaway Slave at Pilgrim's Point, first edn., 8vo, wrappers. *Moxon* (preface dated *Florence*), 1849. This passionate poem, detailing the loves of two slaves, the ruin of the female slave by her master, her anguish and murder of her white babe, and subsequent death, represents the great poetess at her best. It is so rare that even her husband was not aware of its existence till a year or so before his death. When to be had it generally catalogues at six or seven guineas.

Browning (Robt.) Shelley Letters, with Intro. (44 pp.) by R. Browning, cr. 8vo, *Moxon*, 1852. Suppressed, and most copies destroyed, on account of the discovery that nearly all the letters were forgeries. A good copy would be cheap for two guineas — The Keepsake for 1856, contains a Poem by Robt. Browning, "Ben Karshook's Wisdom." 1856.

Bruce (Michael) Ode to the Cuckoo, *Edinb.*, 1770, with Remarks on its Authorship, by David Laing, cr. 8vo, 1873. Scarce. Also attributed to James Logan, Minister of Leith.

Brydall (J., *of Queen's College, Oxford*) Catalogue of the Tracts of Laws, etc., 1711. This item was privately printed, and is excessively rare, not being mentioned by Dr. Bliss in his excellent edn. of Wood's Athenæ Oxon. Market value to-day, half a sovereign or more.

Brydges (Sir Egerton) Libellus Gebensis, Poemata Selecta Latina Mediæ et Infimæ Ætatis, 12mo, *Gebenis*, 1822. Only 37 copies printed (anonymously). 10s.

Brydges (Sir Egerton).—*See* Wither (Geo.).

Brydges (Sir S. Egerton) Memoirs of Peers of England during the Reign of James I., Vol. 1, 4 plates (2 of them portraits), 4to, 1802. 10s. The second volume was not issued.

Brydges (Thos.) A Burlesque Translation of Homer, numerous etchings (curious), 2 vols., 8vo, 1797, best edition, about 15s. Humourous, albeit very coarse, both text and plates. The latter remind one of Gillray.

"**B. T.**"—*See* Brewer (Thomas).

Buchanan (G.) Epithalamium on the Marriage of Francis and Mary, transl. from the Original (by W. Turnbull), 8vo, 1845. Scarce. Ten or twelve shillings.

Buckland (A. C.) Letters on Importance, Duty, and Advantages of Early Rising, frontispiece, 12mo, 1820.

Buckler (Dr. Ben.) Vindication of the Mallard of All Souls' Coll. against the Suggestions of Rev. Mr. Pointer, 2 plates, 8vo, *Oxford*, 1751.

Buckler (Dr.) Stemmata Chicheleana, a Genealogical Account of the Families derived from Thos. Chichele, of Higham Ferrers, 2 vols., 4to, *Oxford*, 1765-75. Rare, 21s. or more.

Buckley (T. A.) Natural History of Tuft Hunters and Toadies, clever illusts., by H. G. Hine, 12mo, wrappers. Uniform with Albert Smith's little "Natural Histories." Diverting Adventures of Mr. S. Greenfinch, first edn., cr. 8vo, pict. wrapps., 1854, illustrated by M'Connell, 5s.

Budgell (Eustace) The Bee, or Universal Weekly Pamphlet. Appeared in parts (in which state it is seldom found now), each having a frontispiece, 1733.

Bugden (Miss L. M.) Episodes of Insect Life, by Acheta Domestica, M.E.S., 108 exquisite coloured illustrations, 3 vols., post 8vo, 1849-51. Scarce, 21s.

Buhl (J. P.).—*See* Hanson (Sir L.).

Buonaparte. Memoirs of an Aristocrat, and Reminiscences of the Emperor Napoleon, by a Midshipman of the "*Bellerophon*," cr. 8vo, 1837. Suppressed and rare, 21s —De C...... J. La Famiglia Bonaparte dal 1183 al 1834, 8vo, *Napoli*, 1840.

Buonarroti (Filippo) Osservazioni Istoriche sopre alcuni Medaglioni Antichi, 38 plates, besides vignettes, thk. 4to, *Rome*, 1698.

Burges (Cornelius) No Sacrilege nor Sinne to Aliene or Purchase the Lands of Bishops or others whose Offices are abolished, by C. B., post 8vo, 1659. Cornelius Burges, the author of this curious work, was a noted pulpit trumpeter in promoting the overthrow of the English Government. See Wood's Athenæ Oxon.

Burgess (James) Lives of Most Eminent Modern Painters who have lived since, or were omitted by M. De Piles, 8vo, 1754. Rare and valuable. 7s. 6d. or more.

Burgess (Bp. Thos., *of Salisbury*) Reasons why a new Translation of the Bible should not be published, etc., 8vo, *Durham*, 1816.

Burke (Edmund) Account of the European Settlements in America, 2 vols., *Dodsley*, 1758. Another edition 1766. Both should have a map. Undoubtedly by E. Burke, though he never acknowledged the authorship.—Thoughts on the Cause of the Present Discontents, 8vo, 1784.—Appeal from the New to the Old Whigs on Discussions in Parliament relating to his "French Revolution," 8vo, 1791.—Thoughts on the Prospect of a Regicide Peace, 8vo, 1796.

Burnaby (C.) The Reformed Wife, a Play, sm. 4to, 1700.

Burnaby (Mrs. F.) High Life and Towers of Silence. (Alpine.) Illustrated, cr. 8vo, 1886. Pubd. at 10s. 6d.

Burnett (G.) Popular Genealogists, or Art of Pedigree Making, cr. 8vo, 1865. Nominal value.

Burney (Fanny).—*See* D'Arblay (Madame).

Burns (R.) The Merry Muses, a choice Collection of Favourite Songs, with Letters, and a Suppressed Poem, *Privately Printed*, 1827. The only copies that have come under my notice have been reprints of above date; which sell at 30s. or more. The volume is of a very erotic nature throughout, and though nominally bearing the name of the great Scottish Poet, it is highly improbable that he had much to do with the authorship.—Poems ascribed to Burns, not contained in any edn of his Works hitherto published, demy 8vo, *Glasgow, Stewart*, 1801.

Burt's (Capt.) Letters from a Gentleman in the N. of Scotland (1726, etc.), Account of the Highlanders, etc., 2 vols, 8vo, 1822. Fifth (and best) edition. Scarce. In addition to Appendix and Notes by Jamieson, contains the History of Donald the Hammerer, communicated by Sir W. Scott.

Burton (Dr. J.) Sacerdos Paroecialis Rusticus, 8vo, *Oxonii*, 1757.

Burton (Sir R. F.) The Kasidah (Couplets) of Haji Abdu al-Yazdi, translated and annotated by his Friend and Pupil, F. B., 4to, 1894. Very rare. Only 100 copies printed. Really composed by Capt. Burton under one of his Eastern *noms-de-plume*. Calling himself the translator was done as a better disguise to the authorship, Francis being his second name, and Baker his mother's family name. It reminds one, more than any other poem, of the Rubáiyat of Omar Khayyam, the Astronomer-Poet of Khorasán, and is of extraordinary power; on Nature and Destiny of Man, Anti-Christian and Pantheistic. Sells at from 25s. to 30s.

Burton (R.) The Anatomy of Melancholy, by Democritus Junior; with Satyricall Preface, folio, *Oxford*, 1638. If with engr. title and portrait, 15s.—Anatomy of Melancholy, 1652. Very rare. The best library edn. is that of 1826, in 2 vols., with facsim. title of the 1652 edn., nicely printed in large type, which can be procured for about 15s.

Bury (Lady Charlotte) Journal of the Heart, first and second series, plates, 2 vols., 8vo, 1830-5.

Buston (G.) The Political Quixote, or Adventures of Don Blackibo Dwarlino (T. Wooler) and his Trusty Squire Seditiono, post 8vo, *Chapple*, 1820.

Bussy-Rabutin, *i.e. Roger de Rabutin, Comte de Bussy*. Amours des Dames Illustres de France sous le Regne de Louis XIV., plates, 2 vols., 12mo, *Cologne, P. Marteau, s.d. (vers* 1737).

Bute (Marquis of) Saint Magnus of the Orkneys, imp. 8vo, 1887.

Butt (G.) A Dialogue between the E. of C——d and Mr. Garrick in the Elysian Shades, 4to, 1785.

" **B.V.,**" *i.e. Bysshe Vanonis*.—*See* Thomson (James).

Byington (Rev. Cyrus) Acts of the Apostles translated into the Choctaw Language, fcap. 8vo, 1839.

Byrne (Mrs. W. P.) Flemish Interiors, frontispiece and vignette title, cr. 8vo, (1854).—Curiosities of the Search Room, a Collection of Serious and Whimsical Wills, by the Author of " Flemish Interiors," thk. 8vo, 1880, 7s. 6d.—De Omnibus Rebus, an Old Man's Discursive Ramblings on the Road of Every-Day Life, by the Author of " Flemish Interiors," 100 illusts., 8vo, 1889. This lady died in 1894.

Byron (Lord) English Bards, etc., first edn., fcap. 8vo, *Cawthorn*, N.D. (1809). Worth now about £2 2s. The *fourth* edn., 1810, is exceedingly common, but there exist a very few copies of a FIFTH edn., which is of the utmost rarity, and worth probably £5. *One* copy, uncut (probably unique) has passed through my hands, and is now, I believe, in the possession of H. Buxton Forman, Esq. I should be glad of a report of any other copy of this fifth edition. It has the words, "Fifth Edition" on title.—The Portfolio, publd. at New York, July, 1814, contains 11 pp. on Byron's "Corsair," and this is a scarce and little known item of "Byroniana."

C. (Marquis de).—*See* Chastelet (Marquis de).

"C. D"—*See* De Morgan.

Calabrella (Baroness de) Evenings at Haddon Hall, with plates by Geo. Cattermole, roy. 8vo, 1857.

Caldecott's Hamlet and As You Like It; a specimen of a new edn. of Shakespeare, thk. roy. 8vo, 1819. Curious and rare, 7s. 6d.

Calprenede (G. de Costes de la) Hymen's Præludia, Love's Masterpiece, trans. by R. Loveday, folio, 1698.

Calver (Edward) Passion and Discretion in Youth and Age Poetry), 4to, 1641. 21s. or more.

Calverley (C. S.) This author is best known by his "Verses and Translations," 1865, and "Fly-Leaves." His most valuable work is perhaps Translations into English and Latin, cr. 8vo, First edn., 1866. 15s.; his Theocritus, First edn., post 8vo, 1869, sells at about 10s.

Cambridge. Musæ Cantabrigiensis; seu Carmina quædam Numismatæ aureo Cantabrigiæ, etc., 1810. Ed. by Bp. Bloomfield and Thos. Rennell.

Camden (W.) Remaines concerning Britaine, sm. 4to, J. Leggat, for S. Waterson, 1714. Good copies are worth 10s. 6d.

Campbell (A.) Lexiphanes, a Dialogue imitated from Lucian, sm. 8vo, 1767.—Another ed., sm 8vo, 1783. Both of trifling value.

Campbell (Duncan).—*See* Defoe (Daniel).

Campbell (Dr. J.) Hist. of Spanish America, and Description of Paraguay, 8vo, 1741. This is the First edn.—Hermippus Redivivus, or the Sage's Triumph over Old Age, etc., 1749.—Memoirs of the Revolution in Bengal (1757), by which Neer Jaffeir was raised to the Government of the Province, with Motives for this Enterprise, and Benefits accrued to the E.I. Co., etc., 8vo, *Lond.*, 1760.

Campbell (J. Francis) Frost and Fire, Natural Engines, Tool Marks, and Chips, with Sketches taken at Home and Abroad, by a Traveller, 2 vols., thk. 8vo, *Edinb.*, 1865. First edn., and scarce. About 12s. 6d.

Campbell (Hon. W. F.) Conversations between a Freshman and Bachelor of Arts, med. 8vo, 1845. A scarce Cambridge item.

Cane (J. V.) The Reclaimed Papist, or Process of a Papist Knight Reformed by a Protestant Lady, with the Assistance of a Presbyterian Minister, 12mo, 1655. In addition to being anonymous, this item is Privately Printed.

Canning (Geo.) The Microcosm, a Periodical Work, by Gregory Griffin, thk. 8vo, *Windsor, C. Knight*, 1797.

Capel (Ed.) Prolusions, or Select Pieces of Ancient Poetry (The Notbrowne Mayde; Edward the Third; Nosce Teipsum, the last by Sir J. Davis), *Tonson*, 1760. Value about 10s. 6d.

Caraccioli (M. de) Le Livre a la Mode, post 8vo, *En Europe chez les Libraires*, 100070060, *i.e.* Paris, 1760. Curious, being *printed throughout in red*; but only realises 3 or 4 shillings.

Carew (R.).—Huarte's (J.) Examination of Men's Wits, Englished by R. C(arew), sm. 4to, 1596. Rare.

Carey (D.) Life in Paris, 21 coloured plates, and 22 woodcuts, by Geo. Cruikshank, First edition, full 8vo, *Fairburn*, 1822. A very tall copy (two plates slightly damaged), 9¾ in., which recently passed through my hands was priced £5 5s., but a really fine copy is worth £7 7s. if on Large Paper.

Carleton (Capt. J. W.) Recreations in Shooting, etc., by "Craven," 9 steel plates after A. Cooper, and 62 cuts by Branston, p. 8vo, 1859. 7s. 6d.

Carlyle (T.) Life of Friedrich Schiller, portrait, 8vo, 1825. Scarce. Present value about 10s.

Carr (Rev. W.) History of the District of Craven, Yorks., 12mo, 1824. First edn. of nominal value. The Second edn. extended to 2 vols., and published 1828, is worth half a sovereign.—The Craven Dialect exemplified in Two Dialogues, p. 8vo, 1825.

Carroll (Lewis).—*See* Dodgson (Rev. C L.).

Carruthers (R.) History of Huntingdon, 8vo, 1824.

Carter (Elizabeth) Poems on Several Occasions, fcp. 8vo, 1789.

Cartwright (T.) Reply to an Answere made against Doctor Whitgift, agaynste the Admonition to the Parliament, 4to, 𝖇𝖑𝖆𝖈𝖐 𝖑𝖊𝖙𝖙𝖊𝖗, 1572. Not *anonymous*, but secretly printed. A good copy would realize 30s.

Casway (R.) Miscellaneous Metaphysical Essay, or an Hypothesis concerning the Formation and Generation of Spiritual and Material Beings; by an Impartial Inquirer after Truth, 8vo, 1748.

Caveat Emptor.—*See* Stephen (Sir G.).

Cavendish.—*See* Jones (Henry).

Cavendish (George) Life and Death of Thomas Woolsey, Cardinal, written by One of his own Servants, portrait, sm. 8vo, 1677. Rare.

"**C. A. W.**"—*See* Wheeler (C. A.).

Caxton (P.).—*See* Lytton (Bulwer).

Cecil.—*See* Tongue (Cornelius).

"**C. H.**"—*See* Constable (Henry).

Chalmers (George) Answer to Edmund Burke's Letter on Affairs of America, with Appendix, 8vo, 1777. Representation of the House of Assembly of the Bahamas to Earl Bathurst, folio, 1817. Printed but not sold. He also pubd. many other small items on America between 1777-1817, all of minor importance.

Chambers (Robt.) Vestiges of the Natural Hist. of Creation; and Sequel to the same, 2 vols., cr. 8vo, 1844-5. Of minor importance.

Chandler (Bishop) Vindication of the Defence of Christianity in Answer to Collins, 2 vols., 8vo, 1728.

Charles (Mrs.) Chronicles of the Schonberg-Cotta Family, illustrated, post 8vo, 1890. Published at 5s.—The Cottage by the Cathedral, and other Parables, by the author of "Schonberg-Cotta Family," cr. 8vo, 1872. Pubd. 6s.

Charles I.—*See* Jane (John) and Milton (J.).

Charleton (Dr. Walter) Natural History of the Passions, 8vo, *In the Savoy*, 1674. Of nominal value.

Chastelet (Marquis de) Traité de la Politique de France, par M. P. H. Marquis de C., *Utrecht, chez P. Elzevier*. La Seconde Partie, *Cologne, chez P. Du Marteau (à la sphère)*, both 12mo, 1670. The author was imprisoned in the Bastile for writing this curious work.

Chatfield (P.).—*See* Smith (Horace).

Chatterton (T.) Poems, supposed to have been written at Bristol, by T. Rowley and others in the XVth Century, with Preface and Glossary, 8vo, 1777. First edition. 7s. 6d.—Poems, supposed to have been written at Bristol in the XVIIth Century, with Appendix proving Chatterton the author, by T. Tyrwhitt, 8vo, 1778.— Another edn. with Commentary by J. Milles, roy. 4to, 1782. Both about 10s. each.—Another edn. (The Best), 2 vols , cr. 8vo, 1842. 7s. 6d.—Another edition, 2 vols., p. 8vo, 1871. 7s. 6d.— His "Ella and other Pieces" interpreted, selections from the Rowley Poems in modern Reading, by J. Glassford, fcp. 8vo, 18—. *Privately Printed*. 5s.

Chelsum (Dr., *Rector of Drosford, Hants.*) History of the Art of Engraving in Mezzotinto from its Origin to the Present Time, including Account of Works of the Earliest Artists, cr. 8vo, *Winchester*, 1786.

Chesney (Sir George) The Battle of Dorking, 1st edn., *Blackwood*, 1871.—The New Ordeal, First edn., post 8vo, 1879. A Pamphlet. now scarce. This author's works have been more in demand since his recent death.

Chester (A.) Schaps-togt van Anthony Chester na Virginia, gedaan in her Jaer, 1620. Beschreeven Door een voornean Reysiger die djese Togt met gedaan heelt, frontispiece, 8vo, *Leyden*, 1707.

Chettle (H.).—*See* Constable.

Chetwood (W. R.) Adventures and Voyages of Capt. R. Boyle, with the Story of Mrs. Villars, with whom he made his Escape from Barbary; also Hist. of an Italian Captive, the Life of Don Pedro Aquilo, etc., fcp. 8vo, 1726. Other edns. 1727-8-35, and 1788. A Fictitious Narrative, published anonymously. Rare, 15s. Many people attribute this work to Daniel Defoe, and these voyages have been translated into French, Italian, Dutch, German, etc.

Chevrier (A.) L'Aciadiade, ou Prouesses Anglaises en Acadie, Canada, etc. (Poetry,, post 8vo, 1758.

Child (D. L.) Political Extracts from a leading Adams Paper, The Massachussetts Journal, 8vo, *s. l. c.*, 1828. The Texan Revolution, with a Letter from Washington, etc., by Protus, 8vo, *Washington*, 1843.

Child (Mrs. D. L.) The First Settlers of New England, etc., by a Lady of Massachussetts, fcp 8vo, 1829.

Child (F. J.) Notice of W. Thaddeus Harris, Esq., 4to, *Boston, U.S.*, 1855.

Child (Sir J.) Britannia Languens: A Discourse of Trade, 12mo, 1680. Very rare.

Childs (O. W.) The Engineer's Report of the Cost of Constructing the Ship Canal of Nicaragua, 8vo, *N. Y.*, 1852.

Chipman (Ward) Remarks upon the Disputed Points of Boundary, under the Fifth Article of the Treaty of Ghent, 8vo, 1839.

Chisholme (David) The Lower Canada Watchman, 24mo, *Kingston*, *s.d.* Rare.

Christian (Chas.) A Brief Treatise on the Police of the City of New York, by a Citizen, 8vo, *N. Y.*, 1812.

Christie (W.) A Speech Delivered at the Grave of the Rev. J. Priestley, LL.D., Feb. 6th, 1804, 8vo, 1804. First edn. of a very scarce Tract.

Christy (David) Cotton is King; or the Culture of Cotton and its Relation to Agriculture, etc., by an American, post 8vo, *N. Y.*, 1856. The last copy of this I catalogued sold for 5s. 6d. The first edn. was pubd. 1855.

Church (Dr. B.) An Address to a Provincial Bashaw (Governor Bashaw), O Shame! where is thy Blush? by a Son of Liberty, 4to, 8 pp., *Boston, U.S.*, 1781. Evidently a reprint of 1769.

Church (E.) The Dangerous Vice (John Adams), a Fragment, etc., by a Gentleman, formerly of Boston, 4to, 1789.

Churchill (John) A Collection of Voyages and Travels, with an immense number of copperplates and maps, etc., 6 vols., folio, *London*, 1704. 97 plates and 11 maps to be complete. Rare. Another Edn , 6 vols., 1732.

Citizen (A.)—*See* Christian (Chas.).

C. J. (De).—*See* Buonaparte.

Clark (Chas.) A few Words on the Subject of Canada, by a Barrister, 8vo, *Longmans*, 1837. Scarce.

Clark (I. G.) Legend of the Chapel of St. Thomas of Acon : a Poem, p. 8vo, 1865.

Clarke (C.) Three Courses and a Dessert, illust. by G. Cruikshank, first edn., 1830, about 25s. 2nd edn., 1830, about 15s; and the edition of 1836, which contains all the illusts., 5s.—The Cigar, by the Author of " Three Courses and a Dessert," illust. by G. Cruikshank, first edn., 12mo, 1835. Rare, 21s There is the companion volume, " The Companion to a Cigar," with 20 cuts by G. C., first edn , 12mo, 1850. Of similar value.

Clarke (H.) The School Candidates : a Prosaic Burlesque, occasioned by the late Election of a Schoolmaster at the Village of Bondinnoir (Stretford), Utopia (Manchester), fcp. 8vo, 1788. Rare, especially if it has the folding plate, usually wanting. Tabulae Linguarum, 8vo, 1793. Of nominal value.

Clarke (Rev. J.) A Letter to Doctor Mather, by One who wishes well to him in common with Mankind, 8vo, 1782.

Clarke (Mary Cowden) Kit Bam's Adventures, 4 full-p. etchings by G. Cruikshank, post 8vo, *Grant*, 1849. First edition, 15s., if a nice copy.

Clavel (Robt.) His Majesties Propriety and Dominion on the British Seas asserted, etc., with coasting map of Gt. Britain and Ireland, by an Experienced Hand, portrait of Chas. II. and map, 8vo, *London*, 1665. Excessively rare.

Cleland (John) Memoirs of Fanny Hill, 8vo, *London*, 1749. Original edition, and exceedingly rare and valuable. There exists, however, a genuine reprint of this edition (issued about 6 years ago), which sells at about two guineas. There are many spurious editions, which are offered at all sorts of prices between 2 and 5 pounds.— Tombo-Chiqui ; or, The American Savage, a Dramatic Entertainment, in 3 Acts, 8vo, *London*, 1758. Excessively rare. 21s. or more.

Cleland.—Specimen of an Etymological Vocabulary to Retrieve the Ancient Celtic, med. 8vo, 1786.

Clemens (S. L., *Mark Twain*) The Celebrated Jumping Frog of Calaveras County, and other Sketches, by Mark Twain, ed. by J. Paul, fcap. 8vo, *N.Y.*, 1867. A rare edn.—The Gilded Age, 3 vols., 1874. First edn. of this popular Novel, written in conjunction with C. Dudley Warner.

Clements (L.) Shooting, Yachting, and Sea Fishing Trips at Home and on the Continent, by Wildfowler, 2 series, cr. 8vo, 1877.

Clifford (Hon. R.) L'Abbé Barruel's Memoirs, illustrating the History of Jacobinism, 4 vols, 8vo, 1797-8. 6s.—Application of Barruel's Memoirs to the Secret Societies of Ireland and Gt. Britain, 8vo, 1798. Very rare, 7s. 6d., or more.

Clive (Mrs. Archer) Poems, by the author of "Paul Ferroll," collected edn., including IX Poems by V., sm. p. 8vo, 1856.

Cluny (Alex.) The American Traveller; or Observations on the Present State, etc., of the British Colonies in America, etc., etc.; in a series of Letters to the Rt. Hon. the E. of *****, by an Old and Experienced Trader, map and plate, 4to, *London*, 1769. These letters were addressed to Pitt, E. of Chatham, and the work is rare and valuable.

Cobbe (F. Power) The Red Flag in John Bull's Eyes, fcp. 8vo, *E. Faithfull*, 1863. Also Rejoinder to Mrs. Stowe's Reply to the Address of the Women of England, fcp. 8vo, *Ib*. Two Tracts of the utmost rarity, practically unknown to the Collector of this Lady's works.

Cobbett (W.) This well-known man has pubd. under the Pseudonym of "Peter Porcupine":—The Bloody Buoy, The American Rush-Light, A Bone to Knaw for the Democrats, The Democratiad and Democratic Judge, Detection of the United Brethren Conspiracy, The Gros Mosqueton Diplomatique, The Guillotina, A Kick for a Bite, Letter to Tom Paine, A Little Plain English, New Year's Gift to the Democrats, The Republican Judge, The Scare-Crow, and many other Pamphlets, including his Monthly Mag.. "Porcupine's Political Censor," 1796, etc. He has also written under pseudonyms of "A Brother of the Birch," "James Quicksilver," etc. All pubd. at the end of last or beginning of this century.

Cobden (R.) England, Ireland, and America, by a Manchester Manufacturer, 8vo, *London*, 1835.—England and America, a Comparison of the Social and Political State of both Nations, 2 vols., med. 8vo, *London*, 1833.

Cobbold (Rev. R.) is best known as the author of "Margaret Catchpole"; his "Geoffrey Gambado, or a Simple Remedy for Hypochondriacism and Melancholy Splenetic Humours, by a Humourist Physician," facetious engravings, sm. 4to, N.D., is very amusing.

Cogan (Thos., *M.D.*) John Buncle, Junior, Gentleman, with vignette, fcp. 8vo, 1776, 5s.

Cockburn (Sir A. J. E.) Charge of the Chief Justice of England to the Grand Jury *re* Regina *v.* Nelson and Brand, ed. by F. Cockburn, 8vo, *London*, 1867.

Cole (F. Sewell) Britain : its Earliest History and Connection with other Nations, med. 8vo, *Chertsey*, 1851.

Cole (Sir H.) Felix Summerley's Pleasure Excursions on Various Railways, 74 engravings, 8vo, 1847. Rare. 7s 6d.—Faery Tales and Ballads, The Sisters, Golden Locks, etc., etc., ed. by F. Summerley, fine coloured plates, cr. 8vo, *Cundall*, 1846.—The Most Delectable History of Reynard the Fox. ed. by F. Summerley, 24 full-page coloured plates, post 8vo, *Cundall*, 1846. First edition.

Colebrooke (Sir G.) Six Letters on Intolerance, including various Religions and Sects, 8vo, 1791. Of nominal value.

Coleridge (S. T.) The Watchman, pubd. by the Author, *Bristol*, 1796. A complete set should comprise 10 numbers, 8vo size. It is rare, and when perfect sells at 21s. and upwards.—The Wild Wreath, p. 8vo, 1804. Contains "The Mad Monk," by S. T. C., not pubd. in any edition of his works. 10s.

Coleridge (S. T.).—*See* Annual Anthology.

Coleridge (H. N.) Six Months in the West Indies in 1825, post 8vo, 1826. First (and only ?) edn.

Coles (B. Coles) Short Whist, its Rise, Progress, and Laws, by Major A., *frontispiece*, fcp. 8vo, 1858.

Collections relative to the Funeral of Mary Queen of Scots, post 8vo, *Edinb.*, 1822. An interesting item. First edition. Only 125 copies were issued. Scarce.

Collegian (A.).—*See* Thomas (W.).

Collier (J.) has pubd. under pseudonym of "Tim Bobbin": View of the Lancashire Dialect, *Manchester*, 1757; another edn., 1770; another, *Leeds*, N.D.; another, *Leeds*, 1787; another, *Warrington*, 1803; another, *Huddersfield*, 1805; another, *Rochdale*, 1819; another, *Preston*, 1823; and another edn. (with Poems), 1845.—Miscellaneous Works, *Manchester*, 1775, portrait and plates; another edn., *Salford*, 1812, portrait and plates; another edn., *London*, 1818, contains Glossary and Life, by Townley, besides curious plates and portrait : another edn., N.D.—Tay Shop Opened, *Manchester* 1763, plates.—Dialect of S. Lancashire, or Tim Bobbin's Tummus and Meary, ed. by Sam. Bamford, first edn., 1850; second edn., 1854.—Tim Bobbin's Lancashire Dialect, with plates by Cruikshank, 8vo, 1833. Best edition, and rare Sells at 21s. The first edition, with portrait and 9 copperplates by Slack, 12mo, *Manchester*, 1793, is worth about ten shillings.—Human Passions

Delineated in above 120 Figures, Droll, Satyrical, and Humourous, designed in the Hogarthian Style, text in verse, folio, (Reprint) 1773, about 7s. 6d. The original is excessively rare.—The Passions, an edn. with port. and cold. plates, 4to, 1810, £2 10s.

Collier (J. Payne) Punch and Judy, illust. by G. Cruikshank, post 8vo, *Prowett*, 1828, first edn., which should have 24 full-page coloured plates (it also exists in plain state) besides woodcuts. Excessively rare coloured. A good copy, £5 at least. The second edition (plates plain), published the same year, 21s.

Collier (Miss) Essay on the Art of Ingeniously Tormenting, post 8vo, 1795. Another edn., the best, with frontispiece, 1811. There are other editions, none of them valuable.

Collins (Anthony) Philosophical Enquiry concerning Human Liberty, etc., 8vo, 1735. Collins was an eminent writer on the side of Infidelity, *vide* Leland's Deistical Writers.

Colman (George) The Fairy Prince, a Masque performed at the T. R., Covent Garden, med. 8vo, 1771.

Colquhoun (J.) Zoë, an Athenian Tale, 12mo, 1824. A very rare little volume, quite unknown to Lowndes. Only *one* copy has passed through my hands.

Combe (Taylor) A Description of the Ancient Terra Cottas in the British Museum, with 49 plates, small paper, 4to. large paper, imp. 4to, 1810. The large paper was pubd. at £2 12s. 6d., but the odd shillings and pence represent its full value now.

Combe (W.) Three Tours of Dr. Syntax: "In Search of the Picturesque," "Consolation," and "A Wife," original editions, *Ackermann*, 1812-20-21. £5 5s. The 3 vols. contain 80 coloured plates by T. Rowlandson; and original copies bear a high price on account of the vast superiority of the plates over those in later issues -- The First Tour of Dr. Syntax, originally appeared in "The Poetical Magazine," 4 vols., 1809-11. A copy of this would realize £3 or more to-day. — History of Westminster Abbey; its Antiquities and Monuments, coloured plates by Mackenzie, Pugin, etc., 2 vols., 4to. *Ackermann*, 1812. Three guineas.—The Dance of Life, by the Author of Dr Syntax, 26 coloured plates by Rowlandson, roy. 8vo, 1817. First edn., £2.—The Wars of Wellington, a narrative Poem, in XV. Cantos, by Dr. Syntax, 6 very fine coloured etchings by W. Heath, 4to, 1821. First edition Rare. £4.— The Diaboliad, a Poem, 4to, 1777. *First editions* of this gentleman's works (and indeed *any* works illustrated by Rowlandson), may always be procured in Collector's state, at moderate prices, from Mr. W. T. Spencer, of 27, New Oxford St., W.C., who holds, probably, the finest stock of books illustrated by T. Rowlandson in the world.

Conder (Josiah) Literary History of the New Testament, thk. 8vo, 1845. Pubd. at 14s.

Constable (Henry) The Forest of Fancy: wherein is contained very pretty Apothegmes and pleasant Histories, both in Meeter and Prose, etc., 4to, *Lond., T. Purfoote, circa* 1580. Most likely (as Warton says) by above Gent., though Ritson ascribes it to Henry Chettle.

Conybeare (W. J.) Church Parties, an Essay, 12mo, 1854.

Cook (Jas., *of Paisley*) A Semi-Botanical Excursion to the Land's End, sm. 12mo, 1875. Besides being anonymous, this is Privately Printed.

Cooke (E.) A Seasonable Treatise wherein is proved that K. William did not get the Crown by the Sword but by the Election and Consent of the People, 8vo, 1689. Of nominal value. The frontis. is generally absent.

Cooke (T.) The Countryman's Guide to London, or Cheats of the Town exposed, med. 8vo, 17—. Rare.

Cooper (E.) Historical and Poetical Medley, or Muses' Library, with Lives of the Authors, 8vo, 1738. 10s. A collection of the best Antient English Poetry from Edward the Confessor to James I.

Cope (H.) Romance of the Chivalric Ages : The Pilgrim Brothers, steel etchings, 2 vols., cr. 8vo, *Bull*, 1833. First edn. The etchings are much like " Phiz," though by Herbert, R.A.

Copleston (J. H.) Reply to *Edinb. Rev.* Calumnies against Oxford, etc., *Oxford*, 1810. A second and third Reply, 1811, should accompany this. Value trifling.

Copley (Lionel) A Letter sent from a Gentleman to Mr. Henry Martin, Member from Worcester, 4to, 1642. A very rare Civil War Tract.

Copywell (J.).—*See* Woty (W.).

Corbet (R.) Papers of the Desires of the Soldiers of the Army, at the General Rendezvous at Newmarket, 4to, 1647. Relates to the Civil War in Cambridge.— Poetica Stromata, a Collection of Sundry Pieces in Poetry, sm. 8vo, 1648. Rare. Two guineas.

Cornet (A.).—*See* Pettigrew (T. L.).

Cornwall (Barry).—*See* Procter (B. W.).

Cornwallis (Mrs) On the State of Man subsequent to the Promulgation of Christianity, 4 vols., fcp. 8vo, *Pickering*, 1851-3. These vols. form part of the set of Pickering's " Small Books on Great Subjects "

Cory (W.) Ionica. FIRST EDITION, p. 8vo, 1858. Very scarce. 21s. —Another edn., *Allen*, 1891. 5s.— Large Paper. Only 100 copies printed. *Ib.* 10s. The author was also known as W. Johnson.

Couch (Quiller) Green Bays, Verses and Parodies, by Q., p. 8vo, 1893.

Coulton (Miss) Our Farm of Four Acres, and the Money we made by it, 12mo, 1859.

Courtier (P. L.) The Pulpit, or Biographical and Literary Accounts of Eminent Popular Preachers by Onesimus, 3 vols., sm. 8vo, 1809-16. This created a reply, "Onesimus Examined," by an Evangelical Minister, which has not come under my notice.

Coventry (Francis) History of Pompey the Little, or Life and Adventures of a Lap Dog, 12mo, 1751. Of this satirical novel Lady M. W. Montagu said that it diverted her more than reading "Peregrine Pickle."

Coxe (Archdeacon) Catalogue of the Manuscripts in the possession of the Earl of Hardwicke, 4to, *Privately Printed (York)*, 1794. Compiled by above gent., and very few copies were struck off.— Sketches of the Lives of Correggio and Parmegiano, portrait of the former, cr. 8vo, 1823. 7s. 6d.

Cozens (Z.) Tour Through the Isle of Thanet, plates, 4to, 1793. Very rare. £4 4s.

Craddock (Jos., F.R S.) Letters from Snowdon, descriptive of a Tour through the N. Counties of Wales, etc., 8vo, 1770.

Cradock (Peter) Papers of the Treatie at a Great Meeting of the Generall Officers of the Army at Putney, 4to, 1647. Carries fine woodcut port. of Prince Charles on title.

Crane (John, *of Bromsgrove*) Bromsgrove Facetiæ (Poems of a very humourous and facetious character), dedicated without permission to John Bull, by a Bard at Bromsgrove, Vol. I. (all pubd. ?), fcp. 8vo, *circa* 1810. Interesting to the local folk-lore collector.

Craven.—*See* Carleton (Capt. J. W.).

Crawley (Thomas) Letters and Dissertations on various Subjects, on the Disputes between Gt. Britain and America, etc., by Author of "Letter Analysis," 1765-76, 8vo, 1776.

Crayon (Geoffrey).—*See* Irving (Washington).

Crithannah (J.) Fifty-one Original Fables, 85 very clever illusts. by G. Cruikshank, 8vo, 1833. Very uncommon. Always catalogues for at least 15s.

Criticus.—*See* Orme (Rev. W.).

Croft (Sir Herbert) Love and Madness, a Story too True, in a Series of Letters, portraits, fcp. 8vo, *Dublin*, 1786, 5s.

Croker (T. Croftou) My Village, *versus* Our Village, post 8vo, 1833. —Barney Mahoney, Fairy Legends of the S. of Ireland, illustrated, 12mo, 1838.

Croly (Dr. G.) Salathiel, a Story of the Past, etc., 3 vols., sm. 8vo, 1828. First edn. of a work which the *Athenæum* characterised as "One of the most splendid productions among the works of fiction that the age has brought forth."

c

Cromwell (Oliver) Shuffling, Cutting, and Dealing in a Game of Picquet, by O. (Cromwell) P[rotector], etc., 1659. An excessively rare pamphlet. £2 2s.

Crosland (Mrs. Newton) Landmarks of a Literary Life, 1890-2, cr. 8vo, 1893.

Cross (Mrs. J. W., *née Marian Evans*) has written under pseudonym of "George Eliot": Scenes of Clerical Life, 2 vols, post 8vo, *Blackwood*, 1858. Worth £7 7s. in cloth uncut.—Silas Marner, p. 8vo, *Blackwood*, 1871, 7s. 6d.—Felix Holt, 3 vols., p. 8vo, *Ib.*, 1866, 10s —Middlemarch, 8 vols., p 8vo, wrapps., *Ib.*, 1871-2, 15s.—Jubal (Legend of), and other Poems, sm. p. 8vo, 1874, 12s 6d. —Daniel Deronda, 8 vols., p. 8vo, wrapp., 1876, 15s.—Theophrastus Such, cr. 8vo, *Ib.*, 1879, 5s.—Above dates are those of first editions. All these used to sell for considerably more, but "George Eliot" is rather down just now. Still, clean uncut copies should always sell. Mr. W. T. SPENCER, the well-known Bookseller, of 27, New Oxford Street, W.C, holds a fine stock of first editions by this popular authoress, all moderately priced. Write for catalogues, or better still, CALL.

Cross (W.) The Disruption, a Scottish Tale of Recent Times, fcap. 8vo, 1846. First edn., now rare, 7s. 6d.

Cross-Buchanan (J.) Edith, a Tale of the Azores, and other Poems, post 8vo, *Pickering*, 1838.

Crossley (James) Sir Thomas Browne's Tracts, new edn., ed. by J. Crossley, 8vo, 1822, 7s. 6d.—Vade-Mecum to Hatton, a Poem, sm. 8vo, 1867. Issued anonymously and Privately Printed.

Crowe (W.) Catalogue of our English Writers on the Old and New Testament, sm. 8vo, 1868.

Croxall (S.) The Royal Sin, or Adultery rebuked in a great King, 8vo, 1738. Curious and rare. 7s. 6d, or more.

"C. S. C."—*See* Calverley (C. S.).

Cruden.—Description of Three Ornamented Bricks found in London and Gravesend, with curious facsimile engravings, 8vo, 1825.

Cruikshank (George and R.).—Numerous works illustrated by these inimitable artists will be found in the "Handbook" under their respective authors, and any Collector desiring to see the finest collection of the same in England should pay a visit to 27, New Oxford Street, W.C., where Mr. W. T. Spencer has, at least, one specimen of every book illustrated by either of these artists.

Crull (J.) Antiquities of St. Peter's, or the Abbey-Church of Westminster, with Inscriptions and Epitaphs on Tombs and Grave-Stones, *plates of tombs, etc.*, 2 vols., 1722.

Cumberland (R.) The Clouds of Aristophanes, acted at Athens in the 2nd year of the Olymp., LXXXIX., Aminias being Archon, post 8vo, *c.* 1797.

Curtis (J.) The Union Collection of Hymns and Sacred Odes, cr. 8vo, *Bristol*, 1827.

Cust (Edward) A Translation of J. H. Meiboni De Flagrorum Usu in Re Veneria et lumborum renumque officio, *Argentorati*, 1657. The above gent. was severely punished by Government for printing this translation, which sells now for about 10s.

C.W.—*See* Wase (C.).

Dalington (Maister Robert) A Survey of the Great Dukes State of Tuscany, 4to, 1605. Rare, though of little commercial value. The volume was printed by Edward Blount, one of the Publishers of the first Folio Shakespeare.

Dalrymple (Sir David, *Lord Hailes*) Opinions of Sarah, Duchess of Marlborough, 1788. This work, which was published *sine loco*, was issued at Edinburgh, and edited by above gent. A good copy can be procured for about 7s 6d.—Ancient Scottish Poems, pubd. from the MS. of Geo. Bannatyne, 1568, 8vo [*Edinb.*, 1770], *Leeds*, 1815.

Dalrymple (Hugh) Rodonto, or the State Jugglers, in verse, 2 Cantos, 8vo, 1763. 5s.

Daniel (J.) A Kick from Yarmouth to Wales, or restricted enjoyment at Oatlands, sm. 8vo, 1812. Curious and rare. Issued "for the Purchaser," still does not command a high price, though suppressed and bought up before publication by order of the Prince Regent.

Daniel (Geo.) Democritus in London, post 8vo, 1852.

Dante.—*See* Vernon (Lord).

D'Arblay (Madame) Evelina, or a Young Lady's Entrance into the World, by Fanny Burney, 3 vols., p. 8vo, *Lowndes*, 1778. 1st edn., £2 2s , or more.—Cecilia, or Memoirs of an Heiress, by the Author of "Evelina," 5 vols., fcp. 8vo, 1782. 15s.—Diary and Letters of Madame D'Arblay, portrait, 7 vols., post 8vo, *Colburn*, 1854.

Darby.—A New Translation of the New Testament, from the Revised Text of the Greek Original, post 8vo, N.D.

Darwin (Erasmus) The Botanic Garden, 2 vols., 4to, 1791. First edn. Should contain amongst the plates two by W. Blake, and 2 of the Portland Vase. 7s. 6d.

Darwin (Capt.).—This gentleman wrote in "*The Field*" under the pseudonym of "High Elms." He published "The Game-Preserver's Manual" in 1866.

Davidson (John) Observations on the Regiam Majestatem, and Remarks on some of the Editions of the Acts of Scottish Parliaments, etc., thin 8vo, 1792.

Davies (John) The Civil Warres of Great Britain and Ireland, an exact History, etc., by an Impartiall Pen, folio, 1661. About 10s.— Epictetus Junior, or Maximes of Modern Morality in Two Centuries, 16mo, 1670. Rare and unknown to Lowndes. Worth 15s.

Davies (Myles) A Critical History of Pamphlets, 8vo, 1715.

Davis (Augusta) Blanche Lisle, and other Poems, by Cecil Home, 12mo, *Camb.*, 1860. Of trifling value.

Davy (Sir Humphry) Salmonia, or Days of Fly-Fishing, by an Angler, 12mo, 1828. Best edn.—Salmonia, or Days of Fly-Fishing, plates by Finden, and cuts, fcp. 8vo, 1832.

Day (Thomas) History of Sandford and Merton, 3 vols, post 8vo, 1791. This edn. is rare, and sells at 10 or 12 shillings. There exists an account of this author by James Keir, which is also scarce.

Deane (Margery) European Breezes, by Marie J. Pitman, fcp. 8vo, *Boston*, 1882. Pubd. 5s.

Deacon (Bp. T., *The Nonjuror*) Compleat Collection of Devotions, Publick and Private, etc., 8vo, 1734. Rare, and always sells for 10s.

Deacon (W. F.) The Exile of Erin, or Sorrows of a Bashful Irishman, 2 vols., cr. 8vo, 1835.

Decker (Sir Matthew) Serious Considerations on the several High Duties which the Nation Labours under, with a Proposal for one Single Tax, 8vo, 1744. This occasioned a reply by Bp. Horsley.

Decker (T.) The Dove and the Serpent, 4to. 1614. Perhaps the rarest of all this author's works. £10 for a good, perfect copy.

Dee.—Ashmole (Elias) Fasciculus Chemicus, or Chymical Collections (by Dr. A. Dee) whereunto is added the Arcanum, or Grand Secret of Hermetick Philosophy (by Juan d'Espagnat), both made English by Jas. Hasalle, 8vo, 1650. Rare, 10s. 6d.

Defoe (Daniel) A Short History of Standing Armies in England, 4to. *Baldwin*, 1698.—Jura Populi Anglicani, or the Subject's Right of Petitioning set forth, etc., 4to, (secretly) Printed in 1701. Rare, —The True Born Englishman, 8vo. *s. l.*, 1701. Reformation of Manners, a Satire, First Edition, 8vo, 1702. Very rare.—The Experiment; or Shortest Way with the Dissenters exemplified, being the case of Abraham Gill, *a Dissenting Minister of the I. of Ely*, 4to, 1705. Rare, about 10s. 6d. Curious account of a vagabond Preacher named Collins, *alias* Gill, who travelled through Norfolk and the I. of Ely with a woman and some children, carrying forged certificates of his Ordination. Also contains Letters from the different towns.—Religious Courtship, etc., 8vo, 1722. About 7s. 6d.—Jure Divino, port. by Vander Gucht, folio, 1st edn., 1870, About 10s.—An edn. by Ross, 1783. Large and small Paper.— Discourse concerning Trouble of Mind arising from Sundry Temptations exemplified in the Life of a Private Gentleman, etc., sm. p. 8vo, 1708. 7s. 6d.—Faction Displayed, a Poem, p. 8vo,

1709.—Secret History of Arlus and Adolphus, p. 8vo, 1710. Attributed to Defoe.—The Allies and the Late Ministry defended against France, etc., two parts, fcp. 8vo, 1712.—Vindication of the Present Ministry from Clamours, etc., on occasion of the New Preliminaries, similar size, 1711. The latter item is *attributed* to Defoe.—The Allies and the Late Ministry defended against France and the present Friends of France; in answer to a Pamphlet, "The Conduct of the Allies," 2 parts, fcp. 8vo, 1712. Attrib. to Defoe.—Reflections upon the Humour of the British Nation in Religion and Politics, p. 8vo, 1713.—History of the Wars of Charles XII., by a Scots Gent. in the Swedish service, med. 8vo, 1715.—Minutes of Negociations of Mons. Mesnager, at the Court of England, etc., 8vo, Printed at the Black Boy and Anchor, 1717.—The Dumb Philosopher, or Account of Dickory Cronke, original edition, 12mo, 1719. Rare, 12s. 6d.—Life and Strange Surprising Adventures of Robinson Crusoe, of York, Mariner, written by Himself, portrait, 8vo, 1719. The first four editions (all necessary to the collector on account of variations) were published in this year, and the First issue is exceedingly valuable; but Collectors must take care that it is a genuine copy. The second edition sells for about £3.—A Journey through England, in Familiar Letters from a Gentleman here to his Friend abroad, 2 vols. A Journey through Scotland, being the volume which compleats Great Britain, together 3 vols (with additions by Saml. Richardson), 8vo, 1732. Rare, 21s. The First edition was 1724-7. A copy of the 6th edn., which I recently catalogued, 4 vols., post 8vo, 1762, was priced 15s.; and a copy of the 1754 edn. (presumably the 5th (the 4th being 1748), 4 vols., 1754, sold at Christie's last March for £1 4s.—Time's Telescope, Universal and Perpetual, fitted for all Countries and Capacities, by DUNCAN CAMPBELL, 8vo, 1734. First edn. 5s.—An Ecclesiastical Hist. of Scotland, from Q. Mary to the Union, 8vo, 1734. The Compleat English Tradesman, 2 vols, fcp. 8vo, 1745.—An Historical Narrative of the Great Plague, 1665, with Account of other remarkable Plagues, &c., 8vo, 1769. 7s. 6d.—History of the Civil Wars in Germany, 1630-5, and Genuine Memoirs of Wars of England, *temp.* Charles I, 8vo, *Newark*, 1782. A doubtful item—Secrets of the Invisible World disclosed; an Universal Hist. of Apparitions, Sacred and Profane, &c., &c., by Andrew Morton, fcp. 8vo, *Oxford*, 1840.

De La Roche (C. F. T.) Giphantia, or a view of what has passed, what is now passing, and during the present Century what will pass in the World. Transl. from the French; post 8vo, 1761. Rare, 7s. 6d. Many of these curious predictions have since become accomplished facts.

Dell (Henry) The Mirrour, a Comedy, 1756-7. This gent. (a Bookseller) wrote several other Facetious pieces.

Dellon (M.) Relation de l'Inquisition de Goa, plates, fcp. 8vo, *Paris*, 1688.

Delony (Thos.) The History of John Winchcomb, usually called Jack of Newbury, the famous Clothier, 1597, 4to, 1859. Only 26 copies printed. 21s. Three Old Ballads on the Overthrow of the Spanish Armada, reprinted from the (unique) originals, 12mo, 1860 Only 30 copies printed. 10s. Both these items were edited by J. O. Halliwell, and they are now very scarce.—Thomas of Reading; or, the Sixe Worthie Yeomen of the West, sm. 4to, *Edinb.* (1812). The original of 1632 I have never seen.

Delta.—*See* Moir (D. M.).

Democritus, Junior.—*See* Burton (R.).

De Morgan (Augustus and Mrs.) From Matter to Spirit, by C. D., sm. 8vo, 1863. Generally catalogues at 10s, or slightly more. It is generally supposed that Prof. De Morgan wrote the Preface only, and his wife the rest of the book, but there is very little doubt that he wrote the greater portion, if not the whole, of it.

Dennis (John) The Character and Conduct of Sir John Edgar, call'd by himself sole Monarch of the Stage in Drury Lane, 8vo, 1720. Rare, 10s. A scurrilous production in which Steele is roundly rated by the author, who was most vindictive.

Dennys (John) Secrets of Angling, 1633. Very rare. The sm. 4to reprint, with Intro. by T. Westwood, 1883, is common. Another edn., ed. by Piscator, 2 vols. in 1, post 8vo, *Privately Printed*, 1885.

De Quincey (T.) Klosterheim: or, The Masque, fcp. 8vo, 1832, First edn. Rare, 7s. 6d.

Derham (Wm.) The Artificial Clock-Maker, a Treatise on watch and clock work, fcp. 8vo, 1734. Should have a folding frontispiece; often absent.

Dering (H.) Reliquiæ Eboracenses, 8vo, 1743. A Latin Poem on the Antiquities of Yorkshire.

Des Periers. Les Joyeuses Aventures et Nouvelles Récréations, &c., 12mo, *Lyon, B. Rigaud*, 1582. Contains 100 Facetious Tales, part of which are selected from the Contes of Des Periers. Exceedingly rare. Probably worth £5.

De St. Cyran (L'Abbé) Question Royalle et sa Decision, fcp. 8vo, *Paris*, 1609. Suppressed. 7s. 6d.

Dibdin (Thos.) Bunyan's Pilgrim's Progress, metrically condensed, in 6 Cantos. First (and probably only) edition, sm. post 8vo, *Harding and King*, 1834. Excessively rare. Only one copy has ever come under my notice. Ten shillings or more.

Dibdin (T. F.) The Director, A Weekly Literary Journal, containing: I. Essays. II. Bibliographiana, III. The British Gallery, 2 vols., 8vo, 1807. The second part was written by Dibdin.—Rational Madness; a Song for Lovers of Curious and Rare Books, &c., 9 verses on 2 leaves. (1813.) Printed in red and black, and rare, only 50 copies having been issued for Private Circulation. Sells at 15s.— Bibliophobia, Remarks on the Present languid and depressed state of Literature and the Book Trade, by Mercurius Rusticus, 8vo, 1832. About 6s.

D'Hancarville. Veneres et Priapi, uti observantur in gemmis antiquis. 70 *plates* (generally on India Paper), 4to, 1888. Rare, and worth £2. Only issued to Subscribers.

Dickens (Chas.) Sketches by "Boz," First and second series, 3 vols., post 8vo, *Macrone*, 1836-7. About £10 10s., if uncut.—The Pickwick Papers, 43 etchings by Seymour and Phiz. A good copy, in the 20 original parts (with the "Buss" plates) £8 8s., *C & Hall*, 1836-7. In cloth, uncut, £3. Half bound, 10s. to 21s., according to condition.—Sunday under Three Heads, by Timothy Sparks (C. D.), illustrated by Phiz, 12mo, *in illustrated wrapper*, 1836. Original edition. £5 5s. The reprint (facsimile) is of merely *nominal* value. The Strange Gentleman; a Comic Burletta, in 2 Acts, by "Boz," first performed at the St. James's Theatre, Thursday, Sept. 29th, 1836, cr. 8vo, 1837. First edition. An uncut copy, £3.—Cleave's Gazette of Variety for Oct. and Nov., 1838, contains Satirical Portraits of many characters in "Nicholas Nickleby" and "Oliver Twist," and forms a scarce item for the Dickens collector. 7s 6d.—The Quarterly Review, 1839, contains an Article on Oliver Twist, by "Boz." 18 pp., 8vo, 1839.—The Library of Romance, a Collection of Tales and Romances by "Boz" (who contributed An Actor's Death), L. Hunt, &c., *frontispiece*, cr. 8vo. 1845.—To be read at Dusk, First Edition, in "The Keepsake" for 1852, also an edition in 4to, illustrated, 1852. The latter realizes 15s.—The unique separate issue was sold by a London Bookseller about 5 years ago for 25 guineas.—The Lamplighter, a Farce by C. Dickens (1838), post 8vo, *Privately Printed*, 1879. First edition. Rare, 30s., perhaps.—Wills of their own, Curious, Eccentric, and Benevolent (includes Will of Chas. Dickens), 12mo, 1879. Trifling value.— The Scrap-Book of Literary Varieties, illust. with 150 engravings, including a complete set of fancy portraits to illustrate "Nicholas Nickleby" by Kenny Meadows, 8vo, *J. Reynolds*, N D. Scarce, 15s., a good copy.—Some well-known Characters from works of; 16 coloured plates, by "Kyd"(J. C. Clark), 4to, N.D. The best edition contains 24 coloured plates, 4to size.—Hughes. A Week's Tramp in Dickens' Land, with personal Reminiscences of the "Inimitable Boz." Illustrated by Phiz, Maclise, Railton, Barnard, &c., 8vo, 1891. Now scarce, 15s.—MR. W. T. SPENCER, of 27, New Oxford Street, W.C., the well-known authority on "Dickens," who has the largest and choicest stock of rare "Dickensiana" in the World, (and to whose ripe experience and knowledge I have been several times indebted for valuable information, cheerfully given, in compiling this work), issues a really bibliographical Catalogue of "Dickens," and other rarities, which is sent Post free to Book-buyers on application, and I can personally recommend him as a conscientious Buyer of First editions of "Dickens" at a high figure.

Diderot (M.) Pensées sur l'Interpretation de la Nature, 12mo, *s.l.*, 1754. Rare, 5s. Cet ouvrage est de M. Diderot, voyez "Journal Encyclopedique" du premier Jan., 1756, page 15, and page 3 du 15e Jan., 1766.—Les Bijoux Indiscrets. 2 vols., 12mo, *Au Monomotapa*, 1772. Rare and highly erotic, 10s. 6d. Another edn., with plates, 2 vols., 12mo, *Bruxelles*, 1881. Of similar value. Only 500 printed.

Digby (Kenelm) Hours with the first falling leaves, *vign. title*, thk. post 8vo, *s. l. et a*. Probably a Privately Printed issue.

D'Israeli (Isaac) Flim-Flams, or Life and Errors of my Uncle and his Friend! &c., 11 humourous plates, 3 vols., fcp. 8vo, 1806. Rare, 15s.

D. J.—*See* Davies (John).

Dilke (Sir C. W.) The Fall of Prince Florestan, of Monaco, frontis., 8vo, 1874, First edition. Of no value.—The Present Position of European Politics, or Europe in 1887, by the Author of "Greater Britain," 8vo, 1887.—The British Army, by the Author of "Greater Britain, 8vo, 1888.

Dillon (Sir J.) Horæ Icenæ, being Lucubrations on the result of the General Election of 1835, 8vo (1836). Anonymous and Privately Printed.

Dinsdale (Dr.) A Glossary of Provincial Words used in Teesdale, Durham, sm. 8vo, *Barnard Castle*, 1849.

Dixon (Henry H.) Saddle and Sirloin, 2 *parts* (1870), Silk and Scarlet, Scott and Sebright, 1862, &c, &c.

Dobell (Sidney) The Roman, a Dramatic Poem, by Sidney Yendys, cr. 8vo, 1850. First edition.—Balder, Part the First, by the author of "The Roman," cr. 8vo, 1854. First edn.

Doblado (Don Leucadio).—*See* White (J. Blanco).

Dockray (Benj.) On Mutual Tolerance, and the Ultimate Test o Truth, by Author of "Remarks on Catholic Emancipation," &c., 8vo, *London*, 1835. Relates to the celebrated Quaker "Beacon Controversy."

Dodd (Chas.).—*See* Tootle (Rev. Hugh).

Dodgson (Rev. C. Lutwidge) Phantasmagoria, and other Poems, fcp. 8vo, 1869 First edn. and Rare, 15s. A Tangled Tale, illusts. by A. B. Frost, 1885. First edn , 7s. 6d.—Through the Looking Glass. 1st edn., 50 *illusts. by J. Tenniel*, 1872. Alice's Adventures in Wonderland, 42 *illusts. by Tenniel*, 1st edn., 1872. These 2 vols. in good condition catalogue at £4 and upwards —The Hunting of the Snark, with 9 illusts. by H. Holiday, sm. 8vo, 1876. First edn., 7s 6d.—The Game of Logic, by Lewis Carroll, cr. 8vo, 1887. First edn., 5s.

Dodsley (Robt.) Chronicle of the Kings of England, written in the manner of the ancient Jewish Historians by Nathan Ben Saddi, 2 parts, 8vo, 1741-2. *Rare*, 12s.—Œconomy of Human Life, with exquisite illusts. by Harding, sm. 8vo, 1795. The most charming edition extant, 7s. 6d.—Œconomy of Human Life; fcp. 8vo, *Leeds* 1797.—Œconomy of Human Life, from an Indian MS., fcp. 8vo, *Eton Printed*, 1796. There are numerous other edns , all of trifling value.

Dodwell (Henry) Christianity not founded on Argument, 8vo, 1743. This gent. (a Barrister) was evidently an ardent Freethinker, and above work created much controversy, evoking replies, amongst others, from Benson, Leland, Randolph, &c.

Dolet (Estienne) Le Maniere de bien Traduire, 1540. Le Second Enfer, 1544. Both post 8vo. The *originals*, issued by Techener, are of the utmost rarity. No copy of either has ever come under my notice, but I am acquainted with the beautiful reprints, issued early this Century, with facsims. of the exquisite Colophons. This author was known as "The Martyr Poet of the Restoration."

Dollinger (Dr.) [and Dr. Friedrich] The Pope and the Council, transl. from the German, cr. 8vo, 1869. Pubd. 7s. 6d.

Donaldson (J.) The Elements of Beauty, also Reflections on the Harmony of Sensibility and Reason, fcp. 8vo, *Edinb.*, 1780. 5s.

Donne (Dr. J.) Poems by J. D [onne] with Elegies on the Author's Death, fcp. 8vo, *Marriott*, 1635. Should have fine frontispiece portrait by Marshall, with verses beneath by I. Walton, and when this is not absent a copy is worth £2 10s.—Poems by J. Donne, with Elegies on the Author's Death, 12mo, *Marriot*, 1639. Very rare, and well worth 21s.

Dorat (M.) Ma Philosophie, 8vo, 1771. Should have full page plate, vignettes and cul-de-lampe after C. P. Marillier, engr by E. De Ghent.—Contes en Vers, contenant La Belle Lyonnaise, ou le Veritable Amour; Le Souper et le Coucher, &c. *Amst.*, 1783.

Dowty (A. A.) Figaro's History of England, by O. P. Q. Philander Smiff, profusely illustrated, p. 8vo, 1873.

Doyle (John, *father of* "*Dick*" *Doyle*) published about 800 Political Sketches (Caricatures) 1832-40. When found complete t ese are now worth about £4 4s. There was a key to these Political Sketches pubd. in 1841 ; also scarce.

D'Oyly (Sir C.) Tom Raw the Griffin, with coloured plates, 8vo, *Ackermann*, 1828. £3 3s., more if in uncut state.

Druid (The).— *See* Dixon (Henry H.).

Dryden (J.) Defense du Beau Sexe, addressée à Eugenie, Dialogue, trad. par une Dame Angloise, 12mo, *Londres*. 1691. Neither Gay nor Lowndes appear to be acquainted with this work, and only one copy has come under my notice.

Du Bois (Edward) My Pocket-Book, or Hints for a Ryghte Merrie and Conceited Tour, to be called "The Stranger in Ireland," by a Knight Errant, folding frontispiece and humourous plates, post 8vo, 1808. An amusing Skit on Sir J. Carr's Travels. Dubois also wrote "Old Nick," edited an edn. of the "Decameron," &c.

Dubreuil (P. Jean) La Perspective Pratique, necessaire à tous peintures, et autres qui se meslent du desseigner, &c.. numerous plates, 3 vols., 4to, *Paris*, 1663. Rare. 25 to 30 shillings.

Dudley (Sir B. and Lady) Passages, &c., on Vortigern and Rowena, 3 vols., 12mo, *s. d.* Trifling in value.

Dudley (Howard) History and Antiquities of Horsham, by the Author of Juvenile researches ; illustrated, 12mo, 1836. Rare, 10s. or more.

Dulaurens (M.) Imirce, ou la Fille de la Nature, post 8vo, Berlin, chez l'Imprimeur Philosophe de Sans Souci, 1765.

Dunkley (H.) Glory and Shame of Britain. Prize Essay on the Working Classes, 8vo, 18—.

Dunton (John, *the Eccentric*) Athenian Sport, or 2000 Paradoxes merrily argued to amuse and divert the Age ; by a Member of the Athenian Soc., thk. 8vo, 1707. 7s. 6d. Perhaps the most diverting book by this heterogeneous character, tho' the style of composition would be considered somewhat coarse in this Century. The subjects treated are, to say the least, curious.—The Athenian Oracle, also the Supplement. Being a Collection of Curious questions, with Answers in the Athenian Mercuries, 4 vols., 8vo, 1710. Only 3 volumes generally turn up ; with the Fourth, the Book catalogues at 10s. or more. It is often placed under "Erotica," and justly so.

Duppa (Brian, *Bp. of Winchester*) Jonsonus Virbius, or the Memorie of Ben Jonson, revived by the Friends of the Muses, 4to, 1638. This volume was *edited* by above gent., the Contributors include T. Sackville, Sir J. Beaumont, Waller, Feltham, Donne, Rutter, Sir T. Hawkins, Coventry, &c. Rare, £2 2s.

Duppa (R.) Life of Raffaello of Urbino, and Characters, &c., by Sir J. Reynolds, post 8vo, 1816.

Durfey (Tom) Butler's Ghost, or Hudibras the fourth Part, with Reflections upon these times, sm. p. 8vo, 1682. First edition, 5s.— Collin's Walk through London and Westminster (a Burlesque Poem). First edition, 1690. This is rare, and cannot be procured under at least 10s.—Wit and Mirth: or, Pills to Purge Melancholy, 6 vols., sm. 8vo, 1719. Messrs. Pearson have issued a Reprint within the last few years which is to all intents and purposes as good as the original.—The Commonwealth of Women. A Reprint, 8vo, 1886. Scarce, only 75 copies issued.

Doubleday (Thos.) The Coquet-dale Fishing Songs, now first collected, and ed. by A North Country Angler, cr. 8vo, 1852. Scarce, 15s.

Dyde (W.) History and Antiquities of the Borough of Tewkesbury from the remotest period to the present time, fcp. 8vo, 1790, with plates. 5s.

Eachard (Dr. J.) Grounds and Occasions of Contempt of the Clergy, &c., 12mo, 1670. First edition.

Eagles (Rev. J.) Journal of Llewellyn Penrose. a Seaman, 4 vols., sm. 8vo, *Murray*, 1815. First edition, 7s. 6d.

Egan (Pierce) Life in London, or Day and Night Scenes of Jerry Hawthorn, and his elegant friend, Corinthian Tom, accompanied by Bob Logic, the Oxonian, in their Rambles and Sprees through the Metropolis, 36 full page coloured plates by G. Cruikshank, besides woodcuts, 8vo, *Sherwood*, 1821. First edition. About £6. The Finish to "Life in London" also contains 36 full page coloured plates, besides woodcuts, by R. Cruikshank, 8vo, *Strange*, N.D. (1830). A good copy is worth £5 5s. There is another edn. with the original illustrations reproduced (in colours), roy. 8vo, *Hotten*, s. d., ca. 1870. Not nearly so valuable as the original. About 15s. A good copy of any of these can be obtained from Mr. W. T. Spencer, 27, New Oxford St., W.C.—Real Life in London, by an Amateur (Pierce Egan), contains 32 full page coloured plates after Alken, Rowlandson, &c., and a First edition, clean in the 14 monthly parts (forming 2 vols.), is of great rarity and should be worth £10 to £12. Pubd. by *Jones*, 1821-2.

Eldridge (R.) Spell Bound. A Tale of Macclesfield Forest, in Verse, post 8vo, 1859.

Elizabeth (Charlotte) The Perils of the Nation, thk. post 8vo, 1843. Also Chapters on Flowers, 1839, &c.

Ellis (John) Maphaeus. The Canto added to Virgil's Æneas, cr. 8vo, 1758.

Elsley (Rev.) Annotations on the Four Gospels and Acts of the Apostles, 3 vols., 8vo, 1812. Pubd. at 18s. Best edition, 3 vols., 8vo, 1824. (24s.)

E. P.—*See* Phillips (E.).

Ephemera.—*See* Fitzgibbon (E.).

Epicure (An).—*See* Saunders (F.).

Erotica. Le Roman de mon Alcove-Aventures Galantes d'une Femme du Monde racontée per Elle même, fcp. 8vo, *s. d.* Privately Printed at Paris, "Au Temple d'Amour." Impression limited to 100 copies. None for sale. 21s. to-day.

Erotica. Quinque Illustrium Poetarum, Ant. Panormitæ; Ramusii, Ariminensis; Pacifici Maximi, Joan Secundi, Lusus in Venerem, &c., 8vo. *Paris,* 1791. Worth a guinea to-day, when to be had. Highly Erotic and Humourous, and by 5 well-known Ancient Latin Poets.

Erotica. Journée de l'Amour, ou Heures de Cythère, 12 engravings (4 full page), designed by Taunay, 8vo, *Gnide,* (Paris), 1776. By The Countess De Turpin, Boufflers, Gaillard, Favart, and l'Abbé de Voisenon. Rare, 21s.

Erskine (Lord) The second part of Armata, 8vo, 1817.

Estienne (C.) Discours des Histoires de Lorraine et de Flandres; au Roy très-Chrestien Henry II., sm. 4to, *Paris, C. Estienne,* 1552. A very rare work. Contains 56 ll. sigs. A—O in fours. Worth £3.

Estienne (H.).—*See* Blount (T.).

Eugenius Philalethes.—*See* Vaughan (Thos.).

Evans (Howard) Our Old Nobility, 2 series, post 8vo, 1878. Now very scarce, and worth 7s. 6d. The originals appeared in Newspaper Articles.

E. V. B.—*See* Boyle (Hon. Mrs.).

Evelyn (John) The Moral Practice of the Jesuits, faithfully rendered into English, sm. 8vo, 1670. Very rare, 10s.

E. W.—*See* Williams (E.).

Ewing (W. C.) Norfolk Lists from the Reformation to the present Time, (including Tradesmen's Tokens), cr. 8vo, *Norwich,* 1837. Scarce, 7s. 6d.

Experienced Hand (An).—*See* Clavel (Robt.).

Eyton (C.) Notes on the Geology of N. Shropshire, sm. post 8vo, 1869. Anonymous, and most likely privately printed.

Facetiæ. Transactions of the Loggerville Literary Society. Woodcuts, 8vo, 1867. Privately Printed and anonymous. Of no commercial value.

Facetiæ. The Wits; or Sport upon Sport, a curious Collection of Drolls and Farces, &c., presented and shewn by Strolling Players, Fools, and Fiddlers, 8vo, 1672. An account of this item will be found in Baker's Biogr. Dramatica. Perfect copies should possess a frontispiece, which is nearly always wanting, and the Book is generally found in poor condition. Perfect, about 21s.

Facetiæ. The Puppet-Show, from March 18th, 1848, to 1849; forms 2 vols. There is also an Almanac This comic weekly failed, and complete sets are now rare. It catalogues at 10 or 12 shillings.

Fane (Julian).—*See* Lytton (Robt. Lord).

Fane (Violet).—*See* Singleton (Mrs.).

Fantosme.—*See* Memoirs, &c.

Father Prout.—*See* Mahony (F. S.).

F. B.—*See* Burton (R. F.).

Fenton (R.) Tour in Quest of Genealogy, through several parts of Wales, &c., fine copper plates, 8vo, 1811.

Ferriar (Dr. J.) The Theory of Dreams, 2 vols., 8vo, 1808. 10s.

Fevre (Raoul Le) The Destruction of Troy (Caxton's translation), with many admirable Acts of Chivalry, 4to, 1684. Printed in 𝔅𝔩𝔞𝔠𝔨 𝔏𝔢𝔱𝔱𝔢𝔯. There are many editions of this Tract, all uncommon.

Fielding (Henry) History of Tom Jones, a Foundling, 6 vols., post 8vo, *Millar*, 1749. Very rare, £2 10s.

Findlay (J. R.) Verses, post 4to, 1874. These anonymous Verses, which were only printed for Private Circulation, possess considerable merit. Should sell at 10s.

Firth (J. F.) Historical Memoranda, Charters, Documents, and Extracts, from the Records of the Corporation and Books of the Cooper's Company, London, 1396—1848, 8vo, 1848. Anonymous and Privately Printed. 21s.

Fisher (Jas., *of Sheffield*) The Wise Virgin, or Wonderful Narration of the various Dispensations of God towards a Childe 11 years old, enabling her when stricken dumb, deaf, and blind, to utter glorious truths to the wonderment of many who came to see her, 12mo, *Rothwell*, 1658. Rare and curious, 21s. The child was Martha Hatfield, of Laughton, Yorks.

Fitzgerald (Edward) Euphranor, a Dialogue on Youth; post 8vo, *Pickering*, 1851. First edition, and has become very scarce, 7s. 6d. —Preciosa. First edition, post 8vo, 1852. Scarce, 7s. 6d.

Fitzgibbon (E.) Ephemera's Handbook of Angling, Fly-Fishing, Trolling, Bottom-Fishing, Salmon-Fishing, &c., frontis. and cuts, post 8vo, 1853.

Fitzpatrick (P. V.) Thaumaturgus (in doggerel verse), fcp. 8vo, 1828. A stupid compilation, issued anonymously, and of not the slightest value either from a Literary or Commercial point of view.

Fitzvictor (J.).—*See* Shelley (P. B.).

F. (L. De).—*See* Fontenelle (Louis De).

Flamank (James) The Natural Influence of Speech in raising Man above the Brute Creation, fcp. 8vo, 1834.

Fletcher (Andrew, *of Saltoun*) A Discourse of Government, with Relation to Militias, *Edinb.*, 1698, 12mo.

Florio (J.).—*See* Montaigne.

Folengo (T.) Orlandino per Limerno Pitocco da Mantua composto, woodcuts, 8vo, *Venet. G. De Gregori*, 1526. A good copy, £2 10s.

Fontenelle (Louis De) Hippocrate dépaysé, ou la Version paraphrasée de ses aphorismes en vers Français par L. de F., 4to, *Paris*, 1654. 10s. 6d.

Forbes (Archibald) War Correspondence of the "Daily News," (Franco-German War), 2 vols., 1871. Also a reprint in 1 volume, same year.

Force (Madlle. Caumons de la) Les Fees, Contes des Contes par Mademoiselle de ***, curious copper plates, sm. 8vo, *Paris*, 1707. Fifteen shillings. Very rare, and ascribed by Barbier (Vol. 2, p. 11) to above author.

Ford (Chas.) London's Resurrection, poetically represented, &c., sm. 4to, 1669. An uncommon "Restoration" item.

Ford (E.) The most famous, delectable, and pleasant History of Parisinus, Prince of Bohemia, 2 parts, each should have old woodcut frontispiece, 4to, 1677 or 1687. An exceedingly rare item, and a good perfect copy is worth at least £2 2s. A notice of this book will be found in the preface to Southey's "Amadis of Gaul."

Foreign Bishop (A.).—*See* Legh (George).

Forester (Frank).—*See* Herbert (H. W.).

Forester (The).—*See* Roberts (Sir R.).

Forrester (A. H.) Der Freischutz Traveste. First edn., roy. 8vo, *Baldwyn*. 1824. Contains 12 etchings by G. Cruikshank, from drawings by An Amateur (A. Crowquill). Perhaps the rarest of all his works. 15s. or more.—(Crowquill) Absurdities in Prose and Verse, 13 coloured plates by the Author, post 8vo, *Hurst*, 1827. First edition. Very scarce. A good copy (with the 13 coloured plates), 30s.—The Sea-Pie; an Omnium Gatherum of Literature and Art, 15 full page plates and numerous cuts by A. Crowquill, 8vo, *Simpkin*, N.D., (1839). First edn., 7s. 6d.—Guide to the Watering Places, 8 full page plates by A. C. First edn., 8vo., wrappers, *Harwood*, S.D., (c. 1837). 7s. 6d.—Nothing to wear, an Episode of Fashionable Life, post 8vo, covers designed by A. C., 1857. Nominal Value.—Dr. Syntax in search of the Picturesque, well illustrated by A. C., p. 8vo, *Ackermann*, 1844. Scarce, Five or Six Shillings.—Leaves from the Memorandum Book of Alfred Crowquill, consisting of 4 parts, oblong 4to, 16 plates containing over 100 designs, *Smith Elder*, 1834-5. Very scarce indeed. Three guineas if clean.—The Vauxhall Papers, (edited by Alfd. Bunn), comical illusts. by Alf. Crowquill, 12mo, 1841. Rare. This was a Daily Journal pubd. at the Roy. Gdns., Vauxhall.

Only 16 of these Nos. appeared. In original state as issued, 10s. 6d.—The Tutor's Assistant, or Comic Figures of Arithmetic, slightly altered and elucidated, from Walking-game, many humourous illustrations by Alf. Crowquill, cr. 8vo, 1843. 10s.—Sketches of Pumps, Handled by R. Cruikshank, with Temperate Spouting by A. Crowquill, 9 illusts. by R. C., 8vo, *Bogue*, 1846. Rare, 15s.—The Wanderings of a Pen and Pencil, by S. P. Palmer and A. Crowquill, illustrated, roy. 8vo, 1846. First edition. 10s. 6d.—Shadow and Substance, by C. H. Bennett and R. H. Brough (of Sir J. Falstaff fame), 30 engravings by Alf. Crowquill, 8vo, 1860. 7s. 6d.—Miss Corner's Cinderella, and Beauty and the Beast, 1854, are both illustrated by Crowquill. Nominal value ; as is Mackenzie's (K. R. H.) Master Tyll Owlglass, 1869.—Surprising Adventures of the Venerable Gooroo Simple and his Five Disciples, coloured frontis. and 50 illustrations by Alfred Crowquill, cr. 8vo, 1881. Publd. at 10s. 6d.—Gold, a Legendary Rhyme, with 12 splendid outline plates (in Alfred Crowquill's happiest style), oblong 4to, N.D. 5s.—Good copies of any of these may be obtained from Mr. W. T. Spencer, of 27, New Oxford St., W.C.

Forsyth (J. S) Demonologia. or Natural Knowledge revealed, folding frontispiece, 8vo, 1827. Rare, 10s. 6d.

Foster (Frank).—*See* Puseley (David).

Foster (W.) Oughtred's (W.) Circles of Proportion, the Horizontal instrument, &c., transl. by W. F., revised and corrected by A. H[aughton], engravings, fcp. 8vo, *Oxford*, 1660.

Fouque (De La Motte) Undine, A Romance, transl. from the German, by G. SOANE, fcp. 8vo, 1818. First edn. of the First English Translation. Scarce, 7s. 6d.

Fox (C. J.) Man in the Moon, or Travels into the Lunar Regions by the Man of the People, 2 vols , sm. 8vo, 1783. A bitter satire against C. J. Fox ; who was evidently not liked by the " Man of the People" (Who ?)

Fox (Geo.) A Battledoor for Teachers and Professors to learn Plural and Singular, sm. 8vo, 1660. Very rare.

Fox (W. J., *M.P.*) The Three Estates, or Household Suffrage in relation to Capital and Labour, by Publicola, thin 8vo, 1880.

F. R.—*See* Raoul (Mademoiselle).

Fraxi (Pisanus).—*See* Ashbee (H. S.).

French (Dr. Nicholas) The Bleeding Iphigenia : an excellent Preface of a Work unfinished, published by the Author's Friend, &c.. Original edition, undated but *circa* 1650 ; there exists a limited reprint. Dr. French was a famous Politician and Prelate.

Frere (J. Hookham) The Monks and the Giants ; prospectus and specimen of an intended National Work, by W. & R. Whistlecraft, fcp. 8vo, 1821. Rare, 10s. 6d.

Frere (Mary) Love's Triumph, 12mo, 1869. A Play, one of Pickering's charming productions.

Froude (J. A.) Shadows of the Clouds, by Zeta, fcp. 8vo, 1847. Formerly catalogued for 21s., now about 10s.

Fry (John, *of Bristol*) Bibliographical Memoranda in illustration of Early English Literature, 4to, *Bristol*, 1816. Privately Printed. 21s. or more.

Fryer (Michael, *Schoolmaster*) Trial and Life of Eugene Aram, with several of his Letters and Poems, and copious notes, med. 8vo, *Richmond (Yorks.)*, 1832.

Fudge Family in Paris and Edinburgh.—*See* Moore (T).

Fulke (W.) A Plain Description of all kinds of Meteors as well Fiery and Ayrie, as Watery and Earthy; by W. F., 12mo, 1655. Curious, but of little value.

Fullarton (John, *of Careltoun*). The Turtle Dove (an Emblem of the New Creature), under the Absence and Presence of her only Choise, or Desertion and Deliverance revived, ushered with the Nicodemian Paradox, seconded with a Survey of the First and Second Death, with a Glimring of the First and Second Resurrection and Generall Judgement, and closing with a Song of Degrees ; by a Lover of the Celestiall Muses, fcp. 8vo, *Edinb* , *A. Anderson*, (1664). Of the greatest rarity. Five guineas at least.

Fuller (Hiram) The Flag of Truce, by A White Republican, cr. 8vo, 52 pp., 1862. Nominal value.

Fuller (Dr T.) Ephemeris Parliamentaria, a faithfull Register of Parliamentary Transactions in the 3rd and 4th years of K. Charles, &c., &c., sm. folio, 1654. 10s. 6d.

G. A.—*See* Gilby (A).

Gall (W. M. W.) Reverberations, Poems. First edn., sm. 8vo, 1849. Scarce. 5s. Contains 9 Poems, including " The People's Petition," and " The Enfranchised Labourer." The author, who published anonymously, appears to have been a Christian Socialist.

Galt (John) The Steam Boat, by the author of " Annals of the Parish," cr. 8vo, 1822.—The Member an Autobiography, by the author of the " Ayrshire Legatees" and " Annals of the Parish," p 8vo, 1832. First editions of this author's works, uncut, are not common.

Garth (Sir Samuel) The Dispensary, a Poem, 8vo, 1706. Another e lition, fcp. 8vo, 1726. The last named has plates.

Gaspey (T.) Richmond, Scenes in the Life of a Bow Street Officer, 3 vols., cr. 8vo, 1827.

Gaston (Rev. Hugh) Common-Place Book, or Companion to the O. & N. Testaments, ed. by J. Strutt, 8vo, 1813. The best edition is that of 1824.

Gataker (T.) Wegelini Sangallenses (B.) De Obedientia Christi perfecta legi divinæ nostro loco præstita, &c., disputatio cum Theologi Angli cujusdam in eandem stricturis, fcp. 8vo, 1653.

Gauden (Dr. J., *of Mayfield*) Eikon Basilike, the Portraicture of His Majesty (Charles I.) in his sufferings, &c., sm. 8vo, 164-. This work, the FIRST EDITION of which is highly prized, is generally attributed to Dr. Gauden.—Portraicture of his Sacred Majestie in his Solitude and Sufferings, 1648, post 8vo, 1824. Rivington's reprint, with a portrait.—Eikon Basilike, &c., 8vo, 1876.—Eikon Basilike, reprinted from the edn. of 1648, cr. 8vo, 1880. With facsimile frontispiece.

Gay. Bibliographie des Ouvrages relatifs à l'Amour, aux Femmes, au Mariage, contenant les titres detailles, les noms des auteurs, un aperçu de leur sujet, leur valeur et leur prix dans les ventes, thk. 8vo, *Paris*, 1864. About 10s. The reissue, extended into 6 volumes, published in 1871, has superseded the 1864 issue; and forms the most valuable Epitome of the Erotic Literature of all Countries extant. Present value about £2 5s.

Gent (Thomas) History of St. Peter's Cathedral, York, folding copper plates. 2 vols., 12mo, *York*, 1768. Another edition, also with plates, 12mo, *Ib* , 1790

Gentleman (A.).—*See* Bedford (H.).

Gentleman (A).—*See* Church (E.).

Gentleman (A).—*See* Copley (Lionel).

Gentleman (A).—*See* Defoe (D.).

Gentleman of the Univ. of Oxford (A).—*See* Shelley (P. B.).

Gentleman (A).—*See* Wallace (J.).

Geoffry Wildgoose (Mr.).—*See* Graves (R.).

Gertrude.—*See* Sewell (E. M.).

Gilbert (W. S.) The Bab Ballads, and More Bab Ballads. Both illust. by the Author. First editions. 2 vols., cr. 8vo, CLOTH, 1869, &c., worth in good condition two guineas or more; having become very scarce.

Gilby (A.) An Answer to the Devilish Detection of Bp. S. Gardiner, &c., sm. 8vo, 1547. Printed in 𝔅lack 𝔏etter, and very rare, selling at 30s. or more to-day.

Gildon (C.) Heliodorus, Adventures of Theagenes and Chariclia intermixed with other Histories, 2 vols., 1717. An exceedingly rare *Erotic* item.

Gillmore (Capt. Parker) Accessible Field Sports, by Ubique, 2 *plates*, p. 8vo, 1869.

Gimcrack (G.).—*See* Gregson (J. S.).

Giraldin (M. de) Promenade, ou Itinéraire des Jardins d'Ermenoville, 24 fine views, 8vo, *Paris*, 1788. 25s.

Glanville (J., *of Witchcraft fame*) A Seasonable Recommendation and Defence of Reason in the Affairs of Religion against Infidelity, Scepticism and Fanaticisms of all sorts, 4to, 1670. First edition. —Lux Orientalis : An Enquiry into the Opinion of Eastern Sages and Rustt's Discourse of Truth, post 8vo, 1682. Should have frontispiece.

Glasse (Mrs. H.) The Art of Cookery made Plain and Easy, which far exceeds any Thing of the Kind yet published, folio, 1747. First edition, and rare. About £5—£6. G. A. Sala's copy sold for £10.—The Art of Cookery made Plain and Easy, which far exceeds anything of the kind yet published, by A Lady, 8vo, 1767. 5s.— The Art of Cookery made Plain and Easy, with 150 new recipes and Index ; by a Lady, 8vo, 1770. 7s. 6d. The 8vo edn. of 1767 is considered the rarest in this size ; and has facsim. autograph on title.

Glazebrook (Mr.) On the practice of what is called "Extempore Preaching" recommended from Scripture, &c., 126 pp , 8vo, *Warrington*, 1794.

Gleig (Rev. G. R.) The Campaigns of the British Army at Washington and New Orleans, 1814-15, by the Author of "The Subaltern," post 8vo, 1836.—Chelsea Hospital and its Traditions, 3 vols., cr. 8vo, 1838. 7s. 6d —Chelsea Hospital and its Traditions, by the author of "The Subaltern," portrait, post 8vo, 1839. 5s.— Life of Warren Hastings, 3 vols., 8vo, 1841. Catalogues at 5s.

Glover (Robt.) Nobilitas Politica vel Civilis, *with plates*, fol., 1608.

Goadby (Mr., *of Selborne*) Illustration of the Holy Scriptures by Notes and Explications on the O. & N. Testaments, 3 vols., folio, 1759 *et seq.*

Godefroy's (Denis) Memoires et Instructions pour servir dans les Negociations et Affairs concernant les Droits du Roy de France, folio, *Paris*, 1665.

Godwin (W.) Cursory Strictures on the Charge delivered by Ld. Chief Justice Eyre to the Grand Jury, Oct. 2nd, 1794, 8vo. First edn , 1794. Of trifling value, though sometimes catalogued at a rather high figure —The Pantheon, with 12 plates by W. Blake, post 8vo, 1806. First Impressions, and rare. Worth 15s.—Cloudesley : a Tale, by the Author of "Caleb Williams," 3 vols., 8vo, 1830. First edition. 10s. 6d.

Godwin (Mrs., *wife of W. Godwin*) A Picture of the new Town of Herne Bay, including particulars of the Roman Town Reculver, by a Lady, map, folding aquatint front. and many engravings, post 8vo, *Macrone*, 1835. Excessively scarce, 7s. 6d.

Goldsmith (O) Life of Richard Nash, Esq., of Bath. 1st edn., 8vo, 1762. Rare, and worth £1, if it contains the portrait, which is generally absent.—Plutarch's Lives abridged, 7 vols., post 8vo, plates, 1762-90. Very rare Three guineas if clean and perfect.— The Vicar of Wakefield, supposed to have been written by Himself,

2 vols., post 8vo, *Salisbury*, 1766. The second edition, (printed for Newbery) was issued the same year, and with the exception of "Printed at Salisbury" on title is identical with the First issue. The second edn. is now worth about £5 5s.; whilst the first realizes ten times this sum.

Gompertz (J.) The Modern Antique, or the Muse in the Costume of Queen Anne, roy. 8vo, 1818. Very few copies Privately Printed, and not Published. This is sometimes catalogued as Large Paper, but I have never seen a smaller size.

Goodby (Robt.) Apology for the Life of Bampfylde Moore Carew, King of the Beggars, sm. 8vo, 1768. Editions of Carew's Life pubd. by J. Barker, *s. d.*, are not by above author, but by T. Price. There is also an anonymous work: "Surprising Adventures of B. M. Carew," sm. 8vo, *Tiverton*, 1812, with portrait and plates.

Goodwin (J.) The Youngling Elder; 1st edn., *c.* 1647. There is an answer to this: "The Blind Guide, or Doting Doctor," 4to, 1648. Both are of trifling account.

Gordon. The Independent Whig. A Defence of Primitive Christianity, &c., 4 vols., fcp. 8vo, 1762.

Gore (Mrs. C. J.) Agathonia, a Romance, 12mo, *Moxon*, 1844. Rather scarce.

Gozzi (G.) Longus. Gli Amori Pastorali di Dafni e Cloe, 2 ports. of the Barziza, and charming vignettes, sm. 4to, 1766. A very scarce Italian edition. Worth 10s.

G. R.—*See* Greene (Robt.).

Grant (James, *Editor of the "Morning Chronicle"*) Random Recollections of the House of Commons, by One of no Party. 8vo, 1836. Includes personal sketches of Cobbett, O'Connell, and Peel. The companion volume on the House of Lords, is by the same author.—Travels in Town, 2 vols., 1839 Chatty and amusing, but very trifling in value.—Portraits of Public Characters, by the Author of "Random Recollections of the Lords and Commons," 2 vols., cr. 8vo, 1841.—Lights and Shadows of London Life, 2 vols., med. 8vo, 1842. An amusing account of Life amongst the lower London orders.—Pictures of Popular People, by the author of "The Great Metropolis," 24 full-p. plates by Gilbert. Imp. 8vo, *Virtue, s. d.* 10s.

Grattan (T C.) Highways and Byways; or Tales of the Roadside, picked up in the French Provinces, by a Walking Gentleman, 2 vols., fcp. 8vo, 1823.

Graves (Rev. R , *of Claverton*) The Spiritual Quixote, or Summer's Ramble of Mr. Geoffrey Wildgoose, a Comic Romance, frontispieces by Grignion. 3 vols., fcp. 8vo, 1792. About 6s.—The Spiritual Quixote, fcp. 8vo, 1816.—Euphrosyne, or Amusements on the Road of Life, (Poems) by the author of "The Spiritual Quixote," sm. 8vo, *London*, 1776.—Columella, or the distressed

Anchorite, a Colloquial Tale, by the Editor of "The Spiritual Quixote," 2 vols., fcp. 8vo, 1779. Should have frontispiece.—Lucubrations: consisting of Essays, Reveries, &c., in Prose and Verse, by the late Peter, of Pontefract, fcp. 8vo, 1786.

Green (Robt.) Alcida: Greenes Metamorphosis, wherein is discovered a pleasant Transformation of Bodies into sundrie shapes, &c., 4to, 1617. Printed in 𝔅lack 𝔏etter. Griffith in his Bibl. Anglo-Poetica prices this curious work at £7 7s.; and it would probably sell at about 3 guineas now.

Green (Robt.) and **Lodge** (Thomas) Lady Alimony, or the Alimony Lady, an excellent new Comedy, duly authorized, daily acted, and frequently followed, sm. 4to, 1659. Rare, 25s.

Greenwood (A. B.) Prize Essay on National Education. 8vo, 1868.

Gregson (J. S.) Gimcrackiana, or Fugitive Pieces on Manchester Men and Manners, vignettes, p. 8vo, *Manchester*, 1833.—A Code of Common Sense; or Patent Pocket Dictionary, by G. Gimcrack, Esq. *Ib.* Both rare. Market value, 7s. 6d. each.

Grenewey (Richd.) The Annales of Cornelius Tacitus, The Description of Germanie, 8vo, 1598.

Grenville-Murray (E. C.) Embassies and Foreign Courts, a History of Diplomacy, post 8vo, 1855.—Pictures from the Battlefield, by the Roving Englishman, 8 *illusts.*, post 8vo, 1856.—People I have met. 54 *tinted plates by F. Barnard.* Imp. 8vo, *Vizetelly*, N.D.

Greswell (Rev. W. Parr) The Monastery of St. Werburgh, A Poem. 8vo, 1823. Anonymous and Privately Printed. 10s. 6d.

Greville (C. C.) Past and Present Policy of England towards Ireland, thk. sm. 8vo. *Moxon*, 1845.

Griffin (Gregory). —*See* Canning (George).

Griffith (A. F.) Bibliotheca Anglo-Poetica, roy. 8vo, 1815. Though, of course, no reliance can be placed to-day on the prices given, still this work (which is really a Catalogue of Messrs. Park & Hill's collection) must always remain a most valuable account of our Early Poets. Sells at about 25s.

Grimm (The Brothers) Popular German Stories, *illus. by G. Cruikshank.* 2 vols. Copies of the original edn. in *boards uncut*, are exceedingly valuable. Another edn. edited by Edgar Taylor, *with all the above spirited plates*, and Intro. by J. Ruskin, thk. cr. 8vo. *Hotten*, N.D. About 7s. 6d.

Grindon (L. H.) Joseph Sidebotham, a Memoir, portrait and photo illustrations, p. 8vo. *Manchester*, 1886. Very few copies Privately Printed.

Gringore (P.) La Quenolle Spirituelle. 23 pp., sm. 8vo, issued without date or place of publication. Printed in 𝔊othic 𝔏etter. Very curious, being a Dialogue between Jesus Christ and a young woman. Composed by Jehan de Lacu, *Canon of Lisle*, and put into verse by P. Gringore. £5.

Grose (Francis, *The Antiquary*) Classical Dictionary of the Vulgar Tongue. 2 vols., 8vo, 1796. 10s. 6d.

Grotius (Hugo) Emblems of Love, Verses in Dutch. 24 circular plates, oblong 8vo, 1656. The plates are curious. Six shillings or more.

Group (The) composed of the most Shocking Figures, though the greatest in the Nation, &c., 4to, 1763. I have been unable to discover the real author of this atrocious Satire, which is directed principally against the E. of Bute.

Guates (M. L'Abbé, Comte de ; *Chanoin de Tournay*) De l'Usage des Statues chez les Anciens, Essai Historique, thk. 4to. *Bruxelles*, 1768. Should have 12 very fine plates. 15s.

Guillim (J.).—*See* Barkham (J.).

Guion (Madame, *the Quietist*) La Theologie du Coeur. Three parts (in 1 vol.) with engraved title, thk. 12mo. *Cologne*, 1697.

Gurdon (Thom., *of Letton*) Essay on the Antiquity of the Castel of Norwich, &c., 8vo. *Norwich*, 1728. This volume was reprinted in 1834.

Gutch (John) Collectanea Curiosa, or Miscellaneous Tracts relating to the History of England, Ireland, &c. 2 vols., 8vo. *Oxford*, 1781. 5s.

G. W.—*See* Whitehead (Geo.).

H.—*See* Halpin (Chas. G.).

Haddington (E. of) Poems on several Occasions, by the Earl of Ha——ton, fcp. 8vo, 1757. Printed for Private Circulation only, and of the greatest rarity. £5.

Haines (J.) History of the Constitution of the Duchy of Cornwall, and its Tenants from 1622. 8vo, 1834. Very scarce.

Halbed (N. H.) and **Sheridan** (R. B.) The Love Epistles of Aristænetus, transl. into English Metre, sm. 8vo, 1781. 6s.

Haldane (Patrick) The Law and Judicatures of Scotland vindicated, post 8vo, 1718.

Haliburton (Dr.) Memoirs of that celebrated Pulpit Hero Mas-John Magopico, with Anecdotes of his Friend Plumbino, 4to, *Edinb.*, 1810. 5s.

Haliburton (Judge, "*Sam Slick*") The Old Judge, or Life in a Colony, 2 vols., cr. 8vo, 1849. First collected edition.—Wise Saws and Modern instances; or Tales of Travellers, 2 vols., 1852. First edition.—Nature and Human Nature, 2 vols., cr. 8vo, 1855. First English edition.—This humourist's works are too well known for more detailed mention to be necessary, it may be noticed however that the best edition of his "Clockmaker" is in 3 vols., with fine plates by Leech, &c.

Hall (John, *of Durham*) An Humble Motion to the Parliament of England concerning the Advancement of Learning and Reformation of the Universities, 4to. *J. Walker*, 1649. 15s.

Hall (Capt. Byng) Lucullus, or Palatable Essays in which are merged "The Oyster," "The Lobster," and "Sport and its Pleasures," by the author of "The Bric-a-Brac Hunter," 2 vols., cr. 8vo, 1878.

Halliwell (J. O.) The Archæologist; ed. by J. O. Halliwell and T. Wright, 8vo, 1841-2. A complete set comprises 10 numbers. Market value, 10s.

Halpin (Chas. G.) Lyrics by the Letter H, *i e.* C. G. Halpin, "Miles O'Reilly," fcp. 8vo, *N.Y.*, 1854. First edn.

Hamilton (Chas.) Metastasio (Pietro) The Patriot : a Tragedy (trans. by C. Hamilton), 8vo, [1784].

Hamilton (Lady Emma) Marriage Rites, Customs, and Ceremonies of the World (by the celebrated Mistress of Lord Nelson), frontispiece, 8vo, 1824. Very scarce, 21s.

Hamilton (Capt. T.) Men and Manners in America, 2 vols., cr. 8vo, 1833.

Hammond (W.) Love Elegies (occasioned by Miss Dashwood), First edn., 4to, 1760. Often reprinted.

Hamst (Olphar).—*See* Thomas (R.).

Hanson (Sir Levett, *Kt.*) An Accurate Historical Account of all Orders of Knighthood at Present existing in Europe, by an Officer of Chancery of the Order of S. Joachim, 2 vols., 8vo, *Hamburgh Printed,* 1802. Rare, 21s. This work, printed abroad, though nominally going under the name of J. P. Buhl, was really written by above gent.

Harbin (Geo.) Hereditary Right of the Crown of England asserted, &c., and the English Constitution vindicated, folio, 1713. Also attributed to H. Bedford, who suffered three years' imprisonment for the supposed authorship, *vide* Bedford, *ante.*

Hardcastle (Ephraim).—*See* Pyne (W. H.).

Hardinge (Geo.) The Essence of Malone, or "Beauties" of that fascinating writer, extracted from his Immortal Work, entitled Some Account of the Life and Writings of John Dryden, 1800.—Another Essence of Malone, or Beauties of Shakespeare's Editor, 1801.— Another Essence of Malone, second part, 1801. All violent attacks.

Hardy (W., *of Wirksworth*) Miner's Guide, or Compleat Miner, with Articles and Customs of the High Peak, &c., &c., 200 pp., 8vo, *Birmingham,* 1762. Very rare. Not mentioned in Lowndes, or any other Bibliographical work with which I am acquainted.

Hare (The Brothers, A. W. & J. C.) Guesses at Truth, 2 vols., post 8vo, 1827.—Guesses at Truth, 2 vols., 1838, &c.—Guesses at Truth, portraits, post 8vo, 1866.—Guesses at Truth, by Two Brothers, *ports.*, fcp. 8vo, 1871.—Guesses at Truth, by Two Brothers. Both series, sm. 8vo, 1878.

Harland (J.) The Ancient Parish Church of Eccles, its Antiquity, Alterations, and Improvements, 8vo, *Eccles*, 1864. 7s. 6d

Harpsfield (N.) Dialogi sex contra Pontificetus Monasticæ vita Sanctorum, Socrarum Imaginum oppugnatores et pseudo martyrs, &c., ab Almo copo, thk 4to, 1566. A fine specimen of the Plantin Press. Should have a large folding plate, usually absent. If containing this, 21s.

Harrington (Jas.) The Commonwealth of Oceana, folio, 1656. First edition, and highly spoken of by Hume. About 10s.

Harvey (W.) Exercitatio Anatomica de Motu Cordis en Sanguinis in Animalibus, with portrait. 1st edn. *Francof.*, 1628. Present market value £20 or more. There was a small reissue, Privately Printed at the expense of G. Moreton, Esq , of Canterbury, in 1894, which is at the time of writing a "remainder" at about 3s. 6d. Though the original is not strictly speaking " anonymous " it has been included in this volume, on account of its insignificant appearance, the uninitiated buyer would probably refuse it at half a sovereign. I have only seen one copy during 15 years' experience as a cataloguer.—I have also seen an edition : " Harveii (Guil.) Exercitationes de Motu Cordis et Sanguinis, curavit T. Hingston, 8vo, 1824 ; worth about 5s.

Hatcher (H.) Richard of Cirencester, the Description of Britain, &c., *maps and facsim.*, 8vo, 1809. About 6s.

Hatton (Edward) New View of London, being a particular Account of the Streets and their Inhabitants. &c., 2 vols., cr. 8vo, 1708. Valued for the 2 old plans, and plates of Arms of the Town and City Companies. The 2 plans are often wanting. A good copy is worth 15s.

Hawarden (Dr.) Charity and Truth, or Catholicks not Uncharitable in saying that none are saved out of the Catholic Communion, by H. E., 8vo, *s. l* , 1728.

Hawker (R. S.) Tendrils, by Reuben (*i.e.*, R. S. Hawker), sm. 8vo, *Cheltenham*, 1821.

Hawkins (Sir C.) Address to the Gentlemen of Cornwall on the present state of Mining in that County, &c., 8vo, 1772. 7s. 6d. Privately Printed in addition to being anonymous.

Hawkins (Sir J.) Probationary Odes for the Laureateship, and criticisms on the Rolliad, 8vo, 1785. These scurrilous publications are generally found together.

Hayward (I.) Lives of the III Normans &c., by H. J., 4to, 1613. About 15s.

Hayward (Sir John) First Part of the Life and Raigne of King Henrie III., &c , sm. 4to, 1599. A rare item, and if with the frontis., (port. of Henry III.), 10s. 6d. Allibone gives a good account of this work, and the offence it caused to Q. Elizabeth.

Hayward (Mrs. Eliza) The Secret History of the Present Intrigues of the Court of Caramania, med. 8vo, 1827. A scandalous publication, "erotic" in every sense of the word. For writing this work, "Pope promoted the authoress to a situation in the Dunciad," according to Drake. A full key to the Characters (all Court Celebrities) is given in Lowndes. Rare, 15s. or more.

Hazlitt (William) Liber Amoris; or the New Pygmalion, vign. port. on title (of S.W.), sm. 8vo, 1823. First edition, and excessively rare, 30s. Reprinted in facsim., 1893, 10s. 6d. There is also a limited private Edition de Luxe of this erotic account of Hazlitt's amours with the servant girl Sarah Walker, with additional matter and Preface by R. Le Gallienne (Gallon), 1894; which is of about the same value as the First edition.—British Galleries of Art, including Matthews's Theatrical Gallery (2 Parts), post 8vo, 1824. Perhaps the rarest of Hazlitt's anonymous works. 15s.

H. B — *See* Doyle (John).

H. E — *See* Hawarden (Dr.).

Head Sir F. B.) Bubbles from the Brunnens of Nassau, by an Old Man, plates on India Paper, post 8vo, 1834. First edition.— Stokers and Pokers, The L. & N. W. Ry., Electric Telegraph, and Railway Clearing House, cr. 8vo, 1849.—A Faggot of French Sticks, 2 vols., med. 8vo, 1852.

Head (R.) The English Rogue, or Life of Jeremy Sharp; with Alphabetical Vocabulary of Gypsies' Cant, to which is added a Narrative of Mary Toft, of an Extraordinary Delivery of 18 Rabbits, performed by Mr. J. Howard, Surgeon, at Guildford, in 1726, 3 vols., sm. 8vo, 1776. Very rare. Catalogues at 25s., and upwards. I have only seen the one copy.

Healey (J.) St. Augustine of the Citie of God, with the Learned of Vives, Englished by J. H., folio, 1610. A good copy, 15s.

Heath (Benj.) A Revisal of Shakespear's Text, wherein the Alterations introduced by Critics are considered, 1765.

Heath (Jas.) Flagellum; or Life and Death of Oliver Cromwell, sm. 8vo, 1669. This is the 4th edn., and only one copy has ever come under my notice.

Heathcote (Ralph) Sylva, or the Wood, A Collection of Anecdotes, Dissertations, Characters, &c., by a Society of the Learned, 8vo, 1786. First edn., 7s. 6d. Another edn., 8vo, 1788.

Helps (Sir A.) The Claims of Labour, an Essay on the Duties of Employers, sm. 8vo, *Pickering*, 1844. First edn.—Companions of my Solitude, fcp. 8vo, *Pickering*, 1851. Second and third edns., 1852. Fourth edn., post 8vo, *Parker*, 1854.—Friends in Council, 2 vols, *Pickering*, 1851. Sells slowly at about 7s. 6d —Organization in Daily Life, med. 8vo, 1862. First edn —Realmah, by the author of "Friends in Council," 2 vols., post 8vo, 1868.— The Rector and his Friends; Dialogues on some of the leading Religious questions of the Day, cr. 8vo, 1869.—Casimir Maremma, 2 vols., cr. 8vo, 1870. First edition. Scarce, 7s. 6d.

Henderson (A.) Life of John, E. of Stair, with Account of the three Rebellions between 1715-45, &c., post 8vo, 1747. Very scarce. Sells at 10s. 6d. or more.

Herbert (H. W.) Fish and Fishing of the U.S.A. and British Provinces of N. America, by Frank Forester, cuts, 8vo, 1849.—Life of Frank Forester (H. W. Herbert), edited by Judd, portrait and plates, 2 vols., cr. 8vo, pubd. at 15s.

Hermit of Marlow (The).—*See* Shelley (P. B.).

Heron (Robert).—*See* Pinkerton (John).

Hett (Rev. Mr.) The York Musical Festival, a Dialogue, 60 pp., *with engraved vignettes*, 4to, *J. Bohn*, 1825. 10s.

Hewlett (J.) Peter Priggins; pubd. anonymously. This author also published College Life, or the Proctor's Note-Book, 3 vols., in 1843, a few years after " Peter Priggins " appeared.

Heylyn (Peter) Microcosmus, or a Little Description of the Great World, a Treatise Historicall, Geographicall, Politicall, Theological (including America), by P. H., 4to, *Oxford, J. Lichfield*, 1622. 7s 6d.—Observations on the Historie of the Reign of King Charles. published by H. L——, Esq., portrait, sm. 8vo, 1656. 7s. 6d.

Heywood (John) A merry Play between Johan Johan, the Husband, Tyb, his Wyfe, and Sir Jhan, the Priest. *Imprinted by W. Rastell*, 1533. Of this exceedingly rare and curious item an excellent reprint was issued from the Chiswick Press, about 1818.

Heywood (Thos.) The Life of Merlin, surnamed Ambrosius. his Prophecies and Predictions, &c., 8vo, 1813. Ed. by T. Heywood, pp. 324.

H. I.—*See* Hayward (I.)

Hickes (Rev. G.) Ravillac Redivivus : A Narrative of the Tryal of J. Mitchell, a Conventicle Preacher, &c., also Trial of Major T. Weir (The Wizard), executed for Adultery. First edn., sm. 4to, 1678. Rare, and the second part very curious, 21s.

Hickman (H.) Bonasus Vapulans ; or some Castigations given to Mr. John Durrell for fouling himself and others in his English and Latin Book, sm. 8vo, 1672. Very rare.

Hieover (Harry).—*See* Brendley (Chas.).

Hierophilos.—*See* McHale (Dr.).

Higgins (John) Sermon taken out of an Oxford Scholar's Pocket, who was found dead in Bishop's Wood, near Highgate, &c., 4to, (with allowance), 1688.

Hillier (G.) Narrative of the attempted escape of Charles I. from Carisbrook Castle, including his Letters to Col. Titus, post 8vo, 1852. With a plan.

Hilman (D.). Ozanam (J.) Introduction to the Mathematics of; done out of the French (by D. Hilman), fcp. 8vo, 1711.

H. J.—*See* Hall (John).

H. J.—*See* Howell (James).

H. N.—*See* Hookes (N.).

Hogg (Cervantes).—*See* Barrett (E. S.).

Hogg (James).—*See* Brown (James).

Holdsworth, Muscipula (by Dr. E. Holdsworth), 8vo, 1709. Original edn., and should have curious frontispiece.—Hoglandiæ descriptio, 8vo, 1709

Hole (Dean) A Little Tour in Ireland. by an Oxonian, 35 sketches by J. Leech, besides large folding coloured frontis. (generally absent), sq. cr. 8vo, 1859. First edn. A good complete copy is worth 15 to 21 shillings.—There also exists a reprint, with all the engravings and folding coloured frontispiece, pubd. 1892. Large Paper, 15s. Small, 7s. 6d.

Holley (Marietta) Poems by Josiah Allen's wife, with illusts by Gibson, sq. fcp. 8vo, 1887. Pubd. at 8s.

Hollingshead (Rev. N. J.) Defence of the Soc. of Sons of the Clergy, &c., 8vo, *Newcastle*, 1812.

Hollingsworth (Rev. Richard) Vindiciæ Carolinæ: or Defence of Eikon Basilike in Reply to Milton's Eikonoklastes, post 8vo, *L. Meredith*, 1692. With portrait of Charles I. by R. White, 10s. Also attributed to John Wilson, author of a Treatise on Necromancy.

Hollinworth (Rev. R.) The Holy Ghost on the Bench, other Spirits at the Barre, sm. 8vo, 1657. Curious and very rare, 10s.

Holmes (Richd.) History of Keighley, past and present, &c., frontispiece, post 8vo, 1858. Contains Accounts of many local Families.

Holt (Dorothy) Address to the Ladies of Great Britain. relating to the most valuable part of Ornamental Manufacture in their Dress, 8vo, 1757.

Holyday (Barten) Comes Facundus in Via: The Fellow Travellei through City and Country, 12mo, 1658. A scarce little anonymous item of Facetiæ, 15s. *See* Wood's Athen. Oxon. There is a quaint allusion to the author at the end of the first advt. to the Reader.

Home (Cecil).—*See* Davis (Augusta).

Home (Henry) Loose Hints upon Education, *Edinb.*, 1782.

Homer.—*See* Blackwell (T.).

Homunculus.—*See* Thackeray (W. M).

Hook (Theodore) John Bull, ed. by this Gent., Vols. 1—3, large folio, 1823. Only worth a few shillings —Personal Narrative of a Journey overland from the Bank to Barnes, by way of Piccadilly, Knightsbridge, &c., with Account of the Inhabitants and Customs of regions E. of Kensington, by an Inside Passenger; also Model for a Magazine, post 8vo, 1829. Excessively rare. Only one copy has passed through my hands. That was uncut! and sold immediately for 10s. 6d.—Births, Marriages, and Deaths, by the Author of "Sayings and Doings," 3 vols., cr. 8vo, *Bentley*, 1839. First edition.—Tentamen, or Essay towards the History of Whittington, some time Lord Mayor of London, by Vicesimus Blenkinsop, portrait on title, sm. p. 8vo, 1820. First and only edn. of this bitter satire on Q. Caroline and Alderman Wood. The D. of Sussex is also roughly handled in the Dedication. Copies rarely occur. 10s.

Hookanit Bee.—*See* Wigram (S. R.).

Hooker (Bishop Richard) A Reproof to the Rehearsal Transposed (Andrew Marvell's work), sm. 8vo, 1673.

Hookes (N.) Amanda, a Sacrifice to an Unknown Goddesse, or a Free Will offering of a loving-Heart to a Sweet-Heart, post 8vo, *H. Tuckey*, 1653. Very rare, 5 guineas. A few copies have a frontispiece by Faithorne. These are worth more. Collation :— Title, Dedication, Commendatory Verses, &c. 11 leaves; 191 pp. (leaves G 5 and H 7 blank).

Hoole (C.) Comenii (Jo.) Orbis Sensualium Pictus, transl. from the Latin by above gent., *with about* 150 *curious vignettes*, 12mo, 1658. A good copy is worth 7s. 6d.

Hope (C.) Anastasius, or Memoirs of a Greek, 3 vols., post 8vo, 1820.

Hopkins (T.) Harold, a Tragedy, post 8vo, *Manchester*, 1843.

Horlock (J. K.) The Master of the Hounds, by "Scrutator," frontispiece, cr. 8vo, 1863.—Letters on the Management of Hounds, by "Scrutator," 8vo.

Horlock (D. W.) D.O.M. The Triune, or new Religion, by "Scrutator," 8vo, 1867.

Hornby (Chas.) A small specimen of the many mistakes in Sir W. Dugdale's Baronage, in 3 Letters, p. 8vo, 1730.

Horne (R. Hengist) Exposition of the False Medium and Barriers excluding Men of Genius from the Public, post 8vo, 1833. With frontispiece.—Orion, an Epic Poem, published at One Farthing. The original edition is very rare, especially in uncut state, and sells at 21s. or more. The *imprint* "One Farthing" appeared in the 2nd and 3rd edns., and a copy of the latter issue, *Miller*, 1843, *cut*, was catalogued at 10s. 6d. recently by a leading London Bookseller.—A New Spirit of the Age, 8 *portraits*, 2 vols., post 8vo, 1844. Undoubtedly his Best Work, and scarce. commands 30s. to-day. It consists of Short Biographies of notable Authors, including Carlyle, L. Hunt, Dickens, Wordsworth, Landor, and T. Barham (Ingoldsby).

Horsley. Hosea, transl. from the Hebrew, with Notes by Samuel [Horsley] Bp. of Rochester, 4to, 1801.

Houghton (Lord).—*See* Milnes (R. Monckton).

Hourd. God's Love to Mankind, 4to, 1633. This occasioned a reply: Davenant's Animadversions upon a Treatise entitled God's Love to Mankind, *Cambridge*, 1641.

Howard (Hy., *E. of Northampton*) A Defensative against the poyson of supposed Prophesies, 4to, 1583. Exceedingly rare, and valuable.

Howell (James) Observations upon Historie, 12mo, 1643.—England's Teares for the Present Wars, &c., 4to, 1644. Rare; and perfect copies should contain a fine portrait of the author, leaning against a tree.—Historie of the late Revolution in Naples, &c, by J. H., fcp. 8vo, 1650. Should have coloured frontispiece. A rare little volume, not mentioned by Lowndes. 7s. 6d.—Philanglus: Some sober inspections made into the Carriage and Consults of the late Long Parliament, &c., fcp. 8vo, 1658. This is the third and best impression, much enlarged.—Dendrologia. Dodona's Grove, or the Vocal Forrest, 1st edn., 1642?; 2nd edn., (the best), containing 2 extra Tracts, sm. 4to, 1644. Both Lowndes and Allibone appear to think that the *third*, with frontis and 2 folding plates, 1645, was the First issue, containing the two extra Tracts "Parables upon the Times," and "England's Teares"; but this is an error. According to Hallam, Harrington's "Oceana" was partly suggested by this work. Present market value of 2nd edn., 12 to 15 shillings.

Howgill (Francis) A Testimony concerning the Life, Death, Trials, Travels, and Labours of E. Burroughs, (Quaker), 4to, *Secretly Printed*, 1663. The subject of this Memoir, a celebrated Quaker, died in prison.

Huarte (J.).—*See* Carew (R.).

Hughes (Thos., *Q.C., M.P.*) The Scouring of the White Horse, or Long Vacation Ramble of a London Clerk, illusts. by "Dick" Doyle, sq. post 8vo, 1859. Original edition, 7s. 6d.

Hull (J., *D.D., B.N.*) The Invisible World discovered, &c., 12mo, 1652. Collation: Title, then Preface (first leaf paged 89-90) continues 91—365 (with two ll. of Contents). Lowndes does not mention it at all. Probably it is by J. Hull, D.D., Bishop of Norwich.

Hume (David) Essays, Moral and Political, fcp. 8vo, *Edinburgh*, 1741. The First edn.; issued anonymously.

Humourist Physician (A).—*See* Cobbold (Rev. R.).

Hunt (Leigh) Classic Tales, 2 vols., fcp. 8vo, 1806-7. First edition, about 10s. 6d.—The Reflector; a Collection of Essays, &c., written by the Editor of the *Examiner*, 2 vols., 8vo, 1810.—The Feast of the Poets, with Notes and other Pieces in Verse by the Editor of the *Examiner*, cr. 8vo, *Cawthorn*, 1814. First edition, 10s.— The Indicator, 2 vols., 1820-1. First edn. Originally pubd. in weekly numbers.—The Liberal, Verse and Prose from the South, 2 vols., 8vo, 1822. Generally bound in 1 vol., 7s. 6d., but more if in the orig. wrappers uncut.—The Companion, 29 Numbers, 8vo, 1828. 7s. 6d.—Christianism : or Belief and Unbelief reconciled, 8vo, (1832). Anonymous, and only 75 copies Privately Printed. The rarest of all this author's works. £4 to £5.—(Hunt (Leigh) and **Powell** (T.)) Florentine Tales with Modern Illustrations, post 8vo, 1847. Really a second edition of "Tales from Boccaccio," and of little value.—The Town ; its Memorable Characters and Events, Illustrated, 2 vols., med. 8vo, 1848. First edn., and if a nice, clean, uncut copy, 30s. or more.—The Religion of the Heart. A Manual of Faith and Duty, fcp. 8vo, 1853. First edition, 10s. 6d.

Hunter (Rev. Joseph, *of Bath*) Who wrote Cavendish's Life of Cardinal Wolsey ? roy. 8vo, 1814. 5s.

Hurdis (Dr.) The Village Curate, a Poem, 8vo, 1797. Privately Printed by the author (who is often called a disciple of Cowper) at his own Press at Bishopstone.

H. T.—*See* Hopkins (T.).

Iconoclast.—*See* Bradlaugh (C.).

Il Musannif.—*See* Mackenzie (Capt. C. F.).

Impartial Inquirer after Truth (An).—*See* Casway (R.).

Impartial Pen (An).—*See* Davies (J.).

Ingoldsby (Thos.).—*See* Barham (Rev. T.).

Innes (Cosmo) Concerning some Scotch Surnames, sm. 4to, 1860. About 5s.

Inside Passenger (An).—*See* Hook (T.).

I. R.—*See* Rhodes (John).

Iram. All sorts, containing Compositions in Verse, &c., by Iram, 12mo. Printed by the Author, at the Roy. Lunatic Asylum, 1856.

Ireland (J.) The Book-Lover's Enchiridion : Thoughts on the Solace and Companionship of Books, selected and arranged by PHILO-BIBLOS, 24mo, (dainty white cloth, r. e.), 1883. First edn., and very scarce, having been withdrawn, 10s. to 12s.—The Book Lover's Enchiridion. Another edn., cr. 8vo, 1883. About 5s. Large Paper copies have several illustrations not in the small ones. 12s. 6d. to 15s. if L. P.

Ireland (W. H.) Stultifera Navis; The Modern Ship of Fools, with curious cut on title by Austin, and very fine coloured frontispiece by Atkinson; much like Rowlandson, post 8vo, 1807. The frontispiece is nearly always missing, but if in the book, a copy is worth 7s. 6d.—The Fisher Boy, a Poem, comprising his several avocations during the four seasons of the Year, by H. C., engraved title, fcp. 8vo, 1808. 5s.— Scribbleomania, or the Printer's Devil's Polichronicon, a Sublime Poem, 8vo, 1815. This author is best known by his "Shakespeare Forgeries." Scribbleomania deals with leading writers of the day, including Dr. Wolcot, Scott, Byron, Wordsworth, &c. The notes are satirical.—Memoirs of Jeanne d'Arc, *port.*, *&c.*, 2 vols., 8vo, 1824. Rare and worth 35s. Large paper copies, roy. 8vo, with port. on India Paper, are rarer still and worth £2 10s.—Memoirs of Henry the Great, &c, 2 vols., 8vo, *Harding and Triphook*, 1824. These vols. should contain a portrait, and the Music of "Charmante Gabrielle." Value 7s. 6d. or thereabouts.

Irishman (A Bashful).—*See* Deacon (W. F.).

Iron (Ralph).—*See* Schreiner (Olive).

Irons (Rev. W. J.) The Preaching of Christ, &c., (Sermons), 8vo, 1858.

Irving (Washington) Salmagundi, Essay and Notes by J. Lambert, 2 vols., 12mo, 1811. First *English* edn., and rare. About 5s.— Bracebridge Hall, or the Humourists, 2 vols., post 8vo, 1822. First edn. Worth about 7s. 6d. Second edn., 1824, 2 vols. About 6s.—Letters of Jonathan Old Style, Gent., 8vo, 1824. Rare. Salmagundi, or Whim Whams, &c., of Launcelot Langstaffe, p. 8vo, 1824.—The Sketch Book of Geoffrey Crayon, Esq., with 2 plates by Leslie, 2 vols., fcp. 8vo, *Murray*, 1838. Also The History of New York, by Diedrich Knickerbocker, of which there are numerous edns., all too well known to need more than mere mention. This remark applies also to the "Sketch Book."

Isla (J. F. de) Historia del famoso predicador Fray Gerundio de Campanzas, *i.e.*, Zotes; escrita por el Licdo. Don Francisco de Salazar, 2 vols., 8vo, 1758-70. Rare, 21s. The first volume was surreptitiously printed, and the second did not appear till 12 years after its publication.—History of the Famous Preacher, Friar Gerund de Campazas, transl. from the Spanish, 2 vols., 8vo, 1772.

J. A.—*See* Astruc (Jean).

Jacob (G.) Poetical Register; or the Lives and Characters of all the English Poets, with Account of their Writings, *cuts of heads*, 2 vols., 1723.

James (Isaac, *of Bristol*) The Remarkable Adventures of Alex. Selkirk, of Largo, Scotland, who lived Four Years by himself on the Island of Juan Fernandez, and was rescued by Capt. Rogers, of Bristol. Map and cuts, cr. 8vo, *Bristol*, 1800. 5s.

Jameson (J. ?) Critical and Practical Exposition of the Pentateuch, with Notes and Dissertations on Mosaic Hist. of the Creation and Destruction of the Seven Nations of Canaan, folio, 1748. Pubd. at 12s., now of trifling value.

Jane (John) The Image Unbroken : A Perspective of the Impudence, Falsehood, Vanitie, and Prophaneness pubd. in a libel, or Portraicture of his sacred Majestie in his Solitude and Sufferings, sm. 4to, 1651. Rare, 10s. 6d.

Janus.—*See* Dollinger (Dr.).

Japp (A. H.) Memoir of Nathaniel Hawthorne, cr. 8vo, 1872.—Thomas De Quincey, by H. A. Page, 2 vols., post 8vo, with portrait, 1879.

J. B.—*See* Burgess (James).

J. D.—*See* Dennys (John).

J. D.—*See* Donne (J.).

Jeans (Thomas) The Tommiebeg Shootings, or A Moor in Scotland, cleverly illust. by Percival Skelton, 8vo, 1860. First edn., and rare, 7s. 6d.

Jefferies (Richard) The Gamekeeper at Home, post 8vo, 1878. 25s.—The Amateur Poacher, post 8vo, 1879. 15s.—Wild Life in a Southern Country, cr. 8vo, 1879. 20s.—Hodge and his Masters, 2 vols., cr. 8vo, 1880. 15s.—Wood Magic, a Fable, 2 vols., cr. 8vo, 1881. 25s.—The Story of my Heart. First edn., cr. 8vo, 1883. 21s.—Round about a Great Estate. 1st edn , 1880. 7s. 6d.—The Open Air. First edn , cr. 8vo, 1885. 5s.—Amaryllis at the Fair, cr. 8vo, 1887. First edn. 10s. 6d. His " Small Farms " first appeared in the *New Quarterly*, 1874 (16 pp.), from which it is sometimes extracted and catalogued separately.—Field and Hedgerow, post 8vo, 1889. 10s. 6d. - A Memoir of the Goddards of North Wilts ; compiled from Ancient Records, Registers and Family Papers, sm. 4to, *s. d.* First edition sells at 15s or more.—Bevis, the Story of a Boy, 3 vols., cr. 8vo, 1882. 30s. Above dates are all those of First editions.—Mr. W. T. Spencer, of 27, New Oxford Street, W.C., has always a set of First editions of this talented writer on hand at moderate prices.

Jeffreys (N.) Facts are stubborn Things ; a Letter to the P. of Wales ; Review of H.R.H.'s Transactions with Mr. Jeffreys, containing much relating to Mrs. Fitzherbert, &c., 8vo, 1806. There also exists on this subject :—Diamond cut Diamond (a review of the above), by Philo-Veritas, 1806, and A Plain Letter to the P. of W. on his plain duties to his wife, child and nation, and a second letter on the same subject. All very curious.

Jenkins (Edward, *M.P.*) Ginx's Baby, his Birth and other Misfortunes, sm. 8vo, 1871.

Jerome (Jerome K.) Weeds, A Story in Seven Chapters, by K. McK., oblong fcp. 8vo, N.D. The first edition is scarce.

Jerram (Chas.) Letters to an Universalist, &c., 8vo, *Clipstone*, 1802. Relates to the controversy between Mr. Vidler and Mr. Fuller.

J. H.—*See* Healey (J.).

J. H.—*See* Howell (James).

J. H.—*See* Hull (J.).

J. M.—*See* Milton (John).

Johnson (Abraham) Lucina sine concubitu, Lettre addressé à la Société Royale de Londres, 1750. Value about 5s. There also exists an edn. in English of 1761 ; and of late years a Reprint by Goldsmid (privately printed at Edinburgh). The two latter are of similar value to the first mentioned.

Johnson (Chas.) Chrysal, or the Adventures of a Guinea, 4 vols., post 8vo, 1783. Still held in high esteem. Catalogues at about 15s.—Another edn. with charming plates by Burney, 3 vols., fcp. 8vo, 1797. Of similar value. Most of these scenes relate to a Society called the "Hell-Fire Club," located at Medmenhand, Buckingham, and the work contains a full Account of the sham order of Monks of St. Francis established at Medenham Abbey by Sir F. Dashwood, Wilkes, and others, with their curious mock rites and orgies.

Johnson (James, *M.D.*) The Recess : or, Autumnal Relaxation in the Highlands and Lowlands ; being the Home Circuit *versus* Foreign Travel, a Serio-Comic Tour to the Hebrides, by Frederick Fay, Esq., of Westminster. Of nominal value.

Johnson (Samuel) A Voyage to Abyssinia, by Father Jerome Lobo, a Portuguese Jesuit, with Continuation of the Hist. of Abyssinia, and Dissertations by Le Grand, from the French (by Saml. Johnson), thk. 8vo, 1735. First edition. 7s. 6d.—The Conduct of a Rt. Hon. Gent. in resigning the Seals of his Office justified by Facts, &c., by a Member of Parliament, 8vo, *Newbery*, 1761. First edn. 5s. A rare Pamphlet.—Life of Richard Savage ; 3rd edition, to which is added the Lives of Sir F. Drake and Admiral Drake, post 8vo, 1767.—The False Alarm, 8vo, 1770.—Thoughts on the late Transactions respecting Falkland's Islands, 8vo, 1771. Taxation no Tyranny, 8vo, 1775.—A Journey to the Western Islands of Scotland, 8vo, 1775. First edition. Issued anonymously. 7s. 6d. Another edition, 8vo, *Edinb.*, 1798. Often reprinted.

Johnston (Mr.) The History of Arbaces, 2 vols., med. 8vo, 1774. Rare, 7s. 6d.

Jones (D.) Life of James II. of England, and the State of his Court at St. Germain's, &c., 5 plates of medals, 8vo, 1702. Of trifling value.

Jones (Griffith) Letter to a Proselyte of the Church of Rome, &c., 4to, 1731. Rare, 10s.

Jones (Henry) Tour in quest of Genealogy through several parts of Wales, Somerset, and Wilts, with Fragments from a MS. ascribed to Shakespeare, 8vo, 1811.

Jones (Henry) Card Essays, Clay's decisions, and Card Table Talk; *portrait*, cr. 8vo, 1879. First edition. His work on Whist is well known and popular.

Jones (Mrs. Herbert) Sandringham Past and Present; and Illustrated Monograph of the Princess Charlotte of Wales; with 12 miniatures. Both recent. The latter is scarce, only 250 having been issued. Sells at 12s.

Jones (John) Epistles of St. Paul to the Colossians, to the Thessalonians, to Timothy and Titus; and the Gen. Epistle of St. James; chiefly from Griesbach's Text; by Philalethes, fcp. 8vo, *London*, 1819.

Jones (S L.) Life in the South, from the commencement of the War (Secession), 2 vols., post 8vo, 1863. First edn. pubd. at 21s.

Jones (T. Percy).—*See* Aytoun (Prof.).

Jones (W.) The Constitutional Criterion, 8vo, 1768.

Journeyman Engineer (A).—*See* Wright (T.).

Journeyman Mason (A).—*See* Miller (Hugh).

J. S.—*See* Sanford (James).

J. T.—*See* Toland (J.).

J. W.—*See* Worledge (J.).

Kames (Lord) Letters from a Blacksmith to Ministers and Elders of the Church of Scotland, &c., 1761. Curious, and scarce.

Katzleben (Baroness de).—*See* Bowles (Caroline).

Keach (Benj.) The Grand Impostor discovered, or Quaker's Doctrine weighed in the Ballance and found wanting, by B. K., 12mo, 1675. Should have a curious frontis. of "Weighing the Bible," generally absent. About 5s. Valued by Griffith in his "Bibl. Anglo-Poet" at £1 10s.

Keddie (H.) The Nut Brown Maid; My Heart's in the Highlands; Wearing the Willow. All post 8vo, 1860-1.

Keepe (Henry) Monumenta Westmonasteriensia: An Historical Account of the Abbey Church of Westminster; by H. K , p. 8vo, 1682. Rare. A good copy, 10s. 6d.

Kellie (Richard) Tragedie of the Lord Boroscho of Poland, from a MS. in the Hunterian Museum, ed. by A. Smith, 4to, *Glasgow*, 1870. Only 50 copies printed.

Kelsey (Richd.) Alfred of Wessex, a Poem (Anglo-Saxon), 2 vols., thk. 8vo, *Battle, Sussex*, 1852. Issued anonymously, and Privately Printed.

Kendal (E. A.) Burford Cottage, First edition, *front. and vign. title by G. C.*, 1835. Also author of " Keeper's Travels."

Kendall (May).—*See* Lang (Mrs. Andrew).

Kennedy (Grace) Dunallan, or Know what you Judge, 2 vols., fcp. 8vo, 1826. Of nominal value.

Keyns (Jas.) Rational Compendious way to convince, without any dispute, all persons whatsoever dissenting from the true Religion, 12mo, *Printed in* 1674. Nominal value.

K. H.—*See* Keepe (Henry).

Khata Phusin.—*See* Ruskin (J.).

Kidgell (J.) The Card, printed for the Maker; coloured playing card on title, 12mo, 1755. There is probably a second volume of this work, which is apparently not noticed by either Lowndes or Allibone.

King (Sir Peter, *Lord Oakham*) Enquiry into the Constitution, Discipline, and Worship of the Primitive Church, 8vo, *London*, 1691. Another edition, 8vo, 1713.

King (W., *Archbp. of Dublin*) State of Protestants in Ireland under King James's Government, 4to. 1691. First edition. 10s. 6d.—The State of the Protestants of Ireland under the late King James's Government, thk. 8vo, 1692. Rare. 6s. A few copies of this edition have a frontispiece.

King (W.) The Dreamer, dealing with :—The Rosicrucians, or Knights of the Rosy Cross, Temple of Hercules. &c., 8vo, *Owen*, 1754. Rare and curious. 7s. 6d.

Kinglake (A. W.) Eothen. Traces of Travel brought home from the East, 8vo, *Ollivier*, 1844. First edition, and should have 2 coloured plates. 6s. Another edn., with 2 coloured plates, 1845. 3s. 6d.—A Month in the Camp before Sebastopol. by a Non-Combatant (A. W. K.), post 8vo, *Longmans*, 1855. First edition and rare. 7s. 6d.

Kingsley (C.) Politics for the People, from No. 1, May 6th, 1848, to No. 17, July, 1848. 17 parts, 8vo. All published. Chas. Kingsley's celebrated Magazine, with all his original " Parson Lot" Articles. It was a remarkable though short-lived publication, and its regular contributors were nearly all University Men, Clergymen of the C. of England, London Barristers, and Men of Science : among them Archdeacon Hare, Sir A. Helps, Prof. Conington, and a well known London Physician. Complete sets are rare. 15s.—Alton Locke, Tailor and Poet, an Autobiography, 2 vols., cr. 8vo, *Chapman and Hall*, 1851.—South Sea Bubbles, by the Earl and the Doctor (The E. of Pembroke and Dr. Kingsley), 8vo, *Bentley*, 1872. Usually considered the best Library edition. About 12s.

Kirkpatrick (J., *of Belfast*) Historical Essay upon the Loyalty of the Presbyterians in the U. K. to 1713, &c., thk. sm. 4to, 1713. A very rare item, issued quite anonymously, the place of publication, and Printer's name being withheld, in addition to that of the author. 15s. or more.

Kitchener (Dr.) Art of Invigorating and Prolonging Life, with Peptic Precepts, &c., p. 8vo, 1822.

K. J.—*See* Keyns (Jas.).

K. McK.—*See* Jerome (J. K.).

Knatchbull-Hugessen (E. II).—*See* Brabourne (Lord).

Knickerbocker (Diedrich).—*See* Irving (W.).

Knight (J.) Dinarbas; a Tale: being a Continuation of Rasselas, Prince of Abyssinia, post 8vo, *Dilly*, 1792. Of nominal value.

Knight Errant (A).—*See* Du Bois.

Kyd.—*See* Clark (J. C.) under " Dickens."

Laclos (Choderlos De) Les Liaisons Dangereuses, Lettres recueillies dans une Société; par C—— de L——, 2 vols., 12mo, 1782. First edition. Another edn, 4 vols, *Neuchatel*, 1782. Another edition, 4 vols., 12mo, *Genève*, 1792. With plates by Le Barbier. Another edition, also with plates, 4 vols., 12mo, 1820. Another edition, 2 vols., 12mo, 1869. Reminds one forcibly of Rousseau's Confessions.—Mémoires de Mme. la'Duchesse de Morsheim, par l'auteur des Liaisons Dangereuses, 2 vols., post 8vo, *s. l.*, 1777. 6s.

Lacu (J. de).—*See* Gringore (P.).

Lacy (John) The Scene of Delusions considered and confuted, sm. 8vo, *circa* 1715. Perhaps the rarest work relating to the French Prophets. Written in answer to Chas. Owen's Scene of Delusions opened. 1712.

Lady (A).—*See* Glasse (Mrs.).

Lady (A).—*See* Godwin (Mrs.).

Lady of Massachussetts (A).—*See* Child (Mrs. D. L.).

Laick (Will.).—*See* Ridpath (Geo.).

Lamb (Chas. and Mary) Mrs. Leicester's School, or History of several young Ladies, related by themselves, post 8vo, 1814. A charming old edition, with frontispiece by Hopwood.—The first edition is of great rarity and valuable —Satan in search of a Wife, with the whole Process of the Courtship and Marriage, and who danced at the Wedding, by an Eye Witness, 6 woodcuts, fcp. 8vo, *Moxon*, 1831. Of the utmost rarity. £5 or more.

Lamb (C.) —*See* under heading Annual Anthology.

Lamb (Rev. R.) Free Thoughts on Many Subjects. A Selection of Articles from " Frazer's Magazine " by a Manchester Man, thk. cr. 8vo, *Manchester* (1866).

Lance (Thos., *of Birkenhead*) Triplicity, 2 vols., p. 8vo, *Liverpool*, 1840.

Landon (Letitia E.) The Golden Violet, with its Tales of Romance and Chivalry and other Poems, sm. post 8vo. 1827. First edition. With frontispiece.—The Improvisatrice and other Poems, by L. E. L., frontis. and vign. title, p. 8vo, 1825.—The Easter Gift, post 8vo, 1832. Fine steel plates. Of nominal value.

Landor (Walter Savage) Count Julian, a Tragedy, 8vo, *Murray*, 1812. Rare. About Two guineas. Also exists on Large Paper (which I have not seen), and in this state is probably worth double above sum.

Landreth (Rev. P.) Legends of Lancashire, 8vo, 1841.

Lane (John) A Perspective of the Impudence in a Libel entitled Eikonoklastes written by John Milton, 4to, 1645.

Lang (Andrew) Much Darker Days, by A Huge Longway, post 8vo, fancy wrapps., 1884. The First edn. is scarce. 5s.—"He," by the author of "Much Darker Days," "It," "K. Solomon's Wives," &c. First edn., post 8vo, *fancy wrappers*, Longmans, 1887.—King Solomon's Wives, by Hyder Ragged, illustrated by Linley Sambourne, cr. 8vo, 1887. Scarce.

Lang (Mrs. Andrew) Poems by May Kendall, post 8vo. VERY SCARCE. 7s. 6d.—Such is Life, by May Kendall, cr. 8vo, *Longman*, 1889. Publ. at 6s., but worth *more* now. Very few people know that "May Kendall" was a pseudonym.

Langland (or Longland) (William, *hic* Robt. W., *a Monk of Malvern*, A.D. 1369) The Vision of Piere Plowman, now first imprynted by Roberte Crowley, dwelling in Ely rentes in Holburne, Anno Domini 1550, 4to, Sigs. A—Ggs., 117 folios, not including title, the Printer to the Reader, and Prologue, 2 ll. Of the utmost rarity. £50 perhaps.—The vision of William concerning Piers Ploughman, with Introduct., Comment. and Glossary, by Rev. T. Dunham Whitaker, 4to, 1813. The companion volume (they are generally found together), Pierce the Ploughman's Crede, 4to, 1814. Two sumptuous volumes, both finely printed in red and black type, 𝔊𝔬𝔱𝔥𝔦𝔠 𝔏𝔢𝔱𝔱𝔢𝔯, by Harding, on very thick Whatman Paper; and illustrated with woodcuts. Only 250 issued. The two vols. are worth £2 2s.—Piers Ploughman's Vision and Creed, ed. from Contemporary MS., with Historical Introduction, Notes, and Glossary, by T. Wright, 2 vols., post 8vo, 1887. Also done on Large Paper. This Religious Allegorical Satire is generally attributed to above gent. who flourished about the middle of the XIVth Century.

Langstaffe (Launcelot).—*See* Irving (Washington).

Langton (Z.) Essay concerning the Human Rational Soul, sm. 8vo, *Liverpool*, 1755. Very early copies have a title page which was suppressed in later issues.

Languet (Hubert) Vindiciæ contra Tyrannos: sive de Principis in Populum, Populique in Principem, legitima potestate, S. J. Bruto Celta, auctore, post 8vo, 1579. Though bearing imprint "Edinburgh," this is a spurious foreign production.

Larwood (Jos.).—*See* Sadler (R. L.).

Latham (J., *Bradwall, Cheshire*) English and Latin Poems, post 8vo, 1853. But few copies done. Not published.

Lathy (Thos. Pike) The Angler (a Poem) by Piscator; with Receipts, &c., cuts, post 8vo, 1819.

Laud (Archbp.) Trial of.—*See* Prynne (W.).

Lauriers (Des) Les Œuvres de Bruscambille, contenant ses Fantasies, Imaginations, et Paradoxes, &c., 12mo, 1629. An exceedingly rare item of "French Facetiæ." Market value, 30s.

Law (John, *of Lauriston*) Proposals and Reasons for constituting a Council of Trades, post 8vo, *Edinburgh*, 1701. I have seen this item incorrectly catalogued with the name of W. Paterson, Founder of the Bank of England, given as the author. It is very scarce, and sells at from 15s. upwards.

Lawrence (J.) Sword and Gown, by the author of "Guy Livingstone," cr. 8vo, 1859.—Guy Livingstone; 3 vols., post 8vo, 1864.—Sans Merci, or Kestrels and Falcons, by author of Guy Livingstone, 3 vols., p. 8vo, 1866.—Breakespeare, or the Fortune of a Free Lance, 3 vols., post 8vo, 1868.—Breaking a Butterfly, by author of "Guy Livingstone," 3 vols., post 8vo, 1869.—Border and Bastille, 8vo, 1863. First edn. realizes about 7s. 6d.

Lawrence (J.) The Empire of the Nairs, or Panorama of Love, *very curious fronts.*, 4 vols., 12mo, 1824. Exceedingly rare. A clean copy of this Picture of Prostitution, Seduction, Gallantry and kindred subjects catalogues at £3 3s.

Lawson (J. P.) Historical Tales of the Wars of Scotland and of the Border Raids, Forays, and Conflicts. 3 vols., post 8vo, 1849. With fine portrait and plates by W. Bell Scott. Scarce. 10s. 6d.

Layman (A).—*See* Taylor (Edgar).

L. B.—The Reformed Monastery. Claustrum Animæ, a Sure, Short, Pleasant, and Easie Way to Heaven, *frontis.*, 2 parts, 12mo, 1677.

Lear's (E.) Book of Nonsense, by Derry Down Derry, *whimsical illusts.*, oblong 4to, *McLean*, 1855. About 7s. 6d. The First edn. is worth much more.

Le Bas (C. H.) Memoir of Henry Vincent Bayley, D.D., 8vo, 1846. Anonymous and Privately Printed.

Le Brunn.—Descriptions de divers ouvrages de Peinture, faits pour Le Roy, fcp. 8vo, *Paris*, 1671.

Lee (P.) Comic Latin Grammar, a facetious Introduction to the Latin Tongue, with 8 etchings and numerous woodcuts by J. Leech, post 8vo, *C. Tilt*, 1840. Rare. 10s.

Lee (Vernon).—*See* Paget (Violet).

Le Gallienne, *i.e.* Gallon (Richard) Three Poems :—The Housemaid, Adultery ad Absurdum, and Julia's Clothes, 4 pp., 8vo. Issued privately, without any printer's name, place, or date ; and of the utmost rarity. Catalogues at about 15s.

Legh (George) The Clergyman's choice of a Wife, delineated in a Letter to Dr. C., in England, by a Foreign Bishop now residing in his Diocese in Terra Incognita (Halifax, Yorks.), 4to, 1738. 10s. 6d. A Privately Printed Poem, highly facetious.

Leighton (John, *of St. Pancras*) Comic Art Manufactures, 64 original designs, collected by LUKE LIMNER, Esq., oblong 8vo, N.D. Issued in an emblematic paper wrapper, and now scarce. 5s.— Madre Natura *versus* the Moloch of Fashion, with 30 illusts. by Luke Limner, sm. 8vo, 1874.

L. E. L.—*See* Landon (Lætitia).

Lennox (Mrs. Charlotte) Shakespeare illustrated, 3 vols., sm. 8vo, 1753-4. Dedication written by Dr. Johnson, also many of the Observations, according to Malone. This lady is also the authoress of "The Female Quixote."

L'Estrange (Hammond) The Reign of King Charles, an History. Faithfully and Impartially delivered and disposed into Annals, folio, 1655. The frontispiece by Faithorne, which includes a fine portrait of the King, is usually absent ; if the vol. contains this, 7s. 6d.

Leti (Gregorio) Il Nipotismo di Roma, or History of the Pope's Nephews, &c., 2 parts, with portrait, fcp. 8vo, *London*, 1669. A very rare little item. 21s.

Lever (Charles) Cornelius O'Dowd. Three series. in 3 vols., 1864-5. Original edn., should be in *green* cloth. Value 25s. For other works by this author *see* the Catalogues issued by Mr. W. T. Spencer, 27, New Oxford Street, W.C. Sent post free.

Leveson (Maj. H. A.) Hunting Grounds of the Old World, by the Old Shekarry, 2 series, tinted lithos., 8vo, 1860, &c. Scarce. 15s. —The Forest and the Field, by "The Old Shekarry," 8 illusts., post 8vo, 1874.—Wrinkles, or Hints to Sportsmen and Travellers, by the Old Shekarry, illustrated, med. 8vo, 1874.

Levinge (Sir Richard) Cromwell Doolan, or Life in the Army, 2 vols., post 8vo, 1849. 6s.

Lewes (G. H.) Ranthorpe ; or a Poet's first struggles, cr. 8vo, 1847. First edition. Scarce. 7s. 6d.

Lewis (John Delaware) Across the Atlantic, by the Author of "Sketches of Cantabs," cr. 8vo, 1851.

Lewis (Richard) The Robin Hood Society, A Satire, with Notes variorum by Peter Pounce, 8vo, 1756. Should have frontispiece. 5s.

Libri.—Catalogue de la Bibliotheque de M. L****, the sale of which occupied 30 days, 8vo, *Paris*, 1847.

Liere (M. Prunelle de) Prophéties d'Isaie, trad. en Français avec des notes, 8vo, *Paris*, 1823.

Lightbrodie (G.) Against the Apple of the Left Eye of Antichrist, or Masse Book of Lurking Darkness, &c., fcp. 8vo, 1638. Very rare. 10s. 6d. or more.

Limner (Luke).—*See* Leighton (John).

Lindsay (T.) Short History of the Regal Succession, &c., &c., 8vo, 1730. The last copy of this work that passed through my hands was formerly the property of the late T. Leveson Gower.

Linton (Mrs. E. Lynn) The True History of Joshua Davidson. There are many edns. of this curious work, which is too well known to need more than mere mention.

Lister (Martin) Johannes Godartius of Insects, done into English, and methodized, with the addition of notes, by M[artin] L[ister], many beautiful folding plates (on copper), 4to, *York Printed*, 1682. Excessively rare. The editor states in the Preface that the "edition consists of 155 copies only, for the curious." About £3.

Lite (Henry, *of Lytescarie*) The Light of Britayne, a Record of the honorable Originall Antiqnitie of Britaine, printed 1588, cuts, 4to, 1814, Large Paper; with portrait of Q. Elizabeth. Very few copies done in this size.

Little (Thomas).—*See* Moore (Thos.).

Livingston (W.) The Conflict in Conscience of a Deare Christian, named Bessie Clarksone Lanerk, fcp. 8vo, *Edinb.*, 1820. A reprint of a rare Early XVIIth Century Tract.

Llewellyn (Dr. Martin) Men Miracles, with other Poems, small 8vo, 1646, First edition. Rare.—Men-Miracles, with other Poems, sm. 8vo. 1655.

Lloyd (C.).—*See* Annual Anthology.

Lloyd (David, *Dean of St. Asaph*) Legend of Capt. Jones, relating to his strange and incredible Adventures by Sea and Land, 2 parts, fcp. 8vo, 1671. With folding plate by Marshall. Valued in Bibl. Anglo-Poetica at £2 12s. 6d.

Lloyd (Thos.) Essay on the Toleration of Papists, 8vo, 1799.

Locke (John) Five Letters concerning the inspiration of the Scriptures, transl. from the French, fcp. 8vo, 1690. First Edition. Of nominal value.

Locker-Lampson (F.) Poems by F. Locker, with frontispiece by Geo. Cruikshank, p. 8vo, 1868. Privately printed and excessively rare. 25s. or more.—Lyra Elegantiarum. First edition, thk. sm. 8vo, *Moxon*, 1867 (suppressed), 25s.—Patchwork (Prose and Verse), with illustrated title by H. S. Marks, sm. post 8vo, 1879. First edition. Ten or twelve shillings. Both are scarce.—London Lyrics, fcp. 8vo, 1881. This edn. (Privately printed) is very rare, and worth 30s. now.

Lockhart (J. Gibson) Peter's Letters to his Kinsfolk. Best Library edn., with numerous steel portraits, 3 vols., 8vo, 1819. Contains interesting particulars of the Edinburgh Literary Society at the beginning of the present century. About 7s. 6d.—Valerius. 3 vols., post 8vo, 1821. First edition.— Songs of the Edinburgh Troop, post 8vo, 1825. Suppressed. Songs of the Edinburgh Squadron, post 8vo, 1839. The first item about 5s., the second is of nominal value.—History of Napoleon Buonaparte, with engravings on steel and wood by Finden and G. Cruikshank, 2 vols., 12mo, 1829. 7s. 6d.—Memoirs of the Life of Sir W. Scott, 7 vols., cr. 8vo., 1837. This, the first, edn. was published anonymously.

Logan (J.).—*See* Bruce (Michael).

London Clerk (A).—*See* Hughes (T.).

Longman (W.) and H. T. Journal of Six Weeks' Adventures in Switzerland, etc., post 8vo, 1856. First Edition. 7s. 6d.

Loudon (J. C.) Green House Companion, etc., coloured frontispiece, 8vo, 1832. Scarce.

Lounger (A).—*See* Porson (Prof.).

Louth (Dr. S.) Rights, Liberties, and Authorities of the Christian Church, sm. 8vo, 1697.

Love (John) Vindication of Mr. G. Buchanan (*i.e.* his Paraphrase of the Psalms), with Appendix, 8vo, *Edin.*, 1749. W. Benson's objections to this paraphrase were so pronounced that he wrote a pamphlet on them, which was answered by T. Ruddiman in 1745. None of these Tracts are valuable.

Loveday (R.).—*See* Calprenede.

Lover of the Celestial Muses (A).—*See* Fullarton (J.).

Lowe (John, *of Manchester*) The Solar Creation and Universal Deluge, 8vo, 18—.

Lowndes (W.) Report containing an Essay for amendment of the Silver Coins, post 8vo, 1695. Of little value.

Lowth (Bp.) Mons. Catharinæ, *Prope* Wintoniam, Poema, 4to, 1760. Now very rare.—Letter to (Dr. Warburton) the Author of the *Divine Legation of Moses*, with a former Literary Correspondence, 144 pp., 8vo, *Oxford*, 1765. Nominal value.

Lubert (Mademoiselle de) Amadis des Gaules, with engraved plates and en-têtes, 4 vols., fcp. 8vo, *Amsterdam* (Paris) *J. F. Jolly*, 1750. Very rare, 10s. 6d.

Lupton (Daniel) The Glory of their Times, or Lives of Ye Primitive Fathers, contayning their Chiefest Actions, Works, Sentences, and Death, sm. 4to, 1640. With a very fine title page and many portraits by Glover, these last in the Text. A good copy is worth 15s.

Lysons (Sam.) Account of Remains of a Roman Villa at Bignor, Sussex. *Plan and 5 coloured plates*, sm. 8vo, 1820.

Lyttleton (Lord) Four New Dialogues of the Dead, 8vo, 1760. Another edn. 8vo, 1765. *Of no value.*

Lytton (Bulwer) What will he do with it? by Pisistratus Caxton, 4 vols., cr. 8vo, *Blackwood*, 1859. First Edition, 7s 6d.

Lytton (Robert, E. of, *Owen Meredith*) Clytemnestra, and other Poems. First edition, sm. 8vo, 1855. Scarce, 21s.—The Wanderer, thk. sm. 8vo, 1859. First edition, £2 10s.—Tannhauser, or Battle of the Bards, by Neville Temple and Edward Trevor (Lord Lytton and Julian Fane), 1st edition, fcp. 8vo, 1861. Rather scarce. The third edn. is very common.—Lucile, by Owen Meredith. 24 *charming illusts. by G. Du Maurier*, sm. 4to, 1868. First issue, sells about 6s.—Lucile. Illustrated Library edn., large 8vo, 1882. About 7s. 6d.—Serbski Pesme, or National Songs of Servia by Owen Meredith, fcp. 8vo, 1861. First edition, 7s. 6d.—The Ring of Amasis. 2 vols., post 8vo, 1863. First edn. Catalogues for 10s. 6d.

Maberley (J.) The Print Collector; with Illustrations, 8vo, *Roxb.*, 1844.

Macfarlane (C.) The Camp of Refuge, c. 1844. The Dutch in the Medway, 12mo, 1845. Saml. Pepys is the chief character in the latter item.

Mackenzie (Capt. A. Sidell) Spain revisited, 2 vols., p. 8vo, 1836.

Mackenzie (Capt. C. F.) The Romantic Land of Hind, by Il Musannif. cr. 8vo, 1882. Pubd. at 6s.

Mackenzie (Colin) Tavern Anecdotes and Reminiscences of the Origin of Signs, Clubs, &c., by One of the Old School, post 8vo, 1825. If containing the portrait of Chris. Brown, and folding frontispiece by Heath, it is valuable; and worth 10s. 6d. or more. Only one copy has ever come under my notice containing the frontispiece which was no doubt suppressed on account of its freedom in illustrating the sign "The Horns," which forms one of the numerous devices it contains.

Macknight (Thos.) The Right Hon. Benjamin Disraeli, M.P., a Literary and Political Biography, 8vo, 1854. Pubd. at 15s., but sells now for about one-fifth of that price.

Macleod (Dr. Norman) The Old Lieutenant and his Son, 2 vols., med. 8vo, 1862. Now scarce and worth 7s. 6d. This author's works "Parish Papers," "The Starling," &c., are all well known.

MacNally (Leonard) Robin Hood, a Comic Opera, 1779. This gent. also pubd. other Operas and Medleys about this period.

Macpherson (Jas.) Fragments of Ancient Poetry, collected in the Highlands and Translated from the Gaelic or Erse Language, thin sm. post 8vo. *Dublin*, 1760. 5s.

MacSarcasm (Sir Archibald).—*See* Shaw (W. D. D.).

M'Taggart (Mrs.) Memoirs of a Gentlewoman of the Old School, by a Lady, 2 vols., cr. 8vo, 1830. 5s.

Madan (M.) Thelyphthora, or Treatise on Female Ruin, its Causes, Effects, Consequences, Prevention, and Remedy, &c., 2 vols., thk. 8vo, 1780. 10s. 6d. If the rare third volume of 1781 accompanies the work, double that amount.

Madden (Rev. Dr. S.) Reflections and Resolutions for Gentlemen of Ireland, &c., 8vo, *Dublin*, 1816. Praised by Dr. Johnson. Worth about 5s.

Maffei (S.) Traddutori Italiani, e Notizia del nuovo Muses in Verone, sm. 8vo, 1720.

Mahony (F. S.) Facts and Figures from Italy, addressed to C. Dickens by Don Jeremy Savonarola, sm. 8vo, *Bentley*, 1847. Rare. About 7s. 6d. Forms an appendix to "Pictures from Italy."

Maidment (J.) Memorials of the Family of Row, sm. 4to, 1828. As only 40 copies were issued this work is rare. Sells at 10s.—Catalogue of Scottish Writers, &c., 8vo, 1833.

Maitland (S. R) Higher Law, a Romance, 3 vols., 1870. First edn. About 5s. He also wrote "The Pilgrim and the Shrine," 8vo, 1869, which is his most popular work; and Descriptive List of Early Printed Books in the Archiepiscopal Library of Lambeth, 8vo, 1843. Privately Printed. Scarce, and worth 10s.

Maittaire (Michael) Senilia, sive Poetica aliquot in Argumentis varii generis Tentamina, roy. 4to, 1742. Only worth 2 or 3 shillings.

Major (J. Henuiker) Letters on Norman Tiles stained with Armorial Bearings, 8vo, 1794. Rare.

Malagrowther (Malachi).—*See* Scott (Sir W.).

Malkin (A. T.) Historical Parallels, 2 vols., post 8vo (sometimes bound in 1 vol. pub. cl.), 1846.

Mall (Thomas) A Cloud of Witnesses, or the Sufferers Mirrour made up of Swanlike Songs, etc., of Martyrs and Confessors to the XVIth Century, etc., 3 vols. (generally bound in 1), sm. 8vo, 1665. Rare. A good copy is worth half a guinea.

Manchester Man (A).—*See* Lamb (Rev. R.).

Manchester Manufacturer (A).—*See* Cobden (R.).

Mandeville (Bernard) Fable of the Bees, or Private Vices Public Benefits, etc., 8vo, 1728. The scarce Second Part, which is rarely met with, and in which the Author "endeavours to illustrate and explain several things, that were obscure or only hinted at in the first," was published in 1729. The two parts together are worth 7s. 6d.

Manley (Mrs. De la Riviere) The Secret History of Queen Zarah and the Zarazians, fcp. 8vo, 1705. There are several other editions, between 1712-45, and Chalmers in his Biographical Dictionary attributes the authorship to above lady. It is, however, very doubtful if she had any hand in the work at all. "Zarah" was of course Sarah, Duchess of Marlborough.

Manning (Anne) Years after, a Tale, sm. p. 8vo. *Parker*, 1849.—The Maiden and Married Life of Mary Powell, afterwards Mistress Milton, cr. 8vo, 1852. 1st edn.—Claude the Colporteur, by the Author of "Mary Powell," post 8vo, 1854. Publd. 7s. 6d.—Some Account of Mrs. Clarinda Singleheart, crown 8vo, 1855. First edn.—Tasso and Leonora, Commentaries of Ser Pantaleone Dagli Gambacorti, Gentleman to the August Madama Leonora d'Este, frontispiece, post 8vo, 1856. First edn.—Helen and Olga, a Russian Tale, cr. 8vo, 1857. First edn.—Belforest, a Tale of Country Life, by the author of "Mary Powell," 2 vols., post 8vo, 1865.—Diana's Descent, by the author of "Mary Powell," 2 vols. (in 1), post 8vo, 1868.—Provocations of Madame Palissy, with beautiful coloured frontis., post 8vo. *Hull*, 1870.—Cherry and Violet, a Tale of the Great Plague, by the Author of "Mary Powell," frontis., cr. 8vo, N.D.—Old Chelsea Bun House, 8vo.—Adventures of the Caliph Haroun Alraschid, 1st edn., 1855. The works of this authoress are still held in high esteem, though they do not command a very high price. Her scarcest and most popular work is the "Old Chelsea Bun House."

Manning (R.) England's Conversion and Reformation compared, etc., 8vo, *Antwerp*, 1725.—Rise and Fall of the Heresy of Iconoclasts, or Image Breakers, 8vo, *Meighan*, 1731. These two Roman Catholic works are very rare, the second item especially. I am unable to trace any mention of either the author or his works in any of the ordinary books of reference.

Manuel.—Chastété (la) du Clergé dévoilée, ou Procès-verbaux des Séances du clérgé chez les Filles de Paris, etc., 2 vols., 8vo. *Rome et Paris*, 1790. Le Bibliophile Jacob says this curious work was edited by Manuel, and that it is of exceeding rarity owing to the Clergy having bought it up. He has only seen two copies of this work, which though well known by name rarely occurs for sale. £2 2s. or more.

Marana (J. P.) Letters writ by a Turkish Spy, etc., 1637-82, portrait, 8 vols., fcp. 8vo, 1718. Used to fetch a high price. Now about 1s. per volume.

Marchandier (L.'Abbé) L'Isle de France, ou la nouvelle Colonie de Venus, precédé d'un Epitre à M***, servant de Preface, sm. post 8vo, *Cologne*, 1758. Rare, 10s. 6d. This curious work is by the above gent., author of " Des Filles femmes, et des Femmes filles."

Marivaux (M. de) Life of Marianne, or Adventures of the Countess of ***, transl. from the French, 3 parts, sm. post 8vo, 1736. First English Translation of this " Erotic " item, and very scarce. 15s.

Markham (Gervase) Cheape and Good Husbandrie for the well ordering of all Beastes, and Fowles, and for the generall cure of their Diseases, etc , with a cut of Fish-Ponds, sm. 4to, 1623, 15s.— Countrey Contentments, or the English Huswife, containing the inward and outward Vertues which ought to be in a Compleat Woman, etc., sm. 4to, 1623. 12s. 6d.

Marriott (Jas., *LL.D.*) Poems written at Cambridge University, with a Latin Oration on the Hist. and Genius of Roman and Canon Law, with engravings, 8vo, *s. l. et. a.* 5s.

Marshall (Mr.) Catalogue of 500 celebrated Authors, 8vo, 1788.

Martin (Sir H.) Murray's (Archbp.) Douay and Flemish Bible and Bordeaux New Testament examined, 12mo, 1850.

Martin (J.) Explication de divers Monumens, etc., avec Traite sur l'Astrologie, plates, 4to, *Paris*, 1739. About 6s.

Martin (John B.) The Grasshopper, being some Account of the Banking House at 68, Lombard St., 8vo, 1874. A very rare Pamphlet. Sells at 7s. 6d. or more. In the following year Mr. F. G. Hilton Price published " Some Account of Ye Marigold, No. 1, Fleet St." (Child's Bank) in which Mr. Martin's claims in " The Grasshopper" are disputed.

Martin (William) published for many years his charming "Peter Parley's Annual." His widow still survives, and I have had the pleasure of hearing many anecdotes of him since my introduction to her.

Martingale.—*See* White (C.).

Marvel (Ik.).—*See* Mitchell (D. G.).

Mary Q. of Scots.—*See* Buchanan (G.), Tytler (W.).

Maseres (Baron) Select Tracts relating to the Civil Wars in England, *temp.* Charles I., by Writers who were Witnesses of the Events, 2 vols., roy. 8vo, 1815. Scarce, 15s. The writers above include Hobbes, Fairfax, May, Holles, etc.

Maskell (Wm.) Bude-Haven, a Pen and Ink Sketch, with portraits of the principal Inhabitants, 2 plates, 8vo, 1863. Anonymous and Privately Printed.

Massey (Isabel) Social Life and Manners in Australia, the Notes of eight years' experience, by a Resident, post 8vo, 1861. Scarce, 5s.

Mather (Cotton) A Faithful Account of the Discipline Professed and Practised in the Churches of New England, 8vo, 1726. Excessively rare. Three guineas.

Mathias (T. J.) The Shade of Alexander Pope on the Banks of the Thames, 8vo, *Dublin*, 1799. — The Pursuits of Literature, a Satirical Poem, with Notes and Appendix, the Citations translated, and Index, 4to, 1812. 7s. 6d.

Matthews (G. K.) Abbotsford and Sir Walter Scott, sm. post 8vo, *Lond.*, 1854. 4s.

Matthews (Col. John) Eloisa en dishabille, being a New Version of that Lady's Epistle to Abelard, 1794 and 1822. Generally ascribed to Prof. Porson, but Moore, in his Life of Byron, says that this piece was really composed by Col. John Matthews, of Hereford shire. Catalogues generally for 15s. and upwards.

Maupertius (M. de) Venus Physique, 12mo, 1746. This rare little Erotic item was privately printed, *sine loco*. Present value, 15s.

Maurice (F. D.) The Kingdom of Christ, etc., 2 vols., post 8vo, N.D.

Maurice (T.) Grove Hill, a Descriptive Poem, with Ode to Mithra, by the Author of "Indian Antiquities," 4to, *Bensley*, 1799. The Large Paper copies are on Whatman paper, and both sizes contain wood engravings by Samuel, engraved by Anderson. 10s.— Richmond Hill, a Descriptive and Historical Poem illustrative of the principal objects viewed from that beautiful eminence, by the author of "Indian Antiquities," 2 large folding plates, 4to, 1807. The plates are seldom to be found, and a copy containing them realizes 7s. 6d.—Westminster Abbey, and Free translation of the Œdipus Tyrranus of Sophocles, 2 views of the Abbey and portrait of Sophocles, impl. 8vo. 1813 Pubd. at 25s Present value about one-fifth of that sum.—Memoirs of the Author of "Indian Antiquities," 2 parts, 8vo. *Privately printed*, 1819-20. Nominal value.

Maxwell (James) Carolonna, a Poem, etc., sm. 4to, s. d. but circa 1714. About 6s.—Prophecies of James Usher, sm. 4to, 1678. Rare, 7s. 6d.

Maxwell (Mrs. John, *formerly Miss Braddon*). This lady is a well-known and voluminous writer. All her works are popular, notably Aurora Floyd, Vixen, and Lady Audley's Secret. Her other works include Lucius Davoren, or Publicans and Sinners, by Miss Braddon, 3 vols., post 8vo, *Lond.*, 1873. First edition.—Strangers and Pilgrims, by Miss Braddon, 3 vols., cr. 8vo, 1873, etc.

Maxwell (W. H.) The Field Book, or Sports and Pastimes of the British Islands, by the Author of "Wild Sports of the West," frontispiece and numerous Nat. Hist. cuts (which remind one forcibly of Bewick), 8vo., 1833. 7s. 6d.—Stories of Waterloo, frontispiece, post 8vo, 1850.

May (Thomas) The Victorious Reign of King Edward III. Written in VII. Books (in Verse) by his Majesty's command, fine portrait, 12mo, *T. Walkley and B. Fisher*, 1635. Very rare. Griffith prices this at £2 5s. in the Bibl. Anglo-Poet., and a good copy with portrait is worth nearly that sum to-day.

M.B.I.D.P.E.C.—*See* Boulanger (M.).

M'Culloch (John) The Art of Making Wine, fcp. 8vo, 1816. Of little value.

McHale (Dr.) Letters of Hierophilos, on Education of Poor in Ireland, and Divorce, with Letters of Bibliophilos, 8vo, *Dublin*, 1821. At the time of publication Dr. McHale was a Maynooth Professor, and afterwards a R. C. Bishop.

McCulloch (J. R.) Catalogue of Books the property of a Political Economist, roy. 8vo, 1862. Anonymous, Privately Printed, and very rare. Three guineas at least when to be had.

Meath (Lord).—*See* Brabazon (Lord).

Mellor (J. W.) Stories and Rhymes, a Book for the Fireside, fcp. 8vo, 1869. Of nominal value.

Melmoth (Courtney).—*See* Pratt (S. J.).

Member of Parliament (A.).—*See* Johnson (Dr.).

Member of the Athenian Soc.—*See* Dunton (J.).

Memoirs of Nobility and Gentry of Thule (England, or the Island of Love, etc.), 2 vols., 12mo, *Lond.*, 1744. Very rare, and full of Court Scandal, *tempus* George II. Sells at about 35s. I have been unable to discover the author.

Menestrier (C. F.) Des Ballets Anciens et Modernes selon les Regles du Theatre, fcp. 8vo, *Paris*, 1684. Rare, 7s. 6d. perhaps.

Mercier (Mons.) L'An Deux Mille quatre cent quarante. Rêves s'il en fût jamais, 8vo, 1772. Full of curious anticipations, many of which have since come to pass. 5s.

Mercurius Rusticus—*See* Dibdin (T. F.).

Meredith (Owen).—*See* "Lytton."

Michault (P.) Le Dance des Aveugles, 𝕷𝖎𝖙𝖇. 𝕲𝖔𝖙𝖇., with curious woodcuts, sm. 4to, *Lyon, M. and B. Chaussart*, N.D. Very rare. The second (and last) copy I have ever seen, sold last year by auction for £11.

Michel (Fernand) The Story of the Stick in all Ages and Lands, by Antony Real, 10 plates by Alfred Thompson, cr. 8vo, *New York*, 1891. About 5s.

Microcosm (The) A Periodical Work, thk. 8vo, *Windsor*, 1787. Written by 4 Eton gentlemen: J. Smith, G. Canning, R. Smith, and J. Frere.

Miller (Hugh) Poems written by a Journeyman Mason, post 8vo, *Inverness*, 1829. Very rare, 15s.

Miller (Mrs. Hugh) The Little Foundling, by Mrs. H. Myrtle, coloured plates, cr. 8vo, *Cundall*, 1836. Of nominal value.—The Water Lily, by Harriet Myrtle, with full-page illusts. by H. K. Browne (Phiz), cr. 8vo, 1854. First Edition. Very scarce. 21s. or more.

Miller (J.) Humours of Oxford, a Comedy, post 8vo, 1730. Rare, 5s. This play brought down on the author's head the vials of wrath of some Heads of Colleges in Oxford, who deemed themselves lampooned in it.

Milman (H. H., *Dean*) History of the Jews, 3 vols., 8vo, 1830.

Milnes (R. Monckton, *afterwards Lord Houghton*) Palm Leaves, 1844. —Poems of Many Years, 1844.—Memorials of a Tour in Greece (chiefly Poetical), 1834, etc., etc. His writings are still esteemed.

Milton (John) The Doctrine and Discipline of Divorce, restor'd for the Good of Both Sexes, from the bondage of Canon Law, etc., the Author, J. M., 4to, *London Printed*, 1644. Very rare, 15s. Written to justify the repudiation of his wife.—Eikonoklastes, in answer to a Book entitled Eikon Bazilike, the portraiture of his Sacred Majesty in his Solitudes and Sufferings, the author J. M., sm. 4to, 1649. First Edition. Rare, two guineas. The reply to this, "Eikon Aklastos," by Joseph Jane (scurrilous and abusive), sm. 4to, 1651, is worth 30s.—School Lawes, or Qui Mihi in English (Verse), by J. M., med. 8vo, 1650. Very rare. Two guineas.

M'Intyre (Duncan) Gaelic Songs. Orain Ghaidhealach, le Dounchadh Macantsoir. 12mo, 1790. Rare, 7s. 6d.

Miniature (The) a Periodical Paper, by Sol. Grildrig, *of Eton College*. 34 numbers. *Windsor*, 1805. Rare, 10s. This interesting serial is one of the earliest publications of the celebrated Chas. Knight, then a Bookseller at Windsor.

Mitchell (D. G.) Dream Life, a Fable of the Seasons, by Ik. Marvel, frontis., post 8vo, *New Y.*, 1851. Also under the same Pseudonym, "Reveries of a Bachelor." Both of minor value.

M. (J. B).—*See* Martin (John B.).

M. L.—*See* Lister (Martin).

Mockett (Dr. Richard) Doctrina et Politia Ecclesiæ Anglicanæ, etc., 4to, *London, J. Bill*, 1617. Nicholson says this work was condemned to the flames and burnt. It is very rare, and sells at from 30s. upwards.

Mogridge (Geo.) has written many juvenile works under the Pseudonym "Old Humphrey."

Moir (D. M. Δ) The Legend of Genevieve, with other Poems, cr. 8vo, *Edinb.*, 1825. First edition.— Sketches of the Poetical Literature of the past Half Century, post 8vo, 1856.—Poetical Works by Δ (Delta), 2 vols., post 8vo, *Blackwood*, 1860.—The Roman Antiquities of Inveresk, post 8vo, 1860.—The Life of Mansie Wauch, Tailor of Dalkeith, writteu by Himself, 8 illusts. by G. Cruikshank, cr. 8vo, *Blackwood*, s. d.

Moll (Prof., *of Utrecht*) On the alleged decline of Science in England, by a Foreigner, with Preface by Prof. Faraday, 8vo, 1831.

Moncrieff (R. H.) A Book about Dominies, p. 8vo, 1867.—A Book about Boys, *uniform*, 1869.

Monro (and Beloe) Alciphron's Epistles, iu which are displayed the Courtesans and Parasites of Greece, now first translated, 8vo, 1791. Curious.

Montague (Lady Mary) Poetical Works of the Rt. Hon. Lady M——y M——e, sm. post 8vo, 1781.

Montaigne (M. de) Essays of, transl. by J. Florio, title page by Martin (with verses facing same), folio, 1632. 15s. to 21s.

Montanus.—*See* Skinner (V.).

Montbron (Fougeret de) Le Canapé, Couleur Feu, par M. de ***, post 8vo, *Amst.* 1761. Rare, 7s. 6d.

Montgomery (James) Prose by a Poet, 2 vols., sm. post 8vo, 1824. First edition, 5s.

Montlyard.—Apule. Les Metamorphoses, ou l'Asne d'Or, curious engravings (full page) by Briot, etc , and Commentaires sur la Metamorphose de l'Asne d'Or, thk. post 8vo, *Paris*, 1648, should accompany this work. £2 2s. This rare edition was translated by Montlyard, and corrected by N. de la Costa, and the Commentaries are very extensive and much esteemed. The engravings by Briot and Crispin de Pas appear here for the first time. Copies rarely occur for sale.

Montmartre (Un Citoyen de).—*See* Sennemaud.

Montreuix (Nicolas de) Les Amours de Cleandre et Domiphille, livre non moins delectable, que profitable à tous vrais amateurs de Chastété, par Ollenix de Mont-Sacré, thk. 12mo, *Paris*, 1598. The pseudonym is an anagram on the Author's name. About 7s. 6d.

Mont-Sacre (Ollenix de).—*See* Montreuix.

Moore (Tom) Poetical Works of Thos. Little, post 8vo, *Chiswick Pr.*, 1817. Many editions exist, all of minor value.—The Fudge Family in Paris, ed. by Thos. Brown the Younger, sm. post 8vo, 1818. Of no value.—The Fudge Family in Edinburgh, post 8vo, *Edinb.*, 1820. First edition.—Memoirs of Captain Rock, the celebrated Irish Chieftain, post 8vo, 1824. 5s.—Travels of an Irish Gentleman in search of a Religion, etc., with Notes and illustrations, 2 vols., fcp. 8vo, 1831.—*See also* Anthologia Hibernica, *ante*.

More (Hannah) Essays on various subjects principally designed for Young Ladies, fcp. 8vo, 1777. Of no value.—Cœlebs in search of a Wife, comprehending Observations on Domestic Habits, Manners, and Morals, etc., 2 vols., post 8vo, 1809. There are many other editions, all of trifling value.—*See also* Shaw (W. D. D.), *supra.*

More (Henry) Discourse of Enthusiasm, written by Philophilus Parresiastes, sm. 8vo, 1656.—Reply to a Late Answer to Dr. Henry Moore, his Antidote against Idolatry, post 8vo, 1672. Of very trifling value.

Moreau (M.) Leçons de Morale et Politique, et de Droit Public, med. 8vo, 1773. 5s.

Morgan (J. Minter) The Revolt of the Bees, fine frontis. by Corbould, post 8vo, 1828.—Hampden in the Ninteenth Century, *plates*, 2 vols., 8vo, 1834.

Morgann (Maurice) Essay on the Dramatic Character of Sir J. Falstaff, 1777. Rare.

Morier (J.) Adventures of Hajji Baba of Ispahan, 3 vols., post 8vo, 1824. Another edition, with steel frontis., post 8vo.—Bentley's Standard Novels, uniform with which are published his Adventures of Hajji Baba in England, Zohrab the Hostage, Ayesta the Maid of Kars (each with frontispiece), 1835-51.

Morley (Countess of) Portraits of the Spruggins Family, etc., arranged by Richd. Sucklethumkin Spruggins, Esq., 45 full p. plates, 4to. *Privately Printed*, 1829. Pubd. anonymously, rare, and highly amusing. 10s. 6d.

Morris (Corbyn) Essay towards fixing the true standards of Wit, Humour, Raillery. etc., with Analysis of the Characters of an Humourist, Falstaff, Sir R. De Coverley, and Don Quixote, 8vo, 1744.

Morris (Lewis) The Epic of Hades, post 8vo, 1878 —Songs of Two Worlds, photo portrait, sm. post 8vo, 1878.

Morris (W.) Letters on Socialism, cr. 8vo, 1894. Very few copies Privately Printed. 21s.

Mortimer (Mrs. Thos) Light in the Dwelling, thk. 8vo, 1846. This lady also pubd. "The Peep of Day," which is a charming book for Children, and commanded a large sale.

Morton (Andrew).—*See* Defoe (D.).

Morton (Thos.) The Grand Imposture of the new Church of Rome manifested, etc., etc., by the Bp. of Coventree and Lichfield, 4to, 162-. Rare, 10s.

Mothe (M. De La) Memorial de quelques Conferences, avec des Personnes Studieuses, 12mo, *Paris*, 1669.

Mottley (John) Scanderbeg, or Love and Liberty, a Tragedy written by the late T. Whincop, with List of all Dramatic Authors, and their Bibliography to 1747, 8vo, 1747. 5s.

Moultrie (Rev. J.) Saint Mary, the Virgin and Wife (Poetry), 8vo, *Rugby*, 1850.

Mozeen (Thomas) Young Scarron, an imitation of the Comicall Romance ridiculing the Foibles of the Itinerant Players or Strollers in England, 1752. A very rare and valuable item. Copies seldom occur, only one having come under my notice in 15 years.

M. T.— *See* Mall (Thos.)

Mudie (Alex.) Scotiæ Indiculum, or Present State of Scotland, with Reflections on the Ancient state thereof, fcp. 8vo, 1682. Should have frontispiece. With this, 7s. 6d.

Mudie (Robert) The Modern Athens (Scotland), by a Modern Greek, 1st edn., cr. 8vo, *Knight and Lacey*, 1825. This curious work was somewhat severely handled in Wilson's Noctes Ambrosianæ.

Muir (T. S.) Pet Jessie-Anne's Exhibition of Unda's Rubbings from Monumental Slabs and Brasses, post 8vo, 1871. Very scarce, 7s. 6d.

Muloch (Miss, *afterwards Mrs. Craik*) John Halifax, Gent. (her most celebrated work). — A Woman's Thoughts about Women, by author of "John Halifax, Gent.," post 8vo, 1858. Pubd. at 6s. — A Life for a Life, the first edition of which was in 3 volumes, 1859. — Our Year, a Child's Book in Prose and Verse, illustrated, cr. 8vo, 1860. — Studies from Life, by the Author of "John Halifax, Gentleman," post 8vo, 1861. — Christian's Mistake, by the author of "John Halifax, Gentleman," post 8vo, 1865. — An Unsentimental Journey through Cornwall, by the author of "John Halifax, Gent.," 35 beautiful engravings, roy. 4to, 1884. 6 or 7 shillings. — Plain Speaking, by the author of "John Halifax," 1882. Pubd. at 10s. 6d.

Munday (Mr.) Needwood Forest, a Poem, with other descriptive County Pieces (Staffs.), 4to, *Lichfield*, 1776.

Munro (Rev. T.) Olla Podrida, a Periodical, published at Oxford, 44 nos., folio, 1787-8. Edited by T. Munro, and the Contributors include Bp. Horne, Rev. Mr. Kett, etc. Of very little value.

Murford (P.) Newes from Southampton, in a Letter to Capt. T. Harrison, discovering a late Plot of the Cavaleering Hoptonians against the said Town, 4to, 1644. I am unable to trace this item as being referred to in the ordinary books of reference. 10 to 15 shillings.

Murray (Rev. J.) Eikon Basilikh, or the Character of Eglon, King of Moab, and his Ministry, by author of "Sermons to Asses," 8vo, *Newcastle*, 1773. — Magazine of the Ants, or Pismire Journal, an original Work concerning the Religion of the Kingdom of Ants, 8vo, *Newcastle*, 1777. Excessively rare. — History of Religion, 4 vols., thk. 8vo, 1764, also Sermons to Asses, 8vo. Best edn., pubd. by the notorious W. Hone, 1819.

Myrtle (Mrs. H.).—*See* Miller (Mrs. Hugh).

Napier (E. H. D. E.) Past and Future Emigration, or the Book of the Cape, ed. by the author of "Five Years in Kaffir Land" (*i.e.* Harriet Ward), map, fcp. 8vo, 1849.

Nares (Dr. Edward) Heraldic Anomalies, or Rank Confusion in our Orders of Precedence, with Disquisitions on all existing Orders of Society, by It matters not who, 2 vols., med. 8vo, 1823. 6s.—I Says, says I, a Novel, by Thinks-I-to-Myself, 2 vols., sm. 8vo, 1812.

Nayler (Sir Geo., *Garter King-at-Arms*) A Collection of Coats of Arms borne by the Nobility and Gentry of Gloucestershire, 62 plates containing hundreds of Coats-of-Arms, 4to, 1792. Rare, 21s., if containing the Introduction (50 pp.) and List of Subscribers.

Naylor (S., *of Maidenhead*) Ceracchi, a Drama, and other Poems, 8vo, 1839. Not published.

N. B.—*See* Baxter (Nathaniel).

Neale (Erskine) Whychcotte of St. John's, or the Court, Camp, Quarter Deck, and Cloister, 2 vols., cr. 8vo, 1833. Of trifling value.

Neale (J. Mason) Ecclesiological Notes on the I. of Man, etc., 12mo, 1848.

Neale (W. J.) is the author of "Cavendish," "Will Watch," etc., all of minor value. His "Paul Periwinkle, or the Press-Gang," *Tegg*, 1841, is very rare, especially in uncut state, and worth to-day £4 or £5. Perfect copies have 40 plates by "Phiz" (H. K. Browne).

Neville (Henry) Plato Redivivus, or a Dialogue concerning Government, wherein by observations drawn from other Kingdoms, etc., an Endeavour is used to discover the present Politick Distemper of our own, with the Causes and Remedies, fcp. 8vo, 1681. Curious, 5s.

Newman (J. H., *Cardinal*) The Catholic University Gazette, Vol. I., roy. 8vo, *Dublin*, 1854-5. Very scarce, easily realizes 10s. 6d. from a Catalogue. It is doubtful if more was published.—Devotions, transl. from the Greek, cr. 8vo, 1848. Another edition, 1856.—Verses on Various Occasions, comprising 172 various Poems, Hymns, etc., dedicated to E. Badeley, sm. post 8vo, *London*, 1868. First edn., scarce, 7s. 6d.

New Testament.—*See* Darby and Taylor (Edgar).

Nichols (John) Collections of all Wills extant of Royalty from William I. to Henry VII., ed. with Notes and Glossary (by J. Nichols), post 4to, 1780. 5s.

Nichols (J. Gough) Accounts of 55 Royal Processions and Entertainments in the City of London; with Bibliographical List of Lord Mayors' Pageants, *frontis.*, 8vo, 1819. 7s. 6d.

Nicholls (J. A.) In Memoriam, a Selection from the Letters of the late John Ashton Nicholls, F.R.A.S., 8vo, 1862. Printed for Private Circulation only.

Nicholls (John) Anecdotes of the late W. Bowyer, Printer, compiled for Private Use, 8vo. Privately Printed, Anonymously, 1778. Of this rare work the entire issue did not, in all probability, exceed 100 copies. 10s. 6d. or more.

Nimrod.—*See* Apperley (C. J.).

Noake (Dorothy) Life and Adventures of the Marchioness Urbino in England, Spain, Turkey, Italy, France, and Holland, 8vo, 1735.

Noblesse Oblige.—*See* Evans (Howard).

Non-Combatant (A).—*See* Kinglake (A. W.).

North Country Angler (A).—*See* Doubleday (T.).

Nugent (Lord and Lady) Legends of the Library at Lilies, by the Lord and Lady there, 2 vols., cr. 8vo, 1822.

Oakley (Peregrine, *of Brighton*) Aureus: or Life and Opinions of a Sovereign, written by himself, med. 8vo, 1824. Trifling value.

Old Bushman (An).—*See* Wheelwright (Horace M.).

Old Humphrey.—*See* Mogridge (Geo.).

Old Maid (An).—*See* Phillips (Miss).

Old Shekarry (The).—*See* Leveson (Maj. H. A.).

Old Sailor (The).—*See* Barker (M. H.).

Old Vicar (An).—*See* Warter (Rev. J. W.).

Oliphant (Mrs.) Passages in the Life of Mrs. Margaret Maitland, o Sunnyside, by herself, 3 vols., post 8vo, *Colburn*, 1849. First edition. Published at 32s.

Ollivant (Henry, *Bp.*) The Condition of Llandaff Cathedral, 4to, *plates*, 1860.

Olmsted (F. L.) Walks and Talks of an American Farmer in England, woodcuts, cr. 8vo, 1852.

One of No Party.—*See* Grant (James).

One of the last Century.—*See* Rose (W. S.).

One of the Old School.—*See* Mackenzie (Colin).

Onesimus.—*See* Courtier (P. L.).

O. P.—*See* Cromwell (Oliver).

O'Reilly (Miles).—*See* Halpin (C. G.).

Orme (Rev. W.) Memoir of the Controversy respecting the Heavenly Witnesses, 1 John v. 7, including critical Notices of the Question by Criticus, fcp. 8vo, 1830. Pubd. at 3s. 6d. Catalogues at more to-day.

Ormerod (O.) Rachde Felley's Okeawnt o' th' Greyt Eggshibishun. Illustrated, 8vo, *Rochdale*, 1856. A curious specimen of the Lancashire Dialect.

Orrery.—Roger Boyle, (*E. of*); Parthenissa ; A Romance, 4to, 1655-6. Best edition and rarely found complete, in which state it should contain 4 parts, and 2 extra (the last very scarce), No 4to edn., is mentioned in the "Bibliographer's Manual." Present market value 10s. or more.

Orwell.—*See* Smith (Walter C.).

Otway (C.) Sketches in Ireland, descriptive of Interesting and hitherto Unnoticed Districts in the North and South, 8vo, 1827. First edition, pubd. at 10s. 6d.

Ouida.—*See* Ramé (Louise de la).

Owen (Henry, *D.D.*) Critica Sacra, or a short Introduction to Hebrew Criticism, with a Supplement, 8vo, *London*, 1774-5.

Owen (Hugh) Some Account of the Ancient and Present State of Shrewsbury, its Ancient and Ecclesiastical Buildings, Domestic Architecture, &c., 560 pp., fcp. 8vo, *Shrewsbury Printed*, 1808. Crammed with valuable Antiquarian matter.

Owen (Jas.) Consecration of Altars and Churches, 4to, 1706.

Paget (E. G.) The Owlet of Owlstone Edge, his Travels, his Experience, and his Lucubrations, sm. post 8vo, 1856.

Paget (Violet) Belcaro, Essays on Æsthetical questions, by Vernon Lee, cr. 8vo, *Satchell* (1880), First collected edn.

Paley (John, *M.P., Father of the Celebrated Philosopher, W. Paley*) The Necessary Knowledge of the Lord's Supper, with Prayers, &c., and Whole Duty of Prayer from Reason and Revelation, 2 vols., 8vo, *Leeds, Printed by J. Hirst*, 1726-30. Both very rare.

Paltock (R.) Life and Adventures of Peter Wilkins, the Flying Man, with plates, 2 vols., post 8vo, 1751. Excessively rare. About £4 10s. The Reprint, with facsim. plates and Preface by Bullen, 2 vols., 1884, sells for 4 or 5 shillings. Humourous Hist. of Dickey Gotham and Doll Clod, 2 vols., sm. 8vo, 1753. Original edition, and rare. Sells at about £2.—Wilkins (Peter, *a Cornish Man*) His Life and Adventures, taken from his own Mouth, in his passage to England from off Cape Horn, in the Ship " Hector," by R. S., fine copper plate engravings, 2 vols., fcp. 8vo, *London*, 1816. Very scarce. 15s. or more.

Pardon (G. F.) Faces in the Fire : by Redgap, *engr. title*, 3 *plates by Nicholson*, (in Leech's style) *and woodcuts*, fcp. 8vo, N.D. A very close imitation of " The Christmas Carol." The plates should be coloured.

Paris.—Philosophy in Sport, &c., cuts by Cruikshank, 3 vols., 1831. Best edition, but of little value. There are numerous reprints in one volume.

Parke (F.) Songs of Singularity : or Lays from the Eccentric, by the London Hermit, 50 illustrations, cr. 8vo. Of trifling value.

Parker (Henry) Dives and Pauper, that is to say the Rich and the Pore. 𝔅𝔩𝔞𝔠𝔨 𝔏𝔢𝔱𝔱𝔢𝔯, folio. Imprinted by R. Pynson at the Temple Barre of London, 1493. An excessively rare volume; and the first of Pynson's publications bearing a date. A clean and perfect copy is worth £30 to £35.

Parker (Henry) The Generall Junto, or the Councell of Union, chosen equally out of England, Scotland, and Ireland, for the better compacting of the three Nations into one Monarchy, &c., sm. folio, A.D. 1642. Rare. £2. Also exists on Large Paper. Ten shillings more in this state. Lowndes mentions no edition before 1643.

Parker (Samuel) Bibliotheca Biblica, a Commentary upon the O. and N. Testaments down to 451, with Discourses on the Authenticity of the Books, time of their being written, &c., 6 vols., 4to, *Oxford*, 1720-35. The notes in this work are generally attributed to Dr. Thos. Haywood.

Parker (T., *of Shincliff*) The Bible, with Notes, 2 vols., 4to, *York*, 1781.

Parks (Fauny) Wanderings of a Pilgrim in Search of the Picturesque, *plates* (some coloured), 2 vols., 8vo, 1850. Scarce. 30s. if a good copy.

Parley (Peter).—*See* Martin (William). His widow still survives, and I have heard many interesting Anecdotes respecting him, since I had the pleasure of being introduced to her.

Parnell (Dr. Thos.) Essay on the different stiles of Poetry, 8vo, 1713. Of no value.

Parson Lot.—*See* Kingsley (C.).

Parsons (Father) A Conference about the next Succession to the Crown of England, 8vo, 1681. An exceedingly rare suppressed item. Perfect copies should contain a large folding genealogical plate (extracted from *most* copies). If perfect, 15s.

Parsons (R.) Elizabethæ Reginæ Angliæ Edictum promulgatum, *Londini*, 29*th Nov.*, 1591, et Philopatri [*i.e.*, Parsons (Robt.)] Responsione, sm. o. 8vo, 1593. Very curious. Sells at 7s. 6d.

Parsons (R.) Leycester's Commonwealth, 4to, *Privately Printed*, 1641. Perfect copies contain a portrait, which is usually wanting in most copies catalogued. Market value from 12 to 15 shillings.

Pascal (Blaise) Les Provinciales, ou Lettres écrites par Louis de Montalte, &c., 12mo, 1689. The rare little Elzevir edition.

Pasquier (E.) The Jesuites Catechisme, or examination of their Doctrine. Published in French, 1602, and now Translated into English, *s. l., (London?)* 1602, 4to size. The Translation is by W. Watson. Very rare. 15s.

Pasquin (Anthony).—*See* Williams (J.).

Patin (Chas.) Thesaurus Numismatum antiquorum et recentiorum, ex Auro, Argento, et Ære, (auctore Carolo Patino, *i.e.*, Chas. Patin), cuts of coins, 4to, *Venet.*, 1633. In addition to the Text illustrations should have very fine engr. title by Dorigni, and vignette title. 7s. 6d.

Patmore (P. G.) British Galleries of Art, post 8vo, 1824. Trifling value.—The Mirror of the Months, post 8vo, 1826. Of no value.

Paton (Sir Noel) Poems by a Painter, cr. 8vo, 1861. Scarce. 10s. 6d.

Paul Pry.—*See* Poole (John).

Pauw (M. de) Recherches Philosophiques sur les Américains, ou Mémoires intéressants pour servir à l'Histoire de l'Espèce Humaine par De P——, 2 vols., sm. 8vo, 1768. First edition. Rare. 10s. 6d.

P. (De).—*See* Pauw (M. De).

Peabody (George) The Battle of Life, or Public Benefactors and their Critics, by an Englishman, post 8vo, 1876.

Peacock (T. Love) Headlong Hall, post 8vo, 1816. Rhododaphne, a Poem, post 8vo, 1818. About 5s. each uncut.

Pearce (G.) Pascal's (Blaise) Provincial Letters, with Essay on Pascal by M. Villemain, trans. (by G. P.) with Memoir, &c., and Appendix, *portrait*, post 8vo, 1847. Pubd. 9s.

Pearson (G. C.) Flights inside and outside of Paradise, by a Penitent Peri, thk. cr. 8vo, *N.Y.*, 1886. Pubd. 5s.

Pegge (Saml.) Anonymiana, ten Centuries of Observations on various Authors and Subjects, 8vo, 1809. First and best edition. Praised by Allibone.

Peletier (J.) Discours non plus mélancoliques que divers, &c., 4to, *Poictiers*, de l'Imp. d'Enguilbert de Marnef, 1556. A good copy is worth £4. This has also been attributed to E. Vinet, whilst Nodier gives Bonaventure des Periers as the author.

Pemberton (H.) A View of Sir I. Newton's Philosophy, *plates*, 4to, 1728. The Initials and vignettes are all engr. by J. Pine. A good copy is worth 10s.—Also exists on Large Paper.

Penn (W.) England's present Interest discovered with Honour to the Prince and Safety to the People, sm. 4to, 1675. Rare. 7s. 6d.—Some Fruits of Solitude, in Reflections and Maxims relating to the Conduct of Human Life, fcp. 8vo, L. *Hinde*, N.D. (*Early Sæc.* XVIII)

Penrose (Llewellyn).—*See* Eagles (Rev. J.).

Penry (John) Marprelate Tract, Epistle to the Terrible Priests of the Convocation House, p. 8vo, 1842. A reprint.

Penton (Stephen) The Guardian's Instruction, &c., 12mo, 1688. First edition.

Percy (Bp.) Five Pieces of Runic Poetry, transl. from the Islandic Language. sm. 8vo, 1763. Scarce. 5s.—Reliques of Ancient English Poetry, consisting of Old Heroic Ballads, Songs, and other Pieces of our earlier Poets, with frontispiece, 3 vols., sm. 8vo, 1765. First edition, and esteemed by Collectors because it is the only edition containing the Poem "The Maid of Bath." 21s. Another Edition, with frontis. by Grignion, and vignettes, 3 vols., sm. 8vo, 1794. 10s. 6d.

Perdita (The Fair).—*See* Robinson (Mrs.).

Pereira (J.) Lectures on Polarised Light, 50 woodcuts, 8vo, 1843. Of nominal value.

Perenas (Le Père) Nouveaux Essais pour determiner les Longitudes en Mer, par les mouvements de la Lune, et par une seule Observation, 4to, *Avignon*, 1768.

Peri (A Penitent).—*See* Pearson (G. C.).

Person of Quality (A).—*See* Settle (E.).

Peter of Pontefract (The late).—*See* Graves (R.).

Peterborough (E. of) Memoirs of Secret Service, by M. Smith, 8vo, 1699. First edn., and was ordered to be burnt by the hangman.

Pettigrew (T. L.) Lucien Greville, by a Cornet in the H.E.I.C.'s Service, 6 full page plates by G. Cruikshank. First edn., 3 vols., sm. 8vo, *Saunders*, 1833. About 30s.

Peyrere (J. La) Præadamitæ, sive Exercitatio super vers XII.—XIV., cap. V., Epistolæ Pauli ad Romanos, quibus inducuntur Primi Homines ante Adamum condi, map, f.p. 8vo, *s.l.* 1655. Exceedingly curious and rare. 10s.

P. H.—*See* Heylyn (P.).

Philalethes.—*See* Jones (John).

Philips (A.) A Collection of Old Ballads, &c., *numerous copper plate engravings*, 3 vols., post 8vo, 1723-25, VERY RARE. Sells at £3 3s. or more. The reprint of 1871 may be procured for 21s.

Phillips (E.) New World of Words, or General English Dictionary, containing the Signification of all Words derived from other Languages, &c., folio, 1678. About 10s.

Phillips (E.) The New World of Words, or General English Dictionary, compartment frontis., containing 10 ports., folio, 1678. 10s. 6d.

Phillips (Miss) My Life and What shall I do with it? A question for young Gentlewomen, by an Old Maid, post 8vo. Of nominal value.

Phillips (Mrs. K., *the Incomparable*) Poems by, 8vo, 1664. 7s. 6d.

Philobiblos.—*See* Ireland (J.).

Philopatri.—*See* Parsons (Robt.).

Philophilus Parresiastes.—*See* More (Henry, *D.D.*).

Philo Scotus.—*See* Ainslie (Philip).

Phiz, *i.e.*, HABLOT K. BROWNE. Works illustrated by this popular Artist will be found classified under their Authors, and all Collectors who read this paragraph are recommended to pay a visit to Mr. W. T. Spencer's shop at 27, New Oxford St., W.C., where, if collecting, they will be sure to meet with some rare item not already in their possession, no matter how good their collection may be, or if, on the other hand, they wish to dispose of Duplicates, or are changing the character of their collections, they will find him a ready buyer at full value of any volumes with which they desire to part.

Picken (A.) The Club-Book, 3 vols., cr. 8vo, 1831. 7s. 6d. Includes tales by Delta, "Gunpowder" James, Galt, The Ettrick Shepherd, &c.

Pierrugues (Chevalier P.) Eroticum Linguæ Latinæ, sive Theogoniæ Legum et morum nuptialum apud Romanos, &c., auct. P. P., 8vo, *Paris, Dupré*, 1826. Some Bibliographers attribute this to Baron de Schoner and Eloi Johannean.

Piers (Henry, *Vicar of Bexley*) Letter in Defence of our Present Liturgy, fcp. 8vo, 1750. Of no value.

Piers Ploughman.—*See* Langland (R.).

Piggott (Charles) The Jockey Club, 3 parts, and The Minor Jockey Club, 8vo, 1792, &c. Issued anonymously and highly scurrilous; the last named item being the rarer. Always ascribed to Charles Piggott.—There exist also Three Scurrilous Pamphlets entitled an Answer to The Jockey Club, by a Member, 1792. A spirited castigation of this Libeller.

P. J.—*See* Pereira (J.).

Pilkyngton (James) Aggeus the Prophete declared by a large Commentarye, sm. 8vo, 1560. **Black Letter.**

Pinchard (Mrs.) The Blind Child; or, Anecdotes of the Wyndham Family, 12mo, 1795, with frontispiece. Nominal value.

Pinio (Jo.) Liturgia Antiqua Hispanica, Gothica Isidoriana, Mozarabica Toletana, mixta, illustrata, adjectis vetustis Monumentis cum Addit. Scholiis, et var. Lectionibus, 2 vols., folio, *Romæ*, 1746. The most sumptuous edition extant.

Pinkerton (John) Letters of Literature (written under Pseudonym Robt. Heron), 8vo, 1785. Nominal value.

Piscator.—*See* Lathy (T. P. .

Pitman (Marie J).—*See* Deane (Margery).

Pitt (William) The Monitor, a Speech in the ——— ———, by the Hon. W—— P——, 12 pp., 8vo, 1755.—Short View of the Political Life and Transactions of a late R.H. Commoner, 8vo, 96 pp., 1766. Neither of these are valuable.

Planta (J.) Catalogue of the MSS. in the Cottonian Library deposited in the British Museum, folio, 1802. About 5s.

Poems by Three Friends (Rev. T. Raffles, of Liverpool, J. Wiffen, and Baldwin Brown), 8vo, 1812.

Poisson (Nic. Jos.) Delectus Actorum Ecclesiæ Universalis seu nova Summa Conciliorum, &c., &c., cum Notis ad Canones, 2 vols, folio, *Lugd. Bat.*, 1706.

Polidori. The Vampyre, A Tale, 8vo, 1819. Always found catalogued under "Byron"; and though formerly commanding a higher figure, can now be procured for 3 or 4 shillings.

Poole (John) Xmas Festivities, with portrait, post 8vo, 1845. About 5s.—Oddities of London Life, by Paul Pry, 2 vols., post 8vo, 1835. First edn., and very rare; easily fetching 30s. to-day. The illustrations are by Pierce Egan, Heath, &c.

Pope (Alex.) The Dunciad in 4 Books, printed according to the complete copy found 1742, 4to, 1743. Exceedingly rare. 21s. or more.

P. P.—*See* Pierrugues (Chev. P.).

Porcupine (Peter).—*See* Cobbett (W.).

Porrinchief (Richd.) Agothocles. The Sicilian Tyrant, or Life of Agothocles, 8vo and sm. 8vo, *i.e.*, L. P. and S. P., 1661. Should have portrait of Agothocles, *i.e.*, Oliver Cromwell inscribed "Tyrranus." There was a Poem published on the Subject in 1683, by T. Hoy.

Porson (Prof.) Eloisha en Dishabille, by a Lounger, 4to, *London*, 1794. Highly facetious and very scarce. Catalogues at 15s. This is put in under "Porson" as being best known by that name, the real author was Matthews (Col. John), which heading *see* in this volume.—The Devil's Walk, with fine plates by Robt. Cruikshank, fcp. 8vo, wrappers. *Marsh*, 1830. Scarce. 6s. This strikingly original Poem has been attributed to both Coleridge and Southey, and was published in the collected works of the former by Pickering, and the Paris edn. of the latter's works.

Potts (Mrs. E. M.) Moonshine, a Collection of Curious, Satyrical, Facetious, and Descriptive Sketches in Poetry and Prose, 2 vols., med. 8vo, 1814. First edition, 5s. The authoress resided in Sloane Street.

Pounce (Peter).—*See* Lewis (R.).

Povey (Chas.) The Visions of Sir Heister Riley, with other Enterteinments (*sic*), &c.. sm. 4to, 1711. Of little value, though extremely curious. The subjects include Vertue, Love and Passion, Beauty, &c.

Powell (Dr. T.) Elementa Opticæ: nova facili, et compendiosa methodo explicata, &c., fcp. 8vo, 1651. A rare and valuable work on Optics. 10s.

Powell (T.) The Repertorie of Records remaining in the 4 Treasuries on the Receipt side at Westminster and the 2 Remembrancers of the Exchequer, with Index to Records of Chancery and the Tower, and Calendar of Records in the latter, sm. 4to, 1631. Rare. About 10s. 6d.

Pownall (H.) History of Epsom, *Surrey*, 8vo, 1825.

Pownall (T.) The great advantage of eating pure and genuine Bread, 8vo, 1773. Of no value.

Praed (W. M.) The Etonian, edited by Praed, contains The King of Clubs, Tales, Poems, On Nicknames, Hair Dressing, Bounce, Essay on Lions, Old Boots, &c., 2 vols., 8vo. Rare. 10 to 12 shillings.

Pratt (S. J.) Travels for the Heart, by Courtney Melmoth, 2 vols., 12mo, 1777.

Prendergast (Paul).—*See* Lee (P.).

Presbytery. The Scotch Presbyterian Eloquence, or the Foolishness of their Teaching discovered from their Books, Sermons, and Prayers, 4to, 1692. Lowndes gives the date of the first edn. as 1693; an error.

Pringle (George) History of Mary Prince, a West Indian Slave, with supplt. by the Editor, also Narrative of Asa-Asa, 8vo, 44 pp., 1831.

Prior (Matthew) The Hind and the Panther transvers'd to the Story of the Country-Mouse and the City-Mouse. On title, "Much Malice mingled with a little Wit Hind. Pan. Nec vult Panthera Domari, Quæ Genus," 4to, *London, printed for W. Davis*, 1687. Exceedingly rare; and unknown to Lowndes. 10s. 6d.

Prior (Matt.) Poems on Several Occasions, 8vo, 1707. First Edition. Excessively rare. Seven or Eight guineas.

Priviledges and Practice of Parliaments in England, collected out of the Common Lawes of this Land, sm. 4to, *s.l.*, 1628. First edition, and secretly printed. When to be had sells for 21s. and upwards.

Procter (B. Waller). This gentleman has published several volumes of Poetry under the title of " Barry Cornwall." notably :—The Flood of Thessaly, Girl of Provence, and other Poems, by Barry Cornwall, 8vo, 1823.—English Songs, &c., by Barry Cornwall, 12mo, *Moxon*, 1844. Another edition, 12mo, 1851.—Essays and Tales in Prose, by Barry Cornwall, portrait, 2 vols., post 8vo, 1853. Scarce. 6s. —Dramatic Scenes and other Poems, by Barry Cornwall, illustrated, sq. 8vo, 1857. 5s.—Charles Lamb, a Memoir, by Barry Cornwall, First edition, post 8vo, *Moxon*, 1866. Scarce. 12s. There was a second issue the same year. 10s. Both are in brown cloth.

Prynne (William) The Land-Tempest; or a Paper-Pellet, Much in a Mouthful, a long Answer to a Short Question, &c., by W. P., 4to, 1644. A very good specimen of the ancient (disused) Gloucestershire Dialect.—Hidden Works of Darkness brought to Publick light. A necessary introduction to the Archbishop's (Laud) Triall, portrait and plates, folio, 1645.—His Defence of Stage Plays, or Recantation of his former book called Histrio-Matrix, 8 pp., 8vo, *Rept. of* 1649. This is a gross forgery and very scarce. Only 100 copies were printed. 5s.—Beheaded Dr John Hewytt's Ghost pleading, yea crying against the arbitrary Injustice of his late Judges and Executioners sitting in Westminster, sm. 4to, 1660. Rare. 10s.

Publicola.—*See* Fox (W. J.).

Puckler-Muskau (H. L. H. Prinz Von.) Aus Mehemed Ali's Reich, vom Verfasser der Briefe eines Verstorbenen, 3 vols., 8vo, *Stuttgart*, 1834. First edition. 5s.

Pullen (W. H.) Modern Christianity, a civilized Heathenism, post 8vo, 1876. Of nominal value.

Puseley (David) has written several works under the Pseudonym of Frank Foster, notably a Journey of Life—and Number one, or the way of the World.

Pyne (W. H.) Wine and Walnuts, by J. Ephraim Hardcastle, 2 vols., sm. 8vo, 1823. First edn. He also published the "Somerset House Gazette," 2 vols., 4to. About 7s. 6d, and the Twenty-Ninth of May, Rare doings at the Restoration, by Ephraim Hardcastle, 2 vols., 8vo, 1825. First and only edn. Dedicated to George IV., and sometimes erroneously attributed to Hazlitt.

Q.—*See* Couch (Quiller).

Quicksilver (James).—*See* Cobbett (W.).

Railton (Jno., *of Cumberland*) The Minister's Practice, or the Female Politician, sm. 4to, 1758. Printed for the Author.

Raine (Rev. J.) Brief Account of Durham Cathedral, with Notices of the Castle, University, City Church, etc. (by Rev. J. Raine), engr. title, fcp. 8vo, *Newcastle*, 1833.

Ralph (James, *Architect*) Critical Review of Publick Buildings, Statues, and Ornaments in London, etc., post 8vo, 1734. Rare.—The Use and Abuse of Parliaments, in two Historical Discourses, 2 vols., 8vo, 1744. 5s.

Rame (Louise de la, *better known as* "*Ouida*"). This talented lady has written many novels, notably "Under Two Flags" (by many considered her *chef d'œuvre*), Folly Farine, Puck, his Vicissitudes, Adventures, etc. First edn., 3 vols., post 8vo, *C. & Hall*, 1870. Scarce. 10s. 6d.—Two Little Wooden Shoes, etc., etc. To my mind her prettiest effort is "The Marriage Plate," a complete short story publd. in a Xmas Number of "St. James's Gazette," now extinct.

Ranchin.—A Review of the Councell of Trent, the Nullities of it, and the Prejudices done by it to Christian Princes, and to the Gallicane Church, transl. by C. L[angbaine], folio, *Oxford*, 1638. Rare. 10s. 6d.

Rands (W. B.) Chaucer's England, by Matthew Brown, portrait and illustrations, 2 vols., cr. 8vo, 1869. An uncommon book, realizes 21s. when it occurs for sale.

Ranyard (Ellen N.) The Missing Link, by L. N. R., Bible Women in the Homes of London Poor, post 8vo, 1860.—The Book and its Story, by L. N. R., frontispiece and woodcuts, fcp. 8vo. Trifling in value.

Ravul (Mademoiselle) Opinion d'une Femme sur les Femmes, par F. R., 72 pp., 12mo, *Paris, An IX.*, i.e. 1801.

Rastell (W.) Collection of all Statutes from Magna Charta to 1557, thk. 4to, *R. Tottyll*, 1559. 𝔅lack 𝔏etter and rare. 21s.

Rathbone (W.) Social Duties, by a Man of Business, cr. 8vo, 1867. First edn.

Rational Mystic (A.).—*See* Belcher (W.).

Raymund (E. ?) Folly in Print, or a Book of Rymes, 12mo, *London*, 1668. Very rare. Three Guineas at least.

R. C.—*See* Carew (R.).

Read (Dr. Andrew) No Fiction, a Narrative founded on Recent and Interesting Facts, 2 vols., post 8vo, 1819. First Edition.

Redding (Cyrus).—*See* Beckford (W.).

Redgap.—*See* Pardon (G. F.).

Red Spinner.—*See* Senior (W.).

Reisch (Geo.) Margarita Philosophica Nova, with woodcuts and music, 4to, *Argent., Gruniger*, 1512. Printed in 𝔅lack 𝔏etter. Rare. Three Guineas.

Reufner (M. H.) Essai sur les Accusations des Templiers et sur le Secret de cet Ordre, avec Dissertation sur l'origine de la Franc-Maçonnerie, etc., fcp. 8vo, *Amst.*, 1784. Rare. 10s. 6d.

Rennell (T.).—*See* Cambridge.

Renwick (W.) The Solicitudes of Absence, 12mo, 1788.

Resident (A.).—*See* Massery (Isabel).

Reuben.—*See* Hawker (R. S.).

Reynolds (Sir J.) Discourses delivered in the Royal Academy by the President, 8vo, 1778. First Edition. 5s.

Reynolds (Miss, *sister of Sir Joshua*) A Dialogue in the Devonshire Dialect (in 3 parts), by a Lady; to which is added a Glossary, by J. F. PALMER, post 8vo, 1837. Very scarce. Six or seven shillings.

Richardson (S.) Clarissa Harlowe, History of a Young Lady, *fronts. by Wale, and plate of Music*, 8 vols., p. 8vo, 1759. About half a Sovereign.—Another Edition, 8 vols., post 8vo, 1792. Of similar value. He also wrote "Pamela, or Virtue Rewarded," etc. There is a beautiful Edn. of Clarissa in French, with an elegant set of engravings, in 7 vols., pubd. at Dresden in 1764; worth now 10 or 12 shillings, if clean and sound in binding.

Ridpath (Geo.) Scot's Episcopal Innocence; or Juggling of that Party with the late King, his present Majesty, the Churches of England and Scotland by W. Laick, sm. 4to, 1694. RARE. 10s. 6d.

Ritson (Joseph) Observations on the three first volumes of the History of English Poetry, by T. Warton, 1782. This has been reprinted. —The Quip Modest, a few Words by way of Supplement to Remarks on Shakespeare, &c., med. 8vo, 1788. 10s. 6d. If a Large Paper copy, of which very few copies were done, double that amount.

Roberts (Rev. Geo.) Speculum Episcopi, the Mirror of a Bishop, p. 8vo, 1848.

Robinson (R., *of Cambridge*) A Political Catechism, cr 8vo, 1782. First edn. and rare. Unknown to Lowndes and Allibone. Worth 7s. 6d.

Robinson.—Memoirs of the late Mrs. Robertson, 12mo, 1801. Rare, and copies with the portrait by Hopwood bring 30s. This lady is known as "The Fair Perdita," from her performance of that part in "The Winter's Tale." She was also the unacknowledged wife of the Prince Regent (afterwards George IV.).

Roby (J.) Jokeby, a Burlesque on Rokeby, by an Amateur of Fashion, p. 8vo, 1813.

Rolewink (Werneto) Fasisculus Temporum, &c., with 18 curious woodcuts (including a large one on back of title), folio, a fine piece of early printing in 𝕲𝖔𝖙𝖍𝖎𝖈 𝕷𝖊𝖙𝖙𝖊𝖗, issued *circa* 1490. 21s.

Rose (*The late* Rev. G.) is the Author of the famous "Mrs. Brown" series, a complete set of which is scarce. "Mrs. Brown on the Tichburg case" is the most uncommon.

Rose (W. Stewart) Thoughts and Recollections, 12mo, 1825.

Ross (Alexander) The Alcoran of Mahomet, transl. into French by the Sieur Du Ryer, and newly Englished (by A. Ross), post 8vo, *London*, 1649. An exceedingly curious volume. 5s.—Arcana Microcosmi, or the Hid Secrets of Man's Body Discovered, with a Refutation of Dr. Brown's Vulgar Errors, Lord Bacon's Natural History, &c., 8vo, 1652.

Ross (John) Civitas Lincolnia, from its Municipal and other Records, post 8vo, *Lincoln*, 1870. Privately printed. 7s. 6d.

Roving Englishman (The).—*See* Grenville-Murray (E. C.).

Rowlands (Sam.) 'Tis Merry when Gossips meet, *John Deane*, 1609. A reprint of this very rare and facetious item was issued in 1818.

Rowlandson (T.) Petticoat Loose, a Fragmentary "Tale of the Castle," 4 full page etchings by T. Rowlandson, 4to, *Stockdale*, 1812. The title conveys some idea of the etchings. Of the utmost rarity. £5 or more.

Roy (William) Rede Me and be not Wrothe, for I say no thing but trothe, (a Satyre against Wolsey), sm. 4to. Arber's reprint of the 1530 edition. 1871. Of nominal value.

Ruddiman (Thomas) A Collection of Scarce, Curious, and Valuable Pieces in Verse and Prose, fcp. 8vo, *Edinburgh*, 1786. Includes the Arts of Dancing, Modern Poetry, Punning, Lying, Angling, and other curious matter. 7s. 6d.

Ruffini (G.) The Paragreens on a Visit to the Paris Universal Exhibition, by the Author of "Lorenzo Benoni" fcp. 8vo, (green cloth), 1856. Illustrated by Leech. If a First Edition, bearing above date, 10s. 6d.—Another Edition, also illustrated by J. Leech, post 8vo, *N. Y.*, 1857.—Lorenzo Benoni, and Doctor Antonio, by the Author of "Lorenzo Benoni," post 8vo, 1855. 3s. 6d.

Ruskin (J.) The Architectural Magazine, ed. by J. C. Loudon, 5 vols, 8vo, 1834-9 contains Ruskin's Poetry of Architecture, First Edition, written under Pseudonym "Khata Phusin," with numerous illustrations; also many other articles and criticisms by Ruskin. Rare. 21s.—Oxford Prize Poems, containing Salsette and Elephanta, by Ruskin, fcp. 8vo, *Oxford*, 1839.—Leoni, a Legend of Italy, thin post 8vo, 1868. Very few copies printed for Private Distribution. A copy would easily realize £5 to-day.—Gold, a Dialogue connected with the Subject of Munera Pulveris, ed. by H. Buxton Forman, cr. 8vo, 1891. Excessively rare. £4 4s. Only 33 copies issued, and none of those for sale.—Several of the volumes of "Friendships Offering" contain Poems, (and one a plate), by J. Ruskin, but they are all of minor value. The contributions are signed J. R. as usual.—A COLLECTION of First Editions by this Author always forms one of the special features in the interesting Catalogues issued periodically by Mr. W. T. Spencer, of 27, New Oxford St., W.C., which are sent post free on application.

Rutland (Duke of) Journal of a Tour round the Southern Coasts of England, plates, 8vo, 1805. Another edition, with 13 plates by J. D. Harding, 4to, 1822. 10s.

R.V.—*See* Verstegan (R.).

Ryder (W. J. D.) Chronicles of the Charterhouse, by a Carthusian, well illustrated, 8vo, 1847.

Saddi (Nathan Ben).—*See* Dodsley (R.).

Sadler and Hotten.—Larwood's (Jos., *i.e.*, R. L. Sadler) and Hotten (J. C.) History of Signboards, 100 facsimile illusts., 8vo, 1867. Rare, 10s. 6d., if on Large Paper.

Sage (John) The Fundamental Charter of Presbytery, as lately established in Scotland, with Preface in Answer to the Vindicator of the Kirk, 8vo, 1697. The Vindicator of the Kirk was Gilbert Rule.

Salvator Rosa.—*See* The Group.

S.A.T.—*See* Taylor (S.A.).

Saunders (Jef.).—*See* Smith (Horace).

Saint Hyacinthe (Le Père de) Le Chef-d'Œuvre d'un Inconnu, etc., etc., par Chrisostome Matanasius, 2 vols., post 8vo, 1732. Should have fine male and female portraits, and folding plate of music. Rare, 15s.

Salmon (N.) History of the Royal Family, 1713.

Salstonstall (W.) Ovid's Heroicall Epistles, Englished by above Gent. (in verse), 24 exquisite little copperplates, 12mo, 1636. Very rare, cheap for half a sovereign.

Saltmarsh (Jo) Poemata Sacra, sm. 8vo, 1636. Poems upon some of the Holy Raptures of David, 8vo, 1636.

Salverte (M. Eusebe) Epitre à une Femme raisonnable, ou Essai sur ce qu'on doit croire, med. 8vo, *Paris*, 1793.

Sanders (Robt.) Complete English Traveller, *with 60 spirited copperplates*, roy. folio, 1773. About 10s.

Sandys (Sir E.) Relation of the State of Religion, and with what Hopes and Policies it hath been framed, and is maintained in the severall States of those Westerne Partes of the Worlde, sm. 4to, 1605. Of nominal value.—Europa Speculum, a view or Survey of the State of Religion in the Westerne Parts of the World, sm. 4to, *London, T. Cotes for M. Sparke*, 1632. Of trifling value.

Sandys (George) Ovid's Metamorphoses Englished, Mythologiz'd, and Represented in Figures, by G. S., fine copperplates, folio, 1632. Rare, 15s —Christ's Passion, a Tragedie, with Annotations, fcp. 8vo, 1640. First edition, rather scarce, 7s. 6d. Second edition, sm. 8vo, 1687, has plates.

Sandford (James) Agrippa (H. Cornelius) Vanitie and Uncertaintie of Arts and Sciences, Englished by J. S., 𝕭𝖑𝖆𝖈𝖐 𝕷𝖊𝖙𝖙𝖊𝖗, folio, 1569. Rare.

Sanscroft (W.) Modern Politics taken from Machiavel, Borgia, and other choice authors, 12mo, 1653.

Saunders (F.) Salad for the Solitary, by an Epicure, first edn., cr. 8vo, 1853. Of trifling value.

Schedel (Hartmanno) Chronicon Nurembergense, beautifully printed in 𝕲𝖔𝖙𝖍𝖎𝖈 𝕷𝖊𝖙𝖙𝖊𝖗, with over two thousand exquisite old woodcuts (some of large size), by M. Wolgemut, Albert Durer's Master, and W. Pleydenwurff, roy. folio, *Nurembergæ, A. Koberger*, 1493. A perfect copy is of the greatest rarity and would represent 20 guineas or more in value to-day.

Schreiner (Olive).—This talented Authoress has published several Works during the last few years, the most notable of which are "The Story of an African Farm," by Ralph Iron, "Dream Life and Real Life," and "Dreams."

Scots Gent (A) in Swedish Service.—*See* Defoe (D.).

Scot (Thos.) Vox Cœli, or Newes from Heaven of a Consultation there held by Henry VIII., Edw. VI., Prince Henry, Q. Mary, Elizabeth, and Anne, wherein Spaine's Ambition and Treacheries are Unmasked, sm. 4to, 1624. Printed in Elysium. Curious and rare. 10s. 6d.

Scott (Sir W.) his first publication :—The Chase, and William and Helen, trans. from Bürger, 4to, *Edinb*, 1796. Rare. 10s. 6d.—Queenhoo Hall, and Ancient Times, a Drama, by J. Strutt, 4 vols., *Edinb.*, 1808. In addition to editing these vols. Scott *finished* Queenhoo Hall. See his general preface to the Waverley Novels. —The Lay of the Scottish Fiddle, 12mo, 1814.—Harold the Dauntless (a Poem), sm. p. 8vo, *Edinb.*, 1817. First edn —The Visionary Nos. 1, 2, and 3. 8vo, *Edinburgh*, 1819. I have never seen any more of this Publication. The three numbers are worth 30s.—Northern Memoirs, by Richard Frank (edited by Sir W. Scott), 8vo, *Edinb.*, 1821. Scarce. About 7s. 6d.—Thoughts on the Proposed Change of Currency : Three Letters on Scottish Affairs by Malachi Malagrowther, 8vo, 1826.—*See* also " Burt."

Scott (W. Bell) Poems by a Painter, by W. Bell Scott, illust. by the author, fcp. 8vo, 1854. First edn. Five or six shillings.

Scott (Dr.) Suggestive Inquiry into the Hermetic Mystery, with Dissertation on the more celebrated of the Alchemical Philosophers, 8vo, 1850. Very rare. A copy sold at Sotheby's in May, 1893, for £5 2s 6d.

Scrutator.—*See* Horlock (J. K.) and (D. W.).

Sealy (T. H) The Porcelain Tower, or 9 Stories of China, by T. T. T., illusts. by J. Leech, p 8vo, 1841. Scarce. 10 or 12 shillings.

Secretary of the Board of Agriculture.—*See* Young (Arthur).

Seeley (Prof. J.) Ecce Homo, a Survey of the Life and Work of Jesus Christ, 8vo, 1866. Library edition.—Another edition, post 8vo, 1868. Pub 6s —Another edition, post 8vo, 1874.

Seeley (R. B) Remedies suggested for some of the Evils which constitute the " Perils of the Nation," p. 8vo, 1844.

Selby (W. D.) The Charters, Ordinances, and Bye-Laws of the Mercer's Company, folio, 1881. Anonymous and Privately Printed. 10s. 6d.

Senior (W.) Waterside Sketches, a Book for Anglers and Wanderers, by " Red Spinner," frontispiece, cr. 8vo, 1875. 5s.

Sennemaud (Le P , *Jésuite*) Pensées Philosophiques d'un Citoyen de Montmartre, 12mo, *La Haye*, 1756.

G

Settle (E.) The Female Prelate, a Tragedy, by a Person of Quality, sm. 4to, 1689. Uncommon, but of little value.

Seward (W.) Anecdotes of Distinguished Persons, 4 vols., 8vo, 1804. 10s.

Sewell (Miss E. M.) Experience of Life, by the author of "Amy Herbert," fcp. 8vo, 1853.—Cleve Hall, by the author of "Amy Herbert," 2 vols., fcp. 8vo, 1855 —Good Old Times, a Tale of Auvergne, cr. 8vo, 1857.—A Glimpse of the World, by the author of "Amy Herbert," fcp. 8vo. 1863 —Gertrude, by the author of "Amy Herbert," fcp. 8vo, 1865.

Sewel (W.) More News from Salisbury, comprising Exam. of the Bp. of Salisbury's Charge Sermon, Vindication of Collier's Ecclesiastical Hist., etc., post 8vo, *E. Curll*, 1714.

Shadwell.—The Fair Quaker of Deal, or Humours of the Navy, 1710. A Comedy.

Shakespeare (W.) A Compendious or Briefe Examination of certayne ordinary Complaints of divers of our Countrymen in these our days (1581), by W. S., 8vo, 1781. Really by W. Stafford, though attributed to Shakespeare. 7s. 6d.

Sharpe (Chas. K.) Six Portraits, by an Amateur, 4to, *s. l.*, 1833. Very rare, not published for sale. Realises 30s. to-day.

Sharpe (Sir Cuthbert) Chronicon Mirabile, or Extracts from Parish Registers, principally in the North of England, 8vo, 1841. Scarce, worth 15s.

Shaw (J. B.) Sonnets and other Poems by Sigma, post 8vo. *Manchester*, 1863. Of nominal value.

Shaw (W., *D.D., Rector of Chelvey*) Life of Hannah More, with Critical View of her Writings by the Rev. Sir Archibald MacSarcasm, Bart , 8vo. *Bristol*, 1802.

Shelley (P. B.) Posthumous Fragments of Margaret Nicholson, ed. by J. Fitzvictor (P. B. Shelley), 4to. Facsimile reprint of 1810.—St. Irvyne, or the Rosicrucian, a Romance by a Gentleman of the University of Oxford, 8vo, 1811. First edn., excessively rare. £10. —Faustus, from the German of Goethe, with Retsch's series of 27 Outlines, all engraved by Moses, and portrait, 4to, 1832. Rare. 25s. The Appendix contains the May Day Night Scene, translated by P. B. Shelley.—"We Pity the Plumage, but Forget the Dying Bird," thin 8vo, *T. Rodd*, N.D. A reprint, but still rare, and worth £1. I have never seen an *original* copy.

Shelley (Mrs.) The Last Man, by the Author of "Frankenstein," 3 vols., med. 8vo, 1826. First edition. 12s. 6d. if uncut.—Lodore, First edn., 3 vols., cr. 8vo, 1835. Very rare, sells at 15s. and upwards. Her "Frankenstein" is too well known to need more than mere mention.

Sheridan (R. B.).—*See* Halbed (N. H.).

Shiells (Alex.) A Hind let Loose, or an Hist. representation of the Testimonies of the C. of Scotland, etc., post 8vo, *s. l.*, 1687. The Printer's name is also absent.

Shirley (E. P.) Historical Memoir of the Lives of the Shirley Brothers, 4to, 1848. Scarce. But few copies were printed for members of the Roxburghe Club. Should sell at 15s.

Shorthouse (J. H.) John Inglesant, a Romance, 2 vols., post 8vo, 1882. 5s. The 8vo Library edn. is worth more.

Shute (John. *Viscount Barrington*) Miscellanea Sacra, 2 vols., 8vo, 1725. Three or four shillings.

Sibson.—A Pinch of Snuff, Curious and Original Anecdotes of Snufftaking, etc., full-page plates by T. Sibson, 12mo, illustrated boards, *Tyas*, 1840. First edition. 10s.

Sigma.—*See* Shaw (J. B.).

Sims (Geo. R.) Balzac's Droll Stories from the Abbey of Touraine, transl. into English, 425 illusts. by G. Doré, thk. cr. 8vo, *J. C. Hotten*, N.D. Scarce, having been rigidly suppressed. Always sells at 10s 6d.

Singer (S. W.) Psalmes of David, with portraits, 8vo, 1823. In addition to the editor being anonymous, only 250 copies were printed. 7s. 6d.

Singleton (Mrs.).—This lady has written several Books under the *nom-de-plume* of "Violet Fane," notably "Denzil Place," the first edn. of which would probably bring £3 3s. to-day; "From Dawn to Noon" (First edn. about £2), and "Sophy, or Adventures of a Savage," original edn. 3 vols., also issued in single volume form, both edns. of minor value.—The Queen of the Fairies, and other Poems, by Violet Fane, post 8vo 1876. First edn., 10s.—Anthony Babington, a Drama, by Violet Fane, post 8vo, 1877. First edn. Scarce. 7s. 6d.—Helen Davenant, 2 vols., cr. 8vo. 1889. First edition.—Margaret de Valois, Q. of Navarre Memoirs of, written by her own hand newly transl. into English, with Intro. and Notes, by Violet Fane, 8 very fine portraits and engr. title, 8vo, 1892. Scarce. A nice copy, 15s.

Skelton (Rev. P.) Ophiomaches, or Deism Revealed, 2 vols., 8vo, 1749. Best edition. 6s.

Skene (J.) Plain Dealing with the Presbyterians, by way of answer from a Gentleman to an M.P. concerning Toleration, in a Letter to a Friend, 4to, 1703. A rare tract. 10s.

Sketchley (Arthur).—*See* Rose (Rev. G.).

Skinner (V.) A Discovery and Playne Declaration of sundry Subtill Practices of the Holy Inquisition of Spayne, by R. G. Montanus (trans. by V. Skinner), sm. 4to, *Ihon Day*, 1568. Printed in 𝕭𝖑𝖆𝖈𝖐 𝕷𝖊𝖙𝖙𝖊𝖗 and rare, examples from the Press of Ihon Day not being common. 21s.

Slick (Sam).—*See* Haliburton.

Smedley (Rev. E.) Lux Renata, a Protestant Epistle, with Notes, by the author of "Religio Clerici," 8vo, 1827.

Smiff (O. P. Q. Philander).—*See* Dowty (A. A.).

Smith (Dr. Angus) Loch Etive and the Sons of Uisnach, *illustrated*, 8vo, 1879. 7s 6d.

Smith (C. Roach) Catalogue of the Museum of London Antiquities, collected by him and in his possession, many plates, roy. 8vo, 1854. Privately Printed 15s. Also 25 copies on Large Paper, seldom met with, about 30s.

Smith (G., *of Kendal*) Compleat Body of Distilling, 8vo, 1749.

Smith (Horace) Zillah, a Tale of the Holy City, by the Author of "Brambletye House," 4 vols., post 8vo, 1828. 7s 6d.—The Tin Trumpet, or Heads and Tales for the Wise and the Waggish, to which are added Poetical Selections by Paul Chatfield, M.D., ed. by Jefferson Saunders, port. of Chatfield, 2 vols., post 8vo, *Whittaker*, 1836. First edition and scarce. 21s.—The Tin Trumpet, or Heads and Tales, ed. by Jef. Saunders, post 8vo, 1869.—Gale Middleton, by author of "Brambletye House," 3 vols., cr. 8vo, *Bentley*, 1883.

Smith (J. and H.) Rejected Addresses, or the new Theatrum Poetarum, sm. post 8vo, 1812. First edition, and rare. 10s. 6d. There exist many editions of this book, but the only one (besides the First) which realizes any price is that issued in 1833, with fine tinted portraits, and humourous engravings by Cruikshank. This commands perhaps 21s.

Smith (J. S.) Mirabeau, a Life History, 2 vols., cr. 8vo, 1848. Now scarce, and sells at 15s.

Smith (M.).—*See* Peterborough (E. of).

Smith (W. C.) The Bishop's Walk, and the Bishop's Time, by ORWELL, fcp. 8vo, N.D.—Hilda among the Broken Gods. First edn, cr. 8vo, 1878.

Smollett (T.) The History and Adventures of an Atom, 2 vols., post 8vo, *Almon*, 1769. Excessively rare. £10—£12 if uncut.

Soane (G.) Specimens of German Romance, selected and translated from various Authors, with fine etchings by Geo. Cruikshank, 3 vols., post 8vo, *Whittaker*, 1826. First edn., very scarce. Two guineas.

Society of the Learned (A).—*See* Heathcote (Ralph).

Solitary Traveller (A).—*See* Atkinson (A.).

Son of Liberty (A).—*See* Church (Dr. B.).

Southey (Robt.) Letters from England, by Don Manuel Alvarez Espriella (Southey), trans. from the Spanish, 3 vols., sm. post 8vo, 1814. Rare. 7s. 6d.

Southey (Mrs.) Chapters on Churchyards. 2 vols., p. 8vo, 1829.

Souza (Catherine De) Osmia, Tragedia de Assumpto Portuguez, sm. 4to, *Lisbon*, 1788. Rare. 7s. 6d. According to Bouterwek this Tragedy is by above Authoress, and doubtless this is correct, though Sismondi says the Countess of Vinciero was the Authoress.

Spannaghel (Phil. Gottfried, Baron Von) Notizia della vera liberta Fiorentina, con la sincera disamina e confutazione delle scritture e testi, etc., 3 vols., folio, (*Milan*), 1724-6. Rare. 21s. This work was secretly printed by order of the Emperor Charles VI, who only had 50 copies printed for the Court of Vienna. Copies very rarely occur for sale.

Sparrow (Antony) Collection of Articles, Canons, &c., of the Church of England, 4to, 1675. Should have frontispiece of Arms. About 7s. 6d.

Spence (Joseph) Moralities, or Essays, Letters, Fables, and Translations, by Sir Harry Beaumont, 8vo, 1753. Of very trifling value. —Crito: A Dialogue on Beauty, by Sir Harry Beaumont, *cut on title*, post 8vo, 17—. Scarce, but of nominal value.

Spencer.—This work is not written with the idea of making it a medium for any "Advertisement Puffs," but having, on many occasions, had the pleasure of inspecting the Stock of Mr. W. T. Spencer, of 27, New Oxford St., W.C., (to say nothing of the information I have gained from the same, duly recorded in this volume, and for which I here tender Mr. Spencer my best thanks), I think it worthy of mention that all Collectors of such authors as Ainsworth, Browning (R. and W.), Dickens, Leigh Hunt, Lamb, Lever, George Meredith, W. Morris, Ruskin, Shelley, Stevenson, Surtees, Tennyson, and Thackeray, or Works illustrated by Alken, Caldecott, Cruikshank, Crowquill, Doyle, Phiz, Seymour, Sibson, &c., should either write for his Catalogues, or, if possible, call and personally inspect his unique stock of the same. Mr. Spencer is also always open to purchase any such works at a good price.

Speranza.—*See* Wilde (Lady).

Sportascrapiana.—*See* Wheeler (C. A.).

Stafford (W.).—*See* Shakespeare (W.).

Steele (Sir R.) The Tatler, Lucubrations of Isaac Bickerstaff, 4 vols., roy. 8vo, 1710. Best large type Library edn. 30s.

Stehelin (John Peter) Traditions of the Jews, with Expositions and Doctrines of the Rabbins contained in the Talmud, &c., and Account of their Religious Customs and Ceremonies, 2 vols., 8vo, 1732-4. First edition. Very rare. Two guineas.

Stephen (Sir G.) Adventures of a Gentleman in search of a Horse, by Caveat Emptor, cuts by Geo. Cruikshank, post 8vo, 1845. First edition. 5s.

Sterndale (Mary) The Life of a Boy, by the author of "The Panorama of Youth," 2 vols., cr. 8vo, 1821. Four or five shillings.

Sterne (Laurence) Sermons of Mr. Yorick, with portrait, 7 vols., fcp. 8vo, 1759-69. First edition 21s.—Life and Opinions of Tristram Shandy, 9 vols., fcp. 8vo, 1760-7. First edn., and carries autograph of author in three of the later vols. £3 3s.—Letters from Yorick to Eliza, [Dedicated to Lord Apsley]. fcp. 8vo, 1775. Rare. 5s. or 6s.—The Koran, &c., by Tria juncta in Uno, M.N.A.; or Master of No Arts, 3 vols. in 1, *Vienna*, 1798. Curious and scurrilous, though of no great value. Also attributed to Richard Griffith.

Stevens (G. A.) Dramatic History of Master Edward (Shuter), Miss Ann (Catley) and others; plates, 8vo, 1785. Very rare. A good copy easily realizes £2.

Stevenson (R. L.) An Inland Voyage, First edn., 1878. Travels with a Donkey, First edn., 1879. Virginis Puerisque, First edn., 1881. New Arabian Nights, First edn., 1882. Familiar Studies in Men, First edn., 1882. A Child's Garden of Verses, First edn., 1885. All rare and exceedingly valuable.—The Broken Shaft, Tales in Mid-Ocean, includes a Contribution by R. L. S., 4to, 1886.

Stirling-Maxwell (W.) Songs of the Holy Land, sq. 8vo, *Ollivier*, 1848. First edn.; very rare. 21s.—Velasquez and his Works, with vign. portrait and title in red and black, post 8vo, orange cloth, *Parker*, 1855. First edition and very scarce. 15s. to 21s., if a nice copy, uncut.

Stockdale (J. J.) The Covent Garden Journal, with 4 views, 8vo, pubd. by the Author, 1810. An amusing History of the O. P. Row, in which John Kemble took a large part.

Stokes (George) Commentary upon the Holy Bible from Henry and Scott, with Notes, maps, &c., 6 vols., fcp. 8vo, 1831-4. About 6s.

Stokes (W.) The Play of the Sacrament, A Middle-English Drama, ed. with Glossary, by W. S., 8vo, *Berlin*, 1862. 5s.

Stonehenge.—*See* Walsh (J. H.).

Stranguage (William) The Historie of the Life and Death of Mary Stuart, Queene of Scotland, with beautiful engr. title, folio. 1624. Issued anonymously, and should have fine portrait of the Queen by Elstracke, which is often absent. 15s. with portrait.

Strutt (Mr.) History and Description of Colchester (the Camulodunum of the Britons and first Roman Colony in Britain), with account of Antiquities of the Borough, fine plates 2 vols., med. 8vo, *Colchester*, 1803. Ten shillings.

Summerley (Felix).—*See* Cole (Sir H.).

Surtees (R. S.) The series of Sporting Novels, Mr. Sponge's Sporting Tour, Handley Cross, etc., illust. with coloured plates by Leech, are too well known to need more than mere mention. First editions are valuable.

Sutcliffe (T.) Crusoniana, or Truth versus Fiction, elucidated in a History of the Islands of Juan Fernandez, plates, 8vo, *Manchester*, 1843. Curious and rare. 7s. 6d.

Swift (Jonathan, *D.D.*) A Tale of a Tub, and Battel between the Ancient and Modern Books in St. James's Library, 8vo, 1704. A rare edn. 15s. There are numerous other issues.—Proposal for correcting, improving, and ascertaining the English Tongue, in a Letter to the E. of Oxford, 8vo, 1712. Nominal value.—Travels into several remote Nations of the World, by Capt. Lemuel Gulliver, 2 vols., 8vo, 1726. With portrait. First edition, and very rare. £5.—Travels into several Remote Nations of the World, in four parts, by Lemuel Gulliver, portrait, and 4 maps, 8vo 1726.—The Hibernian Patriot, being Drapier's Letters to the People of Ireland, with Poems and Songs, 8vo, 1730. 4s.—Political Tracts, by the author of Gulliver's Travels, 2 vols., 8vo, 1737. 7s. 6d.—Complete Collection of Genteel and Ingenious Conversation, by S. Wagstaff (*i.e.*, J. Swift), 8vo, 1738. First edition. Rare. £2 2s.

Swinburne (A. C.) Unpublished Verses by A. C. Swinburne [1866]. 4 pp. Only 20 copies printed.—Dolorida (in French), written in the Album of Adah Isaacs Menken [1813]. 4 pp. Only 50 copies printed. These 2 rare leaflets sold at Sotheby's in May, 1893, for 28s.

Swindon (Tobias) Enquiry into the Nature and Place of Hell, post 8vo, 1714. Exceedingly curious, and this is a very uncommon edition. 5s.

Sykes (A. Ashley) Two Enquiries into the Meaning of Demoniacks in the N.T., by T.P.A.P.O.A.B.I.T.C.O.S., 8vo, 1737.

Symson (Patrick) A Short Compend. of the Hist. of the First Ten Persecutions moved against Christianity, etc., sm. 4to, *Edinburgh, printed by A. Hart*, 1613. 7s. 6d.—A Short Compend. of the Arrian and Eotychian Persecutions, with Compend. of the Romane Autichrist, etc., 4to, *ib.*, 1616. 7s. 6d.

Tabley (Lord de) Rehearsals, a Book of Verses, by J. Leicester Warren, post 8vo, 1870. 5s.

Taylor (Edgar) The New Testament, revised from the Text of Griesbach. by a Layman, thk. cr. 8vo, 1840. One of Pickering's beautiful publications.

Taylor (Sir Henry) Isaac Commenus, a Play, 8vo, 1827. First edition. About 6s.—Natural History of Enthusiasm, Seventh (and best) edn.. 8vo, 1835.—Fanaticism, by the author of Natural History of Enthusiasm, 8vo, 1834. Pubd. 10s. 6d. Two interesting works, always to be procured at from 3s. to 4s. each.

Taylor (John) The Identity of Junius with a distinguished living Character established, with facsimiles of his handwriting. 8vo, 1818. An ingenious attempt to fix Sir Philip Francis as the author of these Letters.

Taylor (S. A.) Cocking and its Votaries, by S. A. T. First edition, 8vo, wrappers, N.D. Very rare. £2 10s.

Taylor (T.) A Cry to the Professor's Conscience, fcp. 8vo, *Leeds*, 1876. Of no value.

Taylor (Thos., *the Platonist*) An Essay on the Beautiful, from the Greek of Plotinus, post 8vo, 1792. First edition, and rare. Eight to ten shillings. The oval nude vignette on title is an exquisite piece of work, worthy of Bartolozzi.—Pausanias, the Description of Greece, etc., maps and plates, 3 vols, 8vo, 1824. Considered the best edition of this valuable book, and sells for about 30s.

Taylor (Tom) Charles Dickens, the Story of his Life, *numerous ports. and facsim.*, 8vo, *Hotten* (1870). Best edition. He has also wrote "Life of Thackeray."

T. B.—*See* Blount (Thos.).

T. B.—*See* Brewer (Thomas).

T. D.—*See* Deloney (Thos.).

Tempest (S., *of Broughton*) Religio Laici, sm. 8vo, 1768.

Tennyson (Alfred, late Lord) Poems, MDCCCXXX.—MDCCCXXXIII., sq. 12mo, wrappers, 1862. Privately printed, and very rare. £4 4s. Probably printed abroad and the publication stopped. It consists of those poems in the volumes of 1830 and 1833, which were suppressed in the subsequent editions.—*THE GEM (an Illustrated Annual) for 1831, has three Poems by the late Lord Tennyson), which are not in his collected works, and cannot (I believe) be obtained elsewhere. (*) Since writing the above, the author of "Tennysoniana" has published a Bibliography of Tennyson (indispensable to all collectors), in which I see a note to the effect that these Poems were contained in "The Lover's Tale," etc., 50 copies of which were Privately Printed in 1875.—The Victim, a Poem, 4to, 1867. Privately Printed at Crawford Manor, on one side of the paper only, with view on title. Would probably realize £4 or £5 to-day.—In the Magazine of Art for 1892 will be found an article " Lord Tennyson," by Theodore Watts, with 7 different portraits of the Poet.

Tennyson (Charles, *i.e.*, Charles Tennyson d'Eyncourt) Eustace, an Elegy, with fine proof plates, large 8vo, 1851. Very scarce, the last copy that passed through my hands sold for 12s. 6d., and a copy sold at the Thomas sale, at Sotheby's, in May, 1891, for £1 6s.—Small Tableaux: Poems by Charles (Tennyson) Turner, fcp. 8vo, 1868. First edition, 15s. Sonnets, Lyrics, and Translations by the same, similar size and value, first edition, 1873. Both very scarce. He was brother to the late Poet Laureate, and one of the authors of "Poems by Two Brothers," 1827.

Tennyson (Frederick), contributed to "Prolusiones Academicæ in cura Cantabrigiensis," etc., 8vo, 1828.

T. F.—*See* Thynn (Fras.).

Thackeray (W. M) The Snob, a Literary and Scientific Journal, not conducted by Members of the University, issued in Numbers, post 8vo size, *Camb.*, 1829. The only *signed* contribution to this Journal by W. M. T., viz., "Timbuctoo" is contained in No. 4. A set is very rare. £10 or more.—The London and Westminster Review, April, 1839, containing a 24-p. contribution by W. M. Thackeray, entitled "Parisian Caricatures," 8vo, 1839. This article is signed "T.," and was afterwards included in his "Paris Sketch Book." Rare, 15s.—The Paris Sketch Book, by M. A. Titmarsh, with 12 full-page engravings and several cuts, all by W. M. T., 2 vols., post 8vo, *Macrone*, 1840. First edn., and very rare. Issued partly cut, but still copies *entirely* uncut do exist, and in such state are probably worth £15.—Essay on the Genius of George Cruikshank, with numerous illusts. and etchings, 8vo, green cloth, *H. Hooper*, 1840. First edition. If uncut, and with the plate "Philoprogenitiveness," often wanting, £2 10s.—Comic Tales and Sketches, by Mr. M. A. Titmarsh, 12 full-p. etchings, by W. M. T., 2 vols., post 8vo, *Cunningham*, 1841. The earliest issue has the gilt lettering in ovals, and should have uncut edges. In this state it realizes £17—£18.—The Irish Sketch Book, by M. A. Titmarsh. numerous illusts. by the author, 2 vols., 8vo, *Chap. and Hall*, 1845.—Mrs. Perkins's Ball, by M. A. Titmarsh, 22 full-page illusts. by the author, sm 4to, pink boards, *C. & Hall*, 1847. First edn. Should have verses underneath frontis. 25s. plain, double that amount coloured.—Our Street, by M. A. Titmarsh, with 16 illusts. by the author, cr. 8vo, pink pictorial boards, 1848. First edition, and if COLOURED, £3 3s., plain copies 25s.—John Bull and his Wonderful Lamp, a new reading of an old Tale, by Homunculus, 6 very clever illustrations by the author, square 8vo, *Petheram*, 1849. Anybody who sees these engravings (the frontispiece especially) cannot help putting down Thackeray as the artist. Rare, 10s. or even more.—The Britannia, a Weekly Journal of News, Politics, etc., 1841 and 3, 2 vols., folio. Contains a long Review of Thackeray's "Second Funeral of Napoleon," "Loose Sketches," etc. Rare. £3 3s.—Rebecca and Rowena, a Romance upon Romance, by Mr. M. A. Titmarsh, with illusts. by R. Doyle. cr. 8vo, pink pict. bds., 1850. First edn., and very scarce. Three guineas, if coloured. Plain copies, 21s.—The Kickleburys on the Rhine, by M. A. Titmarsh, 15 illusts. by the Author, cr 8vo. pink bds., *C. & Hall*, 1850. 1st edn. 21s., plain. £2 2s., coloured.—THE KEEPSAKE (1851), in addition to 12 elegant engravings, contains a Story entitled: "Voltigeur," by W. M. T , sq 8vo, 1851. About 7s. 6d.—The Rose and the Ring, or Hist. of Prince Giglio and Prince Bulbo, by M. A. Titmarsh, full-p. and other illusts. by W. M. T.. pink bds., *C. & Hall*, 1855. Two guineas.—History of Samuel Titmarsh and the Great Hoggarty Diamond, 9 full-page etchings by W. M T., post 8vo, pictorial bds., 1849. First Edn. and Rare, and if UNCUT, £3 10s. Another Edition, post 8vo, yellow wrappers, 1857. 5s. —Kerography. - Specimens of a New Process of Engraving for Surface Printing, by W. J. Linton, illusts., sq. 8vo, *Linton*, 1861. 10s. Includes an experimental drawing by W. M. T., of three figures and some letterpress, viz. :—" Dear Sir,—Will this print in relief? if so, one might write and draw on the same plate. Send me, if possible, a proof of this, and oblige, yours, W. M. T." This illustration by the great Novelist has not appeared in any other way, before or since.—The Victoria Regia, a volume of Original Contributions, ed. by Adelaide A. Proctor, contains ' A Leaf out of a Sketch Book," by W. M. T., and 2 orig. illusts. by him, roy. 8vo, *Faithfull*, 1861. 5s. or 6s.—Thackerayana, Notes and Anecdotes, illust. by nearly 600 Sketches by W. M. Thackeray. First edn., thk. 8vo, 1875. Suppressed and rare. 30s.—" The Grey Friar," a Chronicle in Black and White, by Carthusians, 4to, swd., *printed at the Charterhouse, April,* 1892. Contains Thackeray as a Carthusian, with 12 humourous sketches by W. M. T., drawn when at the School, and reproduced for the first time, also facsim. of a MS. by him, " Holy day Song," dated Aug. 1st, 1826 : also 3 other Portraits of him. Rare. 10s.—Collectors of "THACKERAYANA," or those wishing to dispose of First Editions of Thackeray, or similar standard works, should either write for Mr. W. T. Spencer's Catalogue, issued from 27, New Oxford St., W.C., and sent gratis and post free ; or on the other hand, submit their copies for sale to the same gentleman, when they may rest assured the full market value will be received.

The London Hermit.—*See* Parke (F.).

Thicknesse (P.) Sketches and Characters of the most Eminent and most Singular Persons now Living, Vol. 1, 8vo, *Bristol*, 1770. All published. Rare. 30s.

Thomas (Julian) Cannibals and Convicts, map and portraits, 8vo, 1880.

Thomas (R) Handbook of Fictitious Names, by Olphar Hamst, cr. 8vo, 1868.

Thomas (W.) Prison Thoughts, by a Collegian, p. 8vo, 1821.

Thompson (William) Letters from Scandinavia on the Past and Present State of the Northern Nations of Europe, 2 vols , 8vo, 1796. 5s.

Thomson (Cockburn) Almæ Matres (dedicated, without permission, to the Freshmen and Dons of Oxford), by Megathym Splene, B.A., thk. post 8vo, *Hogg, c.* 1850.

Thomson (J. ?) Dialogues in a Library, sm. 8vo, 1797. Rare. 7s. 6d.

Thomson (Jas.) The City of Dreadful Night. First Edn., cr. 8vo, 1880. The companion volume, Vane's Story, and other Poems, 1881. There were 40 copies each, of these 2 volumes, printed on Large Paper, which sell for 30s. the two, to-day.

Thomson (Richard) Chronicles of London Bridge, by an Antiquary, med. 8vo, 1827. About 12s. 6d. Large Paper Copies, 8vo size, with proof impressions of the vignettes (by W. Harvey) on India Paper. 21s.

Thynn (Francis) The Perfect Ambassador, treating of Antiquities, priviledges, and behaviour of men of that function, by T. F., 12mo, 1652. 5s.

Tilt (C.) The Boat and the Caravan, 7 steel plates (6 by Bartlett and 1 by H. Vernet), 12mo, 1847. Rather scarce, pubd. at 7s.

Timperley (C. H.) Songs of the Press, and other Poems, relative to the Art of Printers and Printing, Authors, Books, Booksellers, Binders, Editors, Critics, Newspapers, &c., with Notes, Biographical and Literary, post 8vo, 1845. Scarce. 7s. 6d.

Tindal (Matthew, *the celebrated Deist*) The Rights of the Christian Church asserted against the Romish and all other Priests who claim an independent power over it, &c., with Preface, 8vo, 1706. Suppressed and very rare.—Christianity as old as the Creation; or the Gospel a republication of the Religion of Nature, 8vo, 1730. There are numerous other editions of this Deistical work, which occasioned much controversy.—A Defence of the Rights of the Christian Church, with some Tracts of Grotius and Hales, 8vo, *London*, 1709. Anonymous and rare.

Tisdale (R.) The Form of Dedication and Consecration of a Church or Chapel, &c., 4to, *J. Hartley*, 1703.

Titmarsh (M. A.).—*See* Thackeray (W. M).

Toland (John) Christianity not Mysterious, or a Treatise shewing there is nothing in the Gospel contrary to Reason, &c., 8vo, 1696. First edition. The second edn., published about 6 years later, is considered the best.—Remarks on the Life of Milton, as published by J. T., with a character of the Author and his party, 8vo, 1699 First edition. Not valuable.—Amyntor, a Defence of Milton's Life, containing Apology for all Writings of that kind, Catalogue of Books attributed in Primitive Times to Jesus Christ, His Apostles, and other Eminent Persons, Complete History of *Eikon Basilike*, proving Dr. GAUDEN and not K. Charles I. to be the Author, &c., &c., 8vo, 1699. First edn. Rare. 10s. 6d.

Tongue (Cornelius) "Cecil's" Records of the Chase, and Memoirs of Celebrated Sportsmen, 2 plates by Herring, post 8vo, 1854.—The Billesdon Hunt, The Belvoir Hunt, The Quorn Hunt, and The N. Warwickshire Hunt, all pubd. under the pseudonym of "Cecil," post 8vo, s. d. (all 1870). Of nominal value.

Tootle (Rev. H.) Secret Policy of the English Society of Jesus, sm. 8vo, 1715. Rare.—Church History of England from 1560-1688, chiefly with regard to Catholicks, 3 vols., folio, *Brussels*, 1737. Rare. About three guineas—Church History of England, by C. Dodd, 5 vols., large 8vo, 1839-43.

Topffer (R.) Beaten Tracks, or Pen and Pencil Sketches in Italy, by the authoress of a "Voyage en Zigzag," numerous illustrations, 8vo, 1866. 7s. 6d —Pictures in the Tyrol and elsewhere, from a Family Sketch Book, by the author of "A Voyage en Zigzag," with a large number of very clever full-page illusts., sq. 8vo, 1867. Scarce. 6s.

Topham (Capt. E.) Letters from Edinburgh, 1774-5, 8vo, 1776. First edition.

Torbuck (J.) A Collection of Welsh Travels and Memoirs of Wales, containing D—n S—t's Journey there; A Trip to N. Wales, by a Barrister; The Welsh School-Master, by Dr. K—g; and Muscipula, or the Mouse-Trap, in Latin and English, collected by J. T., post 8vo, *circa* 1734. 5s.

Toulmin (Camilla).—*See* Crossland (Mrs. Newton).

Tourney (Count de).—*See* Brosses.

Townsend (C.) Winchester, and other Compositions in Prose and Verse, 4to, *Winchester, J. Robins*, 1835. This is a very scarce item, only a few copies having been issued for Private circulation anonymously.

T.P.A.P.O.A.B.I.T.C.O.S.— *See* Sykes (A. A.).

Tracts for the Times. The contributors were John Keble, Isaac Williams, Dr. Pusey, Cardnl. Newman, Thos. Keble, Sir G. Provost, and Rev. R. Wilson, who signed their contributions alphabetically from A. to G., in the order written above.

Traveller (A.).—*See* Campbell (J. F.).

Trelawney (Edw.) Essay concerning Slavery, and the Dangers Jamaica is expos'd to, from the too great number of Slaves, 8vo, 80 pp. (one blank), *c.* 1725.

Trench (Archbp.) Elegiac Poems, 12mo, 1850.

Treuwhard (J.) Abelard to Eloise, a Moral and Sentimental Epistle, with Notes and Illustrations, 8vo, (pub. 1s.), *London*, for the Author, 1820. On the cover of the only copy I ever saw was written: "This Jeu d'Esprit was printed for the use of the author's Friends," and the erotic nature of the Text renders this highly probable. The Printer's name is withheld. Rare. 10s.

Trinity Man (A).—*See* Wright (Thos.).

Trithemii (Jo.) Abbatis Spanhemensis O S.B. Legenda Sanctissimæ Matronæ, Annæ Genetricis Virginis Mariæ metris et Jesu Christi Aviæ, *Impressum Lypsk*, per *Melch. Lotter*. A.D. 1498. XVI. vero Oct. Kalen. feliciter terminatum, 4to. Of the utmost rarity. Sigs. A.—E. iii.

Trye (J) Impartial Inquiry into the Benefits and Damages arising to the Nation from the present great use of low-priced Spirituous Liquors, etc., 8vo, *London*, 1751.

Tryon (T.) Country Man's Companion, or new Method of Ordering Horses and Sheep, so as to preserve Them from Diseases and Casualties, or to Recover them if ill, etc., by Philotheos Physiologus, 12mo, 169-. Rare. 7s. 6d.

T. T. T.—*See* Sealy (T. H.).

Tucker (Miss C. M.) The Young Pilgrim, a Tale illustrative of the "Pilgrim's Progress," by A. L. O. E., fcp. 8vo, 1857.—The Shepherd of Bethlehem, King of Israel, by A. L. O. E., fcp. 8vo, 1863. Pubd. at 4s. 6d. This Lady has pubd. many other works under Pseudonym A. L. O. E.

Turnbull (W. B.) Factum of the E. of Arran, touching the Restitution of the Duchy of Chatelherault, 8vo, 1685-1843. Only 60 copies issued.

Turner (Dawson) Guide to the Historian, Biographer, Antiquary, and Collector of Autographs, towards the Verification of MSS. by reference to engraved facsims. of handwriting, roy. 8vo, *Yarmouth*, 1848. Scarce. 5s. or 6s.

Turner (Dawson) Short History of the Westminster Forum, by the President, 2 vols., 8vo, 1781. 10s. 6d.

Turnley (J.) Reveries of Affection in Memory of the Prince Consort, fine photos, the Text printed within gold borders, *Privately Printed*, 1868.

Twining (Rev. Danl.) A reply to the question (if it should ever be asked) Where and What is Bitteswell? 13 plates, 8vo, 1848. 6s.

Two Brothers.—*See* Hare.

Twogood (Rev. Micajah, *of Exeter*) A Collection of Psalms and Hymns, sm. 8vo, *Exeter*, 1780.

Twysden (Sir Roger) Historical Vindication of the Church of England in point of Schism, as separated and reformed by Q. Elizabeth, 4to, 1657. First and only edition, but of merely nominal value.

Tymme (Tho.) A Silver Watch Bell, the sound whereof is able to win the most prophane Wordling, sm. 8vo, 1617, 𝔅lack 𝔏etter. Rare. 15s.

Tyrrell (E.) A Chronicle of London from 1089 to 1483, written in the XVth Century, and for the FIRST TIME printed from MSS. in the Brit. Museum, with Royal Letters, Poems, &c. (ed. by E. Tyrrell), fine facsimile frontis., 4to, 1827. Only 250 copies printed. 20s. The last copy I catalogued was a Present from E. Tyrrell to Thos. Duffus Hardy, with Inscription, and of course was worth a little more than above amount.

Tytler (W.) Inquiry, hist. and critical, into the Evidence against Mary (Q. of Scots), and Exam. of Robertson and Hume, 8vo, *Edinb*, 1772. 5s.—Inquiry into the Evidence against Q. Mary, &c., 2 vols., 8vo, 1790. Rather scarce, though not of great value.

Ubique.—*See* Gillmore (Capt. P.).

Udall (Nicholas) Ralph Royster Doyster, a Comedy, entered on the Books of the Stationers' Company, 1566, 8vo (78 pp), 1821. The first English Comedy. 5s about.

Urbino (Marchioness).—*See* Noake (Dorothy).

Utterson (E. V.) Select Pieces of Early Popular Poetry, republished principally from early printed copies in Black Letter, 2 vols., 1817. Only 250 issued.

V., Poems by.—*See* Clive (Mrs. Archer).

Vagabond (The).—*See* Thomas (Julian).

Vairasse (D.) History of the Sevarites or Sevarambi, a Nation of the Terræ Australes incognitæ, written by Capt. Siden, 2 parts, 12mo, 1700. Rare, and sells for about 15s.

Vanbrough (Sir J.) A Short Vindication of the Relapse and The Provok'd Wife from Immorality and Prophaneness, 1698.

Van Effen.—Le Conte du Tonneau, contenant tout ce que les Sciences et Les Arts ont de plus sublime et de plus mystérieux, etc., par le Fameux Dr. Swift, trad. de l'Anglais, 2 vols., sm. post 8vo, *La Haye*, 1721. Avec figures, non signées, mais fort curieux. 7s. 6d.

Varley (Isabella) Ivy Leaves. Poems by Mrs. G. Linnæus Banks, cr. 8vo, *Manchester*, 1844. Of trifling value.

Vaughan (Thos.) The Man-Mouse taken in a Trap, by Eugenius Philalethes, sm. 8vo, 1650. Rare. 10s.

Verger de Hauranne (J. Du) Considerations sur les Dimanches et Les Festes, etc., 2 vols., 8vo, *Paris*, 1671. Very rare. £2 2s.

Vernon (Lord) Chiose sopra Dante, testo inedito ora per la Prima Volta Publicato [by Lord Vernon], thk. roy. 8vo (900 pp), *Privately Printed, Firenze*, 1846. A curious point in connection with this production is that it is printed on hand-made paper bearing the Arms of Lord Vernon as watermark on every sheet throughout. Present value 15s.

Vernon (I. R.) The Harvest of a Quiet Eye, many illustrations, 4to. Of little value.

Verstegan (Richard) A Restitution of Decayed Intelligence in Antiquities, concerning the most noble and renowned English Nation, by the Studie and Travails of R. V., very curious cuts, sm. 4to, *Antwerp*, 1605. First edn., 21s. Another edn., sm. 4to, 1638, 7s. 6d to 10s , according to condition.

Viadurre (L'Abbé) Compendio della storia geografica, naturale, e civile del regno de Chile, map and 10 plates, 8vo, *Bologna*, 1776.

Vialart (Ch , *called Saint Paul*) Histoire du Ministere d'Armand Jean du Plessis, Cardinal Duc de Richelieu, sous Le Regne de Louys le Juste (*i e.*, Louis XIII), 2 vols., fcp. 8vo, *Paris (Hollande, Elzevir)*, 1650-55. About 7s. 6d.

Vicars (T.) ΑΣΤΡΟΛΟΓΟΜΑΝΙΑ, The Madness of Astrologers, an Examination of Sir Chris. Heydon's Booke, 4to, 1624. Very rare. 21s. or more.

Vigor (Mrs.) Letters from a Lady, who resided some years in Russia, to her Friend in England, 12mo, 1774. Curious.

Vitis Carolinæ gemma altera, sive Auspicatissima Ducis Eboracensis Genethliaca Decantata ad Vadaisidis, 4to, *Oxon*, 1633. Rare. This is a Collection of congratulatory Poems in Latin and English, in honour of the Birth of James II, by Bp Duppa, J. Prideaux, Parkehurst, C. Herbert, P. Sydney, J. Poulet, J. King, E. Sylvester, &c. Sells at 15s. and upwards. Lowndes does not know it, nor is it mentioned in "*Bibl. Anglo.-Poet.*"

Voltaire (M. de) La Pucelle d'Orleans, Poeme divise en vingt chants, avec des notes, portrait and 20 most spirited and curious plates, 8vo, *sine loco* 1762. This is the rare *first* issue with 20 chapters, the former editions only containing fifteen. A fine old copy which passed through my hands some time ago was sold for 10s., probably less than its value.—La Pucelle d'Orléans, avec des notes, auquel on a joint plusieurs pièces qui y ont rapport, with a very fine vignette, 2 vols, fcp. 8vo, *Londres, (Paris, Casin)*, 1780. A charming and rare edition. 12s. to 15s —Lettres Philosophiques, par M. de V*****, sm. 8vo, *à Rouen*, 1734.

W. A.—*See* Weldon (Sir Anthony).

Waldie (Miss E. A.) Rome in the XIXth Century, &c., 3 vols., p. 8vo, 1822.

Waldron (F. G.) Literary Museum, reprints of Scarce and Curious Tracts, (Gascoigne's Delicate Diet for dainte-mouthde Droonkards, 1576.—Roscius Anglicanus, or an Historical Review of the Stage, 1641-1660, with additions by T. Davies), 1789-92.

Walker (O.) Vulgar Errours in Practice Censured, sm. 8vo, 1659. Rare and curious. 7s. 6d.—Of Education, especially of Young Gentlemen, fcp. 8vo, *Oxford*, 1687. 5s. perhaps.—The Greek and Roman History illust. by Coins and Medals, &c., thk. 8vo, 1692. Of trifling value.

Walker (W.) Jottings of an Invalid in Search of Health, &c., by Tom Cringle, 8vo, *Bombay*, 1865 He also pubd. under above Pseudonym "Hints on House-Building," and "Letters on Practical Subjects."

Walking Gentleman (A).—*See* Grattan (T. C.).

Wallace (J.) Savillon's Elegies, or Poems written by a Gentleman, plates by I. Cruikshank, cr. 8vo, 1795.

Wallis (J.) The Greatest Light in the World, far exceeding the Light of the Quakers, ———, 1674. Attributed to J. Wigan in Smith's Bibliotheca Anti-Quakeristica, but I prefer to attribute the authorship to J. Wallis, D.D.

Walmsley (Bp.) General History of the Christian Church, by Sig. Pastorini, 8vo, 1771.

Walpole (Horace) The Castle of Otranto, a Gothic Story, transl. by W. Marshall Gent, from the Original Italian of Onuphrio Muralto, Canon of the Church of St. Nicholas at Otranto, 4th edn., post 8vo, *Dodsley*, 1782 Lowndes mentions no edition at all between the second and the fifth, and Allibone only mentions 5 editions out of the first 6, excluding the one described above. Very rare. 15s. or more.—The Palace of Otranto, a Gothic Story, 8vo, 1800. A scarce edition, with coloured plates. 6s —The Mysterious Mother, a Tragedy, post 8vo, 1791. This surreptitious edn was the first to appear after the privately printed (50 copies) Strawberry Hill issue. The ground-work of this Tragedy is very similar to the 30th Tale in the " Tales of the Queen of Navarre."

Walpole (Robert) Isabel, from the Spanish of Garcilass de la Vega, with other Poems, &c , 8vo, *Cambridge*, 1805.

Walsh (J. H.) Stonehenge on the Shot-Gun, Sporting Rifle, Dogs, Ponies, Ferrets, etc., illustrated, thk. 8vo, 1859. 5s.— Stonehenge on the Dog, numerous engravings, 8vo, 1859. First edition. 7s. 6d.—The Greyhound, by Stonehenge, illustrated, sq. 8vo 1875, pub. 15s. A good copy about half published price.— Dogs of the British Islands, *engravings*, sq. 8vo, 1882. This author is a well-known authority on the subject, and the illusts. are good. A nice copy is worth 7s. 6d.—The Horse in the Stable and Field, &c., 170 *good engravings*, thk. 8vo, 1866. About the same value as previous item.

Walther (David) VINDICLE BIBLIC.E ; a Series of Notices, and Elucidations of Passages in the Bible misrepresented by the Deistical Writers, 8vo, 1832.

Walton (C.) Notes and Materials for an adequate Biography of the celebrated Divine and Theosopher, William Law (the Nonjuror and Mystic), 8vo, 1854. Privately Printed, without author's name, and very rare.

Warmstry (Thomas) An Answer to Certaine Observations of W. Bridges concerning the Present Warre against His Majestie (Charles I.), whereby he pretends to Justify it, &c., 4to, 1643. Rare and valuable. 10s. 6d.

Warneford (R.) Skedaddle, by "Our own" Special Correspondent, never before printed, post 8vo, *Vickers*, 1865. Of very trifling value.

Warner (Dr.) Metronariston ; or, a New Pleasure, recommended in a Dissertation upon a Part of Greek and Latin Prosody, with fine portrait of Adolphus Mekerchus, post 8vo, *J. Johnson*, 1797. Uncommon, but of trifling value.

Warren (J. Leicester).—*See* Tabley (Lord De).

Warter (Rev. J. W.) The Sea-Board and the Down; or, My Parish in the South, by an Old Vicar, 2 vols., 1860. Scarce. 7s. 6d.

Warton (Thos) The Oxford Sausage, Poems by most Celebrated Wits of the University, post 8vo, *Oxford*, 1772. The scarce illustrated edition, and, in addition to the very quaint cuts, should have portrait of Mrs. Dorothy Spreadbury, Inventress of the Oxford Sausage. This is nearly always abstracted. A perfect copy, 8s. 6d.—Another edition, with cuts by Bewick, post 8vo, 1777.— The Oxford Sausage, or Select Poetical Pieces, written by the most Celebrated Wits of the University, sm. 8vo. *Oxford*, 1821.— Specimen of a History of Oxfordshire, 4to, 1783. 5s.

Warburton (W., *Bp., author of " The Divine Legation of Moses"*) View of Lord Bolingbroke's Philosophy, 8vo, 1756.

Ward (Harriet) Five Years in Kaffir-Land, 8vo, 1846.

Ward (Ned, *author of " The London Spy"*) The Delights of the Bottle; with a South Sea Song upon the late Bubbles, and Spittle-Fields Ballad, 8vo, 1721. Rare, but not exceedingly valuable. Usually catalogues at 7s. 6d. or thereabouts.—Secret History of London Clubs, 2 Parts, 1709. Of this exceedingly quaint account of London Club Life at the beginning of the last Century, there was, till recently, but the solitary issue mentioned above. The compiler of this volume has just issued a limited "Private edition," on Large and Small Paper; the former of which is nearly out of print, only 100 having been done.—Secret History of the Calves Head Club, or the Republican Unmasked, with Thanksgiving Songs for the 30th January (Charles I. commemoration), 4to, 1704. Very rare. 15s.—Another edition, 8vo, 1705.—Another, with the Character of a Modern Whig, 8vo, 1706. 6s.—Vulgus Britannicus, or British Hudibras, the Secret History of the late London Mob, and Wars between High and Low Church, a Continuation of Butler, by the author of the London Spy, five Parts, with a similar number of plates, 8vo, 1710. Rare. 15s.

Ward (R. Plumer) De Vere, or the Man of Independence, by the Author of "Tremaine," 4 vols., post 8vo, 1827. First Edition. 5s.—"Tremaine," 4 vols., is of similar value.

Wase (Christopher) The Electra of Sophocles, presented to Lady Elizabeth, trans. and applied to the Murder of Charles I., and the hoped for Restoration, with an Epilogue, sm. 8vo, *At the Hague*, 1649. Very rare. The writer was expelled from his College (King's, Cambridge) for this production, which, if perfect, should contain 2 ports. (one of Elizabeth and one of Charles II.). If containing these, 21s.

Wassington (Prior) History of the Cathedral Church at Durham, as it was before the Dissolution of the Monastery, containing Rites, Customs, and Ceremonies used therein, Description of Paintings, Translation of St. Cuthbert's Body, etc., 12mo, *Dur., Richardson*, *c.* 1733. 4s. 6d.

H

Watkins (J.) Essay towards a History of Bideford, Devon, 8vo, *Exeter*, 1792.

Watts (Isaac) Philosophical Essays, etc., 8vo, 1733.

W. C.—*See* Worthington (E.).

Webb (Philip Carteret) Short Account of Danegeld, with some further Particulars relating to William the Conqueror's Survey, 1756, thin 4to, 1756. Rare. 10s. 6d.

Weldon (Sir Anthony) Court and Character of King James, written and taken by Sir A. W., sm. 4to, 1650. About £1 10s. The reprint (1817) is of little value.—Aulicus Coquinariæ, in answer to Sir A. W., sm. 8vo, 1650. I take this to be an answer to *Sir A. Weldon's Court and Character of King James*, 1650, the previous item.

Wellesley (Lord) Primitiæ et Reliquiæ, 8vo, *Privately Printed* (issued anonymously), 1840. Formerly scarce, though I have seen a good many copies lately. Nominal value.

Wesley (John) An Account of the Conduct of the War in the Middle Colonies, extracted from a late Author, sm. 8vo, 1780. Of the greatest rarity. 35s. or more.

West (T.) Guide to the Lakes in Cumberland, Westmoreland and Lancashire, 8vo, *Kendal*, 1778. Another edition, *with map*, 8vo, 1812. Numerous other editions, including those of 1784, 1789, 1799, etc. None of any value, with the exception of that of 1811, which has fine map and lovely coloured plate of Grasmere. 7s. 6d. The descriptive portion was reprinted at Kendal, 1802.

Westmacott (C. M.) The Spirit of the Public Journals, 1823-5, with numerous illusts. by Rowlandson, Cruikshank, etc., 3 vols., post 8vo, *Sherwood*, 1824-6. Scarce. 21s.—The English Spy; Portraits of the Illustrious, Eminent, Eccentric and Notorious, drawn from the Life by "Bernard Blackmantle," with coloured plates and woodcuts by R. Cruikshank, 2 vols., 8vo, 1825-6. Excessively rare. £15. if a fine copy.—The Punster's Pocket-Book, or Art of Punning enlarged, by Bernard Blackmantle, author of the English Spy, *with portrait and numerous illusts. by* R. CRUIKSHANK, med. 8vo, *Sherwood*, 1826. Very scarce. A good uncut copy is worth 7s. 6d.—Fitzalleyne of Berkeley, a Romance of the Present Century, by Bernard Blackmantle, engraved titles by G. Cruikshank, 2 vols., post 8vo. Rare. 21s. Withdrawn from sale soon after publication. Written in illustration of the well-known connection of Miss Foote with Col. Berkeley, the late E. of Fitzhardinge.

Weston (Mr. and Mrs., *of West Horsley Place, Surrey*) The Amulet, Truth in Absence, a Collection of Poems, post 8vo, 1852. Privately Printed at Brixton. 5s.

W. F.—*See* Fulke (W.).

W. G.—*See* Withers (George).

Whately (Archbp.) Scripture Revelations concerning Angels, sm. 8vo, 1851. Of trifling importance.

Whateley (Thos.) Remarks on some of the Characters of Shakespeare, 1785. Scarce.

Wheeler (C. A.) Sportascrapiana, Cricket, Shooting, Pedestrianism, Lion Hunting, etc., by Celebrated Sportsmen, ed. by C. A. W., cr. 8vo, 1867.

Wheelwright (Horace M.) Bush Wanderings of a Naturalist, by an Old Bushman, illustrated, fcp. 8vo, 1862. Of nominal value.— A Spring and Summer in Lapland, by "An Old Bushman," 6 coloured plates, post 8vo, 1871. 5s.

Whistlecraft (W. & R.).—*See* Frere (J. Hookham).

Whitaker (T. D.) A Description of Browsholme Hall, and of the Parish of Waddington, Yorks, also Collection of Letters from original MSS. in the Reigns of Chas. I. and II., and James II., in the possession of T. Lister Parker, plates by Buckler, pedigree, facsimile autographs, etc., 4to, 1815. Anonymous, and privately printed. Rare. 21s.

White (C.) English Country Life, post 8vo, 1843.

White (J.) A Rich Cabinet, with Variety of Inventions, unlocked and opened, for Recreation of Ingenious Spirits at their vacant hours, collected by J. W., many cuts, post 8vo, 1668. With curious frontis. by T. Cross. 7s. 6d.

White (James) Adventures of Sir Fizzle Pumpkin; Nights at Mess, etc., illusts. by G. Cruikshank, post 8vo, 1836. First edn., and of great rarity. Value £2.

White (J.?) Sporting Scenes and Country Characters, by Martingale, many woodcuts after T. Landseer, Alken, etc., 8vo, 1840. Fifteen shillings.

White (James) Aristophanes, The Clouds, now first entirely translated into English, with Notes, fcp. 8vo, 1759. Whether this is really the first complete translation is possibly open to question. It is of little commercial value in any case.

White (J. Blanco) Letters from Spain, by Don Leucadio Doblado, 8vo, 1825. Best edition. Recommended in Ticknor's Spanish Literature.

White (Thomas) Monumethan Excantatus, sive Animadversiones in Libellum Famosum auctore Thoma Anglo, ex Albiis East Saxonum, 12mo, *Rotomagi*, 1659. A rare little item. 7s. 6d.

White (Rev. T. H.) A Pilgrim's Reliquary, 8vo, 1845. Of little value.

Whitehead (George) An Unjust Plea Confuted; an Answer to Moses and Aaron, by Daniel Pointell, a Kent Minister, sm. 4to, 1659. Rare, but of nominal value.—An Epistle of Consolation from the

Fresh Springs of Life and Flowings of the Father's Love, 4to, 1664. Secretly printed. This vigorous old Quaker of Orton (Westmoreland) spent the greater portion of his life in prison. Other pieces of his which I have not met with were secretly printed about the same time; though I have made careful search amongst items from the library of J. Smith, of Whitechapel, a good portion of whose collection lately passed through my hands.

Whiter (W.) A Specimen of a Commentary on Shakespeare, containing Notes on "As you like it," &c. 1794.

White Republican (A).—*See* Fuller (Hiram).

Whitty (J.) Tales of Irish Life, 6 plates by G. Cruikshank, 2 vols., post 8vo, *Robins*, 1824. Rare. A good copy of this (First) edn. is worth 35s.

Wicks (F.) A Ready-Made Family, 3 vols., cr. 8vo, 1871. Three or four shillings.

Wigram (S. R.) Flotsam and Jetsam, A Cargo of Xmas Rhyme (including Leaves from the Arabian Nights), by Hookanit Bee, Esq., cr. 8vo, 1853. Scarce. 5s.

Wilbraham (Roger) Three Letters concerning the Surrender of many Scotch Lords to the High Sheriffe of the Co. of Chester, &c., 4to, 17—. Contains a very full list of Officers and Soldiers of 20 Regiments, who were taken prisoners at Warrington Bridge. About 12s. 6d.

Wilde (Lady, *mother of Oscar*) Ugo Bassi, a Tale of the Italian Revolution, by Speranza, post 8vo. 1857.—Sidonia the Sorceress, translated from the German of William Meinhold by Francesca Speranza (Lady Wilde). The best edition of this book is 4to size, 1893. It is rare and worth between £3 10s. and £4.

Wildfowler.—*See* Clements (L.).

Wilkes (John) The North Briton, 2 vols., fcp. 8vo, J. Williams, 1763.—Origin and Progress of Despotism in the Oriental and other Empires of Africa, Europe, and America, post 8vo, *Amsterdam*, (*i.e.*, the Private Press of the author), 1764 (1763 really). Rare. 7s. 6d.

Wilkie (Wm) The Epigoniad, a Poem, post 8vo, *Edinburgh*, 1757. Of trifling value though very curious.

Wilkins (Bishop) The Discovery of a World in the Moone, or a Discourse tending to prove that there is probably another habitable world there ; diagrams, fcp. 8vo, 1638. Should also have frontispiece, sometimes wanting, but even with this it is of trifling value.—Mercury; or the Secret and Swift Messenger, shewing how a Man may with Privacy and Speed communicate his Thoughts to a Friend at any Distance. fcp. 8vo, 1641. First edition and rare. A good perfect copy is worth 10s. to 12s.

Wilkinson (W.) On the Orbits described by Bodies revolving in given Planes round immoveable centres of Forces, 4to, 1816.

Willes (John) The Present Constitution and the Protestant Succession vindicated, in answer to a late Book "The Hereditary Right of the Crown of England asserted," 8vo. 1714. Of nominal value. The author was a Justice of the Common Pleas.

Willet (Andrew) Synopsis Papismi, that is a general view of Papistrie, 2 vols., 4to, 1594. First edition. There are several other edns in folio, worth 5s. or 6s. each.

Williams (C. Hanbury) Isabella, or the Morning and other Poems, sm. post 8vo, 18—. About 5s.

Williams (E. W.) Virginia, more especially the South part thereof, richly and truly valued; the second edn. with the Discovery of Silkworms, &c., by E. W.; woodcuts and maps, sm. 4to, *London*, 1650. Very Rare. Two guineas or more.

Williams (Isaac) The Cathedral, 12mo, *Parker*, 1858.—The Seven Days, or Old and New Creation, by the author of "The Cathedral," *Oxford*, 1850—The Baptistry, or Way of Eternal Life, 8vo, *Parker*, 1842. Contains 24 very curious plates.

Williams (J.) A Liberal Critique of the present Exhibition of the Royal Academy, by Anthony Pasquin, 8vo, 1794. Of nominal value.

Williams (John) The New Brighton Guide, by Anthony Pasquin, 8vo, 1796. 5s.

Williams (John, *i e., Anthony Pasquin*). Poems. Humourous and Satirical, 2 vols., 1789. Pin Basket to the Children of Thespis, 1797.

Williams.—Annals of the Founders' Company, plates, 8vo, *Privately Printed*, 1867. Very rare. 15s.

Willis (Browne) The Ladies Calling, cr. 8vo, *Oxford*, 1673. Should have a frontispiece. One of the most uncommon of this author's works.

Willis (H Norton) Biographical Sketches of Eminent Persons whose portraits form part of the D of Dorset's Collection at Knole, *Kent* (by H. N. W.), with Description of the Place (by J. Bridgman), 8vo, 1795. Perfect copies have 2 views. 5s.

Wilson (Harriette, *the Notorious Courtezan*) Clara Gazul, or Honi Soit qui mal y pense, 3 vols., post 8vo, 1830. Printed for and pubd. by the author, 16, Trevor Sq., Knightsbridge. Of the greatest rarity. 30s. in the original boards.

Wilson (T.) Catalogue raisonné of the Select Collection of Engravings of an Amateur, with India Proofs of the Engravings by G. Cruikshank, 4to, 1828. Anonymous and Privately Printed. Very rare. £2 10s.

Wilson (W.) The Post Chaise Companion, or Traveller's Directory through Ireland, plates, med. 8vo, *Dublin*, 1788. According to " Lowndes " nearly the whole of this work was included by Gough in his edition of " Camden's Britannia."

Wilton (C) Histoire des Voyages des Papes depuis Pape Innocent I., A.D 409, jusqu'à Pie VI., A D. 1782, avec des notes, 8vo, *Vienna*, 1782.

Winstanley (W., *Jesuit*) England's Worthies, Select Lives of most Eminent Persons of the English Nation from Constantine the Great down to these Times, thk. sm. 8vo, 1684. Curious and rare, though of very trifling value.

Winston (Chas.) Inquiry into the Difference of Style observable in Ancient Glass Paintings, especially in England, with Hints on Glass Painting, by an Amateur, many illusts by P. H. Delamotte, 2 vols , 8vo, *Oxford, Parker,* 1847. In most copies many of the illustrations are coloured. About 35s.

Wise (John R., *Author of " The New Forest "*) is the author of the Text to W. Crane's " May Day," the latter gent being only the illustrator, and Mr. Wise paid him £700 for his work. For this information I am indebted to R. White, Esq , of Worksop, who also sends me other valuable information, which unfortunately arrived too late for incorporation in this edition.

Wiseman (Cardinal) Fabiola, or The Church of the Catacombs, with frontis. and engr. title, post 8vo, *c.* 1860. Scarce. 5s.

Wither (Geo.) Fides Anglicana, a Plea for the Publick Faith of these Nations, sm. 8vo, 1660 —Speculatum Speculativum, or a Considering Glass. sm 8vo, 1660.—Shepherds Hunting [edited by Sir Egerton Brydges], 1814. Only 100 copies printed.—Wither's Motto, *Birmingham*, 1814.—Hymns and Songs of the Church, with Preface by the Editor [Sir E. Brydges], 1815. Only 100 copies issued, and many of these were destroyed by fire.— Another edition, with Intro. by E. Farr, *portrait*, 1856 —Fair Vertue, the Mistress of Philarete and the Shepherd's Hunting, from the 1622 edn. (by J. M. Gutch). 8vo, *Bristol*, 1840. 5s.

Withers (Geo.) Respublica Anglicana, or Historie of the Parliament in their late Proceedings, etc., sm. 4to, 1650. A rare Tract 5s.

Withers (R.) Description of the Grand Signor's Seraglio, &c., ed. by J. Greaves, 12mo, 1650. First edn. of this very curious little Book. Well worth 10s. 6d.

W. J.—*See* Wigan (J.).

W. L.—*See* Longman (W.).

Wolcot (Dr. J.) Bozzy and Piozzi a rare edition, with Rowlandson's plates, 4to. 1786.—Peter Pindar's commiserating Epistle to James Lowther, Earl of Lonsdale and Lowther, with engraving, 4to, 1791. Rare, but not valuable.—Poetical Works, with fine portrait (generally wanting), 5 vols., 8vo, 1795. Best Library edition. Ten or twelve shillings.—Peter Pindar's Hair Powder, a Plaintive Epistle to Mr. Pitt, with Frogmore Fete, and Ode for Music, 4to, 1795. With port. of Dr Wolcot.—Peter Pindar's Tears and Smiles, a Miscellaneous Collection of Poems, frontis. by Corbould, 12mo, 1801.—The Eldest Chick of the Royal Brood, 8vo, *Lond.*, 1812.—The R—l Brood, or an Illustrious Hen and her Pretty Chickens, a Poem, 8vo, 1813.—Suppressed Evidence, or R—l Intriguing, Hist. of a Courtship, Marriage and Separation, &c., 8vo, *Wilson*, 1813.

Wollaston (J.) The Religion of Nature delineated, 4to, 1731. There are numerous other editions, none of them valuable.

Womock (Laurence) Moses and Aaron, the King and the Priest, sm. 4to, 1675.

W. O.—*See* Walker (O.).

Wood (Basil) Stereometry; or Art of Solids demonstrated, fcp. 8vo, 1707. Scarce. 6s.

Woodhouse (J. C., *D.D.*) Short Account of Lichfield Cathedral, frontispiece, 8vo, 1823-4. Other editions, none valuable.

Woodrofte (Dr) Feckenham Charity, founded by Sir T. Cookes, Discourse to Trustees, on management of this Charity, 4to, *Oxford*, 1700.

Woodward (J.) Account of Roman Urns, &c., digg'd up at Bishopsgate, 8vo, 1715. One of E. Curll's curious publications.

Woolcombe (Thos.) Notices of Sir W. Molesworth, portrait, cr. 8vo, 1857. Anonymous and Privately Printed.

Woolston (Thos.) A Letter to Dr. Bennet upon this Question, whether Quakers do not the nearest of any other Sect in Religion, resemble the Primitive Christians in Principles and Practice, by Aristobulus, 8vo, *London*, 1720.

Woorell (A.) The Resolution of the Army concerning the King's Majestic's going to Richmond (Surrey), &c , 4to, 1647.

Wordsworth (C.) The College of St. Mary, Winton, near Winchester. 4to, 1848.

Worledge (J.) Systema Agriculturæ, the Mystery of Husbandry Discovered, with Kalendarium and Dictionarium Rusticum, folio, 1681. 15s.

Worthington (E.) Reason and Religion, or the certain Rule of Faith, where the Infallibility of the Roman Catholick Church is asserted, against Atheists, Heathens, Jewes, Turks, and all Sectaries; with Refutation of Stillingfleet's many gross errours, thk. 4to, *Antwerp*, 1672. Rare. A good copy. 21s.

Woty (W) Shrubs of Parnassus, a Variety of Poetical Essays, by J. Copywell, of Lincoln's Inn, fcp. 8vo, 1760. Rare. 7s. 6d.

W. P.—*See* Prynne (W.).

Wright (Thos.) Alma Mater, or Seven Years at the University of Cambridge, by a Trinity Man, 2 vols., cr. 8vo, 1827.

Wright (T.) The Great Unwashed, by the Journeyman Engineer, cr. 8vo, 1868. First edn. 5s.—Johnny Robinson, the Story of the School Days of an Intelligent Artisan, by a Journeyman Engineer, 2 vols., cr. 8vo, 1868. Pubd. at 21s.

Wright (Thos).—*See* Halliwell (J. O.).

W. S.—*See* Stokes (W.).

Yarrell (T) Gardens and Menagerie of the Zoological Society delineated, hundreds of fine illustrations, 2 vols., 8vo, *Chiswick*, 1830. Pubd. £2 8s. Yarrell the eminent Naturalist contributed a great deal of valuable matter to these volumes.

Yelverton (T.) Teresina in America, by Therese Yelverton (Viscountess Avonmore), 2 vols , thk. cr. 8vo, 1875. First edition, scarce. 5s.

Yendys (Sidney).—*See* Dobell (Sidney).

Yonge (Charlotte M.) History of Sir Thomas Thumb, illust. by J. B., 8vo. *Edinb.*, 1855. First edn. of a very uncommon Book by this popular Authoress. The illustrations are good, and remind one somewhat of Doyle.—The Six Cushions, by the author of "The Heir of Redcliffe," post 8vo, 1867. First edition —The Pupils of St. John the Divine, by the author of "The Heir of Redclyffe," illustrated, post 8vo, *Macmillan*, 1868.

Young (Arthur) Six Weeks' Tour in the Southern Counties of England and Wales, describing particularly the Agriculture, Manufactures, Prices of Labour, Country Seats, &c , plates, 8vo, 1769. Rare. 15s —General View of Agriculture of Essex, drawn up by the Secretary of the Board of Agriculture, coloured map and plates, 2 vols., thk. 8vo, 1807 —View of the Agriculture of Oxfordshire, by the Secretary of the Board of Agriculture, 8vo, 1809. Pubd. at 12s. With folding coloured map and 28 full-page plates. 5s.— A Farmer's Tour through the East of England, being the Register of a Journey through the various Counties of this Kingdom to enquire into the State of Agriculture, 4 vols., 8vo, with plates. Very rare. 30s. or more.

Young (Sir G. C.) Privy Councillors and their Precedence, 8vo, 1860. Anonymous and privately printed, but of little value.

Zabrochi (Count de Brody) A Pilgrimage of the Freemasons and their Mission, with Account of their Persecution, by P. Le Bell and Clement V., 8vo, *Bath*, N.D , 184-.

Zeta.—*See* Froude (J. A.).

Index to Titles.

Index to Titles.

N.B.—With respect to the titles of anonymous works described in the Index, the definite article has either been excluded or placed at the end of title—thus " The Heir of Redclyffe" will be found under " Heir of Redclyffe," and Pseudonyms with Christian Names will nearly always be found under the second name, thus " Bernard Blackmantle," vide Blackmantle (B.).

A.—*See* Arnold (Matthew)
A. (Major).—*See* Coles (B. Coles)
Abbatis Spanhemensis.—*See* Trithemii (Jo.)
Abbotsford and Sir W. Scott.—*See* Matthews (G. K.)
Abelard to Eloise.—*See* Treuwhard (J.)
Absurdities, &c.—*See* Forrester (A. H.)
Accessible Field Sports.—*See* Gilmore (Parker)
Account of European Settlements in America.—*See* Burke (E.)
Account of Roman Remains. - *See* Lysons (Sam.)
Account of Roman Urns, &c.—*See* Woodward (J.)
Account of the Conduct of the War.—*See* Wesley (J.)
Accounts of 55 Royal Processions.—*See* Nichols (J. Gough)
Acheta Domestica.—*See* Bugden (Miss L. M.)
Across the Atlantic.—*See* Lewis (J. D.)
Acts of the Apostles, &c.—*See* Byington (Rev. C.)
Address to a Provincial Bashaw.—*See* Church (Dr. B.)
Address to the Ladies.—*See* Holt (Dorothy)
Adventures of a Gentleman, &c.—*See* Stephen (Sir G.)
Adventures of an Atom.—*See* Smollett (T.)
Adventures of Caliph Haroun Alraschid.—*See* Manning
Adventures of Capt. Boyle.—*See* Chetwood (W. R.)
Adventures of Hajji Baba.—*See* Morier (J.)
Adventures of Sig. Gaudentio de Lucca.—*See* Berkeley (Bp.)
Adventures of Sir Frizzle Pumpkin.—*See* White (Jas.)
ΑΣΤΡΟΔΓΟΜΑΝΙΑ.—*See* Vicars (T.)
A F. F.—*See* Arbuthnot (F. F.)
Against the Apple of the Left Eye.—*See* Lightbrodie (G.)
Agathonia.—*See* Gore (Mrs.)
Aggeus the Prophete.—*See* Pilkyngton (J)
Agothocles.—*See* Porrinchief (R.)
Agrippa's Vanitie, &c.—*See* Sanford (James)
A. H.—*See* Anderson (H.)
A. K. H. B.- *See* Boyd (Rev. A. K. H.)
Albert Lunel.—*See* Brougham (Lord)
Alcida.—*See* Greene (Robt.)

Alciphron's Epistles.—*See* Monro
Alcoran des Cordeliers.—*See* Albère (E.)
Alcoran of Mahomet.—*See* Ross (Alex.)
Alexander's Expedition.—*See* Beddoes (Dr.)
Alfred of Wessex.—*See* Kelsey (R.)
Alice through the Looking Glass, and Alice in Wonderland.—*See* Dodgson (Rev. C. L.)
Allies (The) and the late Ministry.—*See* Defoe (D.)
All Sorts, &c.—*See* Iram
Alma Mater.—*See* Wright (T.)
Almæ Matres.—*See* Thomson (Cockburn)
Almerinde.—*See* Asserino (L.)
A. L. O E.—*See* Tucker (Miss C. M.)
Alpine Lyrics.—*See* Bainbridge (W.)
Alton Locke.—*See* Kingsley (C.)
Amadis des Gaules.—*See* Lubert (Mlle.)
Amanda, a Sacrifice. &c.—*See* Hookes (N.)
Amaryllis at the Fair —*See* Jefferies (R)
Amateur (An).—*See* Egan (Pierce)
Amateur (An).—*See* Sharpe (C. K.)
Amateur (An).—*See* Winston (C)
Amateur of Fashion (An).—*See* Roby (J)
Amateur Poacher (The).—*See* Jefferies (R.)
American (An).—*See* Christy (David)
American Traveller (The).—*See* Cluny (A.)
Amours de Cleandre &c.—*See* Montreuix
Amours des Dames illustres.—*See* Bussy-Rabutin
Amours d'Ismene et d'Ismenias.—*See* Beauchamp (De)
Amours and Gallantry.—*See* Amours
Amulet (The).—*See* Weston (Mr. and Mrs)
Amy Herbert —*See* Sewell (E. M.)
Amyntor —*See* Toland (J.)
Ananga Ranga.—*See* Arbuthnot (F. F.)
Anastasius —*See* Hope (C.)
Anatomy of Melancholy —*See* Burton (R.)
Ancient Parish Church of Eccles.—*See* Harland (J)
Ancient Scottish Poems.—*See* Dalrymple (Sir D.)
Anecdotes of Distinguished Persons.—*See* Seward (W.)
Anecdotes of W. Bowyer.—*See* Nicholls (J.)
Angler (An).—*See* Davy (Sir H.)
Angler (The).—*See* Lathy (T. P.)
Anna.—*See* Bennet (Mrs.)
Annals of Cornelius Tacitus.—*See* Grenewey (Richard)
Annals of the Founders Company.—*See* Williams
Annals of the Parish - *See* Galt (John)
Annotations on the Gospels.—*See* Elsley (Rev.)
Annual Anthology.—*See* Lloyd (C.)
Anonymiana.—*See* Pegge (Saml.)
Anser Pen-Dragon —*See* Ireland (W. H.)

INDEX TO TITLES.

Answer to W. Bridges.—*See* Warmstry (T.)
Answer to Where are your Arguments, etc ?—*See* Bolton (R.)
Answer to Bp. Gardiner.—*See* Gilby (A.)
Anthony Babington.—*See* Singleton (Mrs.)
Antiquary (An) —*See* Thomson (R.)
Antiquities of St. Peter's.—*See* Crull (J.)
Autony (Real).—*See* Michel (Fernand)
Apology for Carew, King of Beggars.—*See* Goodby (R.)
Appeal to the Whigs, etc.—*See* Burke (E)
Apule. Les Metamorphoses.—*See* Montlyard
Arcana Microcosmi.—*See* Ross (A.)
Archæologist (The).—*See* Halliwell (J. O.)
Architectural Mag —*See* Ruskin (J.)
Aristobulus.—*See* Woolston (Thos)
Aristophanes, The Clouds of.—*See* White (J.)
Armata.—*See* Erskine (Lord)
Artemus Ward.—*See* Browne (C. F.)
Artificial Clock-Maker (The).—*See* Derham (Dr.)
Art of Cookery.—*See* Glasse (Mrs. H.)
Art of Ingeniously Tormenting.—*See* Collier (Miss)
Art of Making Wine —*See* M'Culloch (J.)
Art of Prolonging Life.—*See* Kitchener (W.)
Ashmole, Fasciculus Chemicus.—*See* Dee (Dr. A.)
Athenian Oracle (The).—*See* Dunton (J.)
Athenian Sport.—*See* Dunton (J.)
Augustine (St.) of the Citie of God.—*See* Healey (J.)
Aulicus Coquinariæ.—*See* Weldon (Sir A.)
Aureus, etc.—*See* Oakley (P.)
Aus Mehemed.—*See* Puckler-Muskau (H. L H)
Autumn Holidays of a Country Parson.—*See* Boyd (A. K. H.)
Avonmore (Viscountess) —*See* Yelverton (Therese)
A. W.—*See* Allen (William)
A. W.—*See* Weldon (Sir A)
Ayesha, the Maid of Kars.—*See* Morier (J.)
Ayrshire Legatees (The).—*See* Galt (John)

Bab Ballads, and More Bab Ballads.—*See* Gilbert (W. S.)
Balder.—*See* Dobell (Sidney)
Balzac's Droll Stories.—*See* Sims (G. R.)
Banks (Mrs. Linnæus).—*See* Varley (Isabella)
Baptistery (The). - *See* Williams (Isaac)
Bard (A).—*See* Crane (J)
Barnabee's Journal.—*See* Braithwaite (R.)
Barney Mahoney —*See* Croker
Barrister (A).—*See* Clark (Chas.)
Barruel's Memoirs.—*See* Clifford (Hon. R.)
Battle of Dorking.—*See* Chesney (Sir G.)
Battle of Life.—*See* Peabody (G.)
Battle of Waterloo.—*See* Booth (J.)

Battledoor (A) for Teachers, etc.—*See* Fox (Geo.)
Bayley (H. V.) Memoir of.—*See* Le Bas (C. H.)
Beaten Tracks.—*See* Topffer (R.)
Beaumont (Sir Harry).—*See* Spence (Joseph)
Beau Nash.—*See* Goldsmith (O.)
Beauty and the Beast, and Cinderella.—*See* Forrester (A. H.)
Bee (The).—*See* Budgell (Eustace)
Belcaro.—*See* Paget (Violet)
Beheaded Dr. Hewytt's Ghost, etc.—*See* Prynne (W.)
Belforest.—*See* Manning (Anne)
Bell (Currer).—*See* Bronté (C.)
Bell (Ellis).—*See* Bronté (E. J.)
Bell (Acton).—*See* Bronté (Anne)
Bellenden.—*See* Ballantyne (J.)
Bevis, the Story of a Boy.—*See* Jefferies (R.)
Bible (The).—*See* Brett (T.)
Bible (The).—*See* Burgess (Bp.)
Bible (The).—*See* Martin (Sir H.)
Bible (The).—*See* Parker (T.)
Bibliographical Memoranda.—*See* Fry (J.)
Bibliography des Ouvrages relatifs à L'Amour, etc.—*See* Gay
Bibliophobia.—*See* Dibdin (T. F.)
Bibliosophia.—*See* Beresford
Bibliotheca Anglo-Poetica.—*See* Griffith (A. F.)
Bibliotheca Biblica.—*See* Parker (S.)
Bickerstaff (I.).—*See* Steele (Sir R.)
Biographical Memoirs, etc.—*See* Beckford (W.)
Biographical Sketches, etc.—*See* Willis (H. N.)
Bipeds and Quadrupeds.—*See* Brendley (C.)
Births, Marriages, and Deaths —*See* Hook (Theodore)
Bishop's Walk, etc. (Poetry).—*See* Smith (W. C.)
B. K.—*See* Keach (Benjamin)
Blackmantle (Bernard) —*See* Westmacott (C.)
Blacksmith (A).—*See* Kames (Lord)
Blanche Lisle.—*See* Davis (Augusta)
Bleeding Iphigenia (The).—*See* French (Dr.)
Blenkinsop (Vicesimus).—*See* Hook (Theo.)
Blind Child (The).—*See* Pinchard (Mrs.)
Bloomfield (Bp.).—*See* Cambridge
Boat and the Caravan.—*See* Tilt (C.)
Bobbin's (Tim) Works, various.—*See* Collier (J.)
Boece (Hector) Hist. of Scotland.—*See* Ballantyne (J.)
Bolingbroke's Philosophy.—*See* Warburton (Bp.)
Bonasus Vapulans.—*See* Hickman (H.)
Bon Gaultier.—*See* Aytoun and Martin
Book about Boys.—*See* Moncrieff (H.)
Book about Dominies.—*See* Moncrieff (H.)
Book of Ballads.—*See* Aytoun and Martin
Book of Nonsense.—*See* Lear (E.)

Book and its Story.—*See* Ranyard (Mrs.)
Book-Lover's Enchiridion.—*See* Ireland (J.)
Border and Bastille.—*See* Lawrence (Major G. A.)
Botanic Garden (The).—*See* Darwin (E.)
Boy of Bilson (The).—*See* Baddeley (R.)
Boz.—*See* Dickens (C.)
Bozzy and Piozzi.—*See* Wolcot (Dr. J.)
Bracebridge Hall.—*See* Irving (W.)
Braddon (Miss M. E.).—*See* Maxwell (Mrs. J.)
Brambletye House.—*See* Smith (Horace)
Bramhall.—*See* Bromwell (J.)
Breaking a Butterfly.—*See* Lawrence (J.)
Breakspeare.—*See* Lawrence (J.)
Brereley (J.).—*See* Anderton (J.)
Breton (Nich.).—*See* Baxter (N.)
B. R. F.—*See* Arbuthnot and Burton
Brief Treatise on N. Y. Police.—*See* Christian (C.)
Britain, its Earliest Hist.—*See* Cole (F. S.)
Britannia (The).—*See* Thackeray (W. M.)
Britannia Languens —*See* Child (Sir J.)
British Army (The).—*See* Dilke (Sir C.)
British Galleries of Art.—*See* Hazlitt (W.)
Broken Shaft (The).—*See* Stevenson (R. L.)
Bromsgrove Facetiæ.—*See* Crane (J.)
Brother of the Birch (A).—*See* Cobbett (W.)
Brown (Baldwin).—*See* Poems by Three Friends
Brown (Pisistratus).—*See* Black (W.)
Brown (T., the Younger).—*See* Moore (Tom)
Browne (Matt.).—*See* Rands (W. B.)
Browne (Sir T.).—*See* Crossley (J.)
Brydges (Sir E.).—*See* Wither (Geo.)
Bubbles from the Brunnens, etc.—*See* Head (Sir F. B.)
Bude-Haven.—*See* Maskell (W.)
Buhl (J. P.).—*See* Hanson (Sir L.)
Bunyan's Pilgrim's Progress.—*See* Dibdin (T.)
Buonaparte.—*See* Anti-Gallican (The)
Burford Cottage.—*See* Kendal (E. A.)
Burke (Edmund) Answer to.—*See* Chalmers G.)
Burlesque Translation of Homer.—*See* Brydges (Thos.)
Burney (Fanny).—*See* D'Arblay (Madame)
Burroughs (E. Quaker).—*See* Howgill (F.)
Butler's Ghost.—*See* Durfey (Tom)
B. V., " Bysshe Vanolis."—*See* Thomson (J.)

C. (Marquis de).—*See* Chastelet
Caleb Williams.—*See* Godwin (W.)
Camp of Refuge.—*See* Macfarlane (C.)
Campaigns of the British Army, etc.—*See* Gleig (Rev. G. R.)

INDEX TO TITLES.

Campbell (Duncan).—*See* Defoe (D.)
Cannibals and Convicts.—*See* Thomas (Julian)
Canning (G.)—*See* Microcosm (The)
Card (The).—*See* Kidgell (J.)
Card Essays.—*See* Jones (Henry)
Carolonna.—*See* Maxwell (James)
Carroll (Lewis).—*See* Dodgson (Rev. C. L.)
Casimir Maremma.—*See* Helps (Sir A.)
Castle of Otranto.—*See* Walpole (H)
Catalogue de la Bibliotheque, etc.—*See* Libri
Catalogue of Books, etc.—*See* McCulloch (J. R.)
Catalogue of Cottonian MSS.—*See* Planta (J.)
Catalogue of English Writers.—*See* Crowe (W.)
Catalogue of 500 Authors.—*See* Marshall
Catalogue of Hardwicke MSS.—*See* Coxe (Archdeacon)
Catalogue of London Antiquities.—*See* Smith (C. Roach)
Catalogue of Scottish Writers.—*See* Maidment (J.)
Catalogue of the Tracts of Laws, etc.—*See* Brydall (J.)
Catholic University Gazette —*See* Newman (Cardnl.)
Cat's Tail (The).—*See* Bowles (C)
Caveat Emptor.—*See* Stephen (Sir G.)
Cavendish.—*See* Jones (Henry)
Cavendish.—*See* Neale (W. J.)
C. A. W.—*See* Wheeler (C. A.)
Caxton (P.).—*See* Lytton (Bulwer)
C. D.—*See* De Morgan
Cecilia.—*See* D'Arblay (Madame)
Cecil.—*See* Tongue (C.)
Ceracchi, a Drama.—*See* Naylor (S.)
Certain Odes of Horace.—*See* Ashmore (J.)
C. H.—*See* Constable (H.)
Chapters on Churchyards.—*See* Southey (Mrs.)
Chapters on Flowers.—*See* Elizabeth (C.)
Charge of the Chief Justice, etc.—*See* Cockburn (Sir A)
Charity and Truth.—*See* Hawarden (Dr.)
Charles I —*See* Jane (John)
Charles II.—*See* Vitis Carolinæ
Charters, etc., of Mercers' Company.—*See* Selby (W. D.)
Chase (The) and William and Helen.—*See* Scott (Sir W.)
Chase, Turf, and Road.—*See* Apperley (C.)
Chastété (La).—*See* Manuel
Chatfield (Paul).—*See* Smith (Horace)
Chaucer's England.—*See* Rands (W. B.)
Cheape and Goode Husbandrie.—*See* Markham (G.)
Chef-D'Œuvre d'un Inconnu.—*See* Saint Hyacinthe
Chelsea Hospital.—*See* Gleig (G. R.)
Cherry and Violet.—*See* Manning (Anne)
Chettle (H.)—*See* Constable (H.) ..
Child's Garden of Verses.—*See* Stevenson (R. L.)

Chiose sopra Dante.—*See* Vernon (Lord)
Christianity as old, etc.—*See* Tindal (M.)
Christianity not founded, etc.—*See* Dodwell (H.)
Christianity not Mysterious.—*See* Toland (J.)
Christian's Mistake.—*See* Muloch (Miss)
Christmas Festivities.—*See* Poole (John)
Christ's Passion.—*See* Sandys (G.)
Chronicle of Kings of England.—*See* Dodsley (R.)
Chronicle of London.—*See* Tyrrell (E.)
Chronicles of the Charterhouse.—*See* Ryder (W. J. D.)
Chronicles of London Bridge.—*See* Thomson (R.)
Chronicles of Schonberg-Cotta Family.—*See* Charles (Mrs.)
Chronicon Mirabile.—*See* Sharpe (Sir C.)
Chronicon Nurembergense.—*See* Schedel (H.)
Chrysal.—*See* Johnson (Charles)
Church History of England.—*See* Tootle (Rev. H.)
Church Parties.—*See* Conybeare (W. J.)
Cigar (The).—*See* Clarke (C.)
Cigar, Companion to.—*See* Clarke (C.)
Citizen (A).—*See* Christian (Chas.)
City of Dreadful Night.—*See* Thomson (J.)
Civil War (Charles I.).—*See* Copley (L.)
Civil War, Charles I.—*See* Cradock (P.)
Civil War, Charles I.—*See* Woorell (A.)
Civil Warres of G. Britain.—*See* Davies (J.)
Civitas Lincolnia.—*See* Ross (John)
C. J. (De).—*See* Buonaparte
Claims of Labour.—*See* Helps (Sir A.)
Clara Gazul.—*See* Wilson (Harriette)
Clarissa Harlowe.—*See* Richardson (S.)
Clark (J. C.).—*See* Dickens (C.)
Classic Tales.—*See* Hunt (Leigh)
Classical Dictionary Slang).—*See* Grose (F.)
Claude the Colporteur.—*See* Manning (Anne)
Cleave's Gazette.—*See* Dickens (C.)
Clergyman's Choice of a Wife.—*See* Legh (G.)
Cleve Hall.—*See* Sewell (E. M.)
Clockmaker (The).—*See* Haliburton
Cloud of Witnesses (A).—*See* Mall (T.)
Cloudesley.—*See* Godwin (W.)
Clouds of Aristophanes.—*See* Cumberland (R.)
Club-Book (The).—*See* Picken (A.)
Clytemnestra.—*See* Lytton (Robt.)
Cocking and its Votaries.—*See* Taylor (S. A.)
Code of Common Sense (A).—*See* Gregson (J. S.)
Cœlebs in Search of a Wife.—*See* More (Hannah)
Colchester, Hist. of.—*See* Strutt (J.)
Cole (Sir H.).—*See* Summerley (Felix)
Coleridge (S. T.).—*See* Annual Anthology

Collectanea Curiosa.—*See* Gutch (J.)
Collection of Articles, Canons, &c.—*See* Sparrow (A.)
Collection of Coats-of-Arms.—*See* Nayler (Sir G.)
Collection of Old Ballads.—*See* Philips (A.)
Collection of Psalms and Hymns.—*See* Twogood (Rev. M.)
Collection of Royal Wills.—*See* Nichols (J.)
Collection of Statutes.—*See* Rastell (W.)
Collection of Verse and Prose.—*See* Ruddiman (T.)
Collection of Voyages and Travels.—*See* Churchill (J.)
Collection of Welsh Travels.—*See* Torbuck (J.)
College of St. Mary, Winton.—*See* Wordsworth (C.)
Collegian (A).—*See* Thomas (W.)
Collins' Walk through London.—*See* D'Urfey (Tom)
Columella.—*See* Graves (Rev. R.)
Comes Facundus, &c.—*See* Holyday (Barten)
Comic Art Manufactures.—*See* Leighton (J.)
Comic Latin Grammar.—*See* Lee (P.)
Comic Tales and Sketches.—*See* Thackeray (W. M.)
Commenius.—*See* Hoole (C.)
Common-Place Book —*See* Gaston (Rev. H.)
Commentary (Bible).—*See* Stokes (Geo.)
Commonwealth of Oceana.—*See* Hannington (J.)
Commonwealth of Women.—*See* Durfey (T.)
Companion (The).—*See* Hunt (Leigh)
Companion to the Playhouse.—*See* Baker (David Erskine)
Companions of my Solitude.—*See* Helps (Sir A.)
Compendio della storia, etc.—*See* Viadurre (L'Abbé)
Compendious or Briefe Exam., etc.—*See* Shakespeare (W.)
Compleat Body of Distilling.—*See* Smith (G.)
Compleat Collection of Devotions.—*See* Deacon (Bp. T.)
Compleat English Tradesman.—*See* Defoe (D.)
Complete Collection of Conversation.—*See* Swift (J.)
Complete English Traveller.—*See* Sanders (Robt.)
Concerning some Scotch Surnames.—*See* Innes (C.)
Condition of Llandaff Cathedral —*See* Ollivant (H.)
Conduct of a Rt. Hon. Gent.—*See* Johnson (Dr.)
Conference about the Crown of England —*See* Parsons (Fa.)
Confession de Mademoiselle Sapho.—*See* Anandria
Conflict in Conscience, etc.—*See* Livingstone (W.)
Consecration of Altars.—*See* Owen (Jas.)
Considerations sur les Dimanches —*See* Verger de Hauranne (J. Du)
Constitutional Criterion (The).—*See* Jones (W.)
Contes en Vers —*See* Dorat
Conversations between a Freshman, etc.—*See* Campbell (Hon. W. F.)
Copywell (J.).—*See* Woty (W.)
Coquet-dale Fishing Songs.—*See* Doubleday (T.)
Cornelius O'Dowd.—*See* Lever (C.)
Cornet (A).—*See* Pettigrew (T. L.)
Cornwall, Address to Gent. of.—*See* Hawkins (Sir C.)

Cornwall, Duchy of.—*See* Haines (J.)
Cornwall (Barry).—*See* Procter (B. W.)
Correggio and Parmegiano.—*See* Coxe (Archdeacon)
Cotton is King.—*See* Christy (David)
Council of Trent.—*See* Ranchin
Count Julian.—*See* Landor (W. S.)
Country Contentments.—*See* Markham (G.)
Country Man's Companion.—*See* Tryon (T.)
Countryman's Guide to London.—*See* Cooke (T)
Court Convert (The).—*See* Anderson (H.)
Court and Character of K. James.—*See* Weldon (Sir A.)
Covent Garden Journal.—*See* Stockdale (J. J.)
Craven.—*See* Carleton (Capt. J. W)
Craven Dialect (The).—*See* Carr (Rev. W.)
Crayon (Geoffrey).—*See* Irving (W.)
Critica Sacra.—*See* Owen (Henry)
Critical Exposition of the Pentateuch.—*See* Jameson (J.)
Critical History of Pamphlets.—*See* Davies (Myles)
Critical Review of Public Buildings, &c.—*See* Ralph (J.)
Criticisms on the Rolliad.—*See* Hawkins (Sir J.)
Criticus.—*See* Orme (Rev. W)
Crito, a Dialogue.—*See* Spence (J.)
Cromwell Doolan.—*See* Levinge (Sir R)
Crowquill (A).—*See* Forrester (A. H)
Cruise in the "Eothen."—*See* Brassey (Lady)
Crusoniana.—*See* Sutcliffe (T.)
Cry to the Professor's Conscience.—*See* Taylor (T.)
C. S. C.—*See* Calverley (C. S.)
Culte des Dieux Fétiches.—*See* Brosses
Curate of Cranston (The).—*See* Bradley (Rev.)
Cursory Strictures on the Charge, &c.—*See* Godwin (W.)
C. W.—*See* Wase (C.)

Dance of Life.—*See* Combe (W.)
Dangerous Vice (The).—*See* Church (E.)
Daniel Deronda.—*See* Cross (Mrs.)
Dante.—*See* Vernon (Lord)
Davenant's Animadversions.—*See* Hourd
Defence of the Clergy, &c —*See* Hollingshead (N. J.)
Defence of Stage Plays.—*See* Prynn (W.)
Defensative against Prophecies.—*See* Howard (H.)
Defense du Beau Sexe.—*See* Dryden (J.)
Defoe (D.).— *See* Chetwood (W. R.)
Deity's Delay, &c.—*See* Bolton (R.)
Delectus Actorum Ecclesiæ.—*See* Poisson (N.)
Delights of the Bottle, &c.—*See* Ward (Ned)
De l'Origine &c. de la Maçonnerie.—*See* Bertola
Delta.—*See* Moir (D. M.)

De l'usage de Statues, &c.—*See* Guates
Democritus in London.—*See* Daniel (G.)
Demonologia.—*See* Forsyth (J. S.)
Dendrologia, Dodona's Grove.—*See* Howell (J.)
Denzil Place.—*See* Singleton (Mrs.)
De Omnibus Rebus.—*See* Byrne (Mrs. W. P.)
De Quincey.—*See* Japp
Der Freischutz Traveste.—*See* Forrester (R. H.)
Des Ballets Anciens, etc.—*See* Ménestrier (C. F.)
Description Générale de l'Hosp. des Invalides.—*See* Boullencourt
Description of Browsholme Hall.—*See* Whitaker (T. D.)
Description of the Seraglio.—*See* Withers (R.)
Description of Three Bricks, etc.—*See* Cruden
Description of Terra Cottas.—*See* Combe (Taylor)
Descriptions de Divers, etc.—*See* Le Brunn
Des Periers (P.).—*See* Peletier (J.)
Destruction of Troy.—*See* Fevre (R. Le)
De Vere —*See* Ward (R. Plumer)
Devil's Walk (The).—*See* Porson (Prof.)
Devotions.—*See* Newman (J. H.)
Diaboliad (The).—*See* Combe (W.)
Dialogi sex contra Pontificatus.—*See* Harpsfeld (N.)
Dialogue (A), etc.—*See* Butt
Dialogue in the Devonshire Dialect.—*See* Reynolds (Miss)
Dialogues in a Library.—*See* Thomson (J.)
Diana's Crescent.—*See* Manning (Anne)
Diary and Letters.—*See* D'Arblay (Madame)
Dickens (Chas.).—*See* Taylor (Tom)
Dinarbus —*See* Knight (J.)
Director (The).—*See* Dibdin (T. F.)
Discours des Histoires de Lorraine.—*See* Estienne (C.)
Discours non plus, etc.—*See* Peletier (J.)
Discourse against Transubstantiation —*See* Barrow (I.)
Discourse against Purgatory.—*See* Barrow (I.)
Discourse concerning Trouble of Mind.—*See* Defoe (D.)
Discourse deld. in the Roy. Academy.—*See* Reynolds (Sir J.)
Discourse of Divine Assistance.—*See* Allen (W.)
Discourse of Enthusiasm.—*See* More (H.)
Discourse of Government.—*See* Fletcher (A.)
Discovery of a World in the Moone.—*See* Wilkins (Bp.)
Discovery of the Inquisition.—*See* Skinner (V.)
Dispensary (The).—*See* Garth (Sir S.)
Disraeli (Benj.).—*See* Macknight (Thos.)
Disruption (The).—*See* Cross (W.)
Diverting Adventures —*See* Buckley
Dives and Pauper.—*See* Parker (Henry)
D. J —*See* Davies (J.)
Doblado (Don Leucadio).—*See* White (J. Blanco)
Doctor Antonio.—*See* Ruffini (G.)

Doctrina et Politia Ecclesiæ.—*See* Mochett (Dr.)
Doctrine and Discipline of Divorce.—*See* Milton (J.)
Dodd (C.)—*See* Tootle (Rev. Hugh)
Dodona's Grove.—*See* Howell (J.)
Dogs of the British Islands.—*See* Walsh (J. H.)
D. O. M., The Triune.—*See* Horloch (D. W.)
Dove and the Serpent (The).—*See* Decker (T.)
Dramatic Hist. of Mast. Edward, etc.—*See* Stevens (G. A.)
Dramatic Scenes, by B. Cornwall.—*See* Procter (B. W.)
Dream Life.—*See* Mitchell (D. G.)
Dreamer (The).—*See* King (W.)
Druid (The).—*See* Dixon (H. H.)
Drunken Barnaby's Four Journeys.—*See* Braithwaite (R.)
Dugdale's Baronage (Corrections to).—*See* Hornby (Chas.)
Dumb Philosopher (The) —*See* Defoe (D.)
Dunallan —*See* Kennedy (Grace)
Dunciad (The).—*See* Pope (Alex.)
Durham Cathedral.—*See* Raine (Rev. J.)
Dutch in the Medway.—*See* Macfarlane (C.)

Easter Gift (The).—*See* Landon (L. E.)
Eastern Archipelago (The).—*See* Adams (W. D.)
Ecce Homo.—*See* Seeley (Prof. J.)
Eccles Church, etc.—*See* Harland (J.)
Ecclesiastical Hist. of Scotland.—*See* Defoe (D.)
Ecclesiological Notes, etc.—*See* Neale (J. Mason)
Edith, a Tale of the Azores.—*See* Cross-Buchanan (J.)
Eikon Basilikh.—*See* Gauden (Dr. J.)
Eikon Basilikh.—*See* Murray
Eikonoklastes and Eikon-Aklastos (the reply).—*See* Milton (J.)
Elementa Optica.—*See* Powell (Dr. T.)
Elements of Armories.—*See* Bolton (Ed.)
Elements of Beauty —*See* Donaldson (J.)
Electra of Sophocles.—*See* Wase (Christopher)
Elegiac Poems.—*See* Trench (Archbp)
Elizabethæ Reginæ, etc.—*See* Parsons (R.)
Eloisa en Dishabille —*See* Matthews (Col. J.)
Eloisha en Dishabille —*See* Porson (Prof.)
Embassies and Foreign Courts.—*See* Grenville-Murray (E. C.)
Emblems of Love.—*See* Grotius (Hugo)
Empedocles on Etna.—*See* Arnold (M.)
Empire of the Nairs.—*See* Lawrence (J.)
Engineer's Report on Nicaragua Canal.—*See* Childs (O. W.)
England, Ireland, and America.—*See* Cobden (R.)
England's Conversion.—*See* Manning (R.)
England's present Interest discovered.—*See* Penn (W.)
England's Teares —*See* Howell (J)
England's Worthies.—*See* Winstanley (W.)

English Bards.—*See* Byron (Ld)
English Country Life.—*See* White (C.)
English and Latin Poems.—*See* Latham (J.)
Englishman (An).—*See* Peabody (G.)
English Rogue (The) —*See* Head (R.)
English Songs, etc.—*See* Procter (B. W.)
English Spy (The).—*See* Westmacott (C. M.)
Enquiry into the Constitution —*See* King (Sir P.)
Enquiry into the Soul —*See* Baxter (A.)
Enquiry respecting Hell —*See* Swindon (T.)
Eothen.— *See* Kinglake (A. W.)
E. P.—*See* Phillips (E.)
Ephemera's (Handbook of Angling).—*See* Fitzgibbon (E.)
Ephemeris Parliamentaria.—*See* Fuller (Dr. F.)
Epic of Hades.—*See* Morris (Lewis)
Epictetus Junior.—*See* Davies (J.)
Epicure (An).—*See* Saunders (F)
Epigoniad (The). — *See* Wilkie (W.)
Episodes of Insect Life.—*See* Bugden (Miss L. M.)
Epistle of Consolation.—*See* Whitehead (G.)
Epistles of St. Paul.—*See* Jones (John)
Epistle to J. Lowther.—*See* Wolcot (Dr.)
Epithalamium, etc.—*See* Buchanan (G.)
Epitre à une Femme, etc.—*See* Salverte (E.)
Eroticum Linguæ Latinæ.—*See* Pierrugues (P.)
Espriella (Don M. A.).— *See* Southey (R.)
Essai sur les Accusations, etc.— *See* Renfner (M. H)
Essay concerning Slavery.— *See* Trelawney (E.)
Essay concerning the Soul.—*See* Langton (Z.)
Essay on Cruikshank.—*See* Thackeray (W. M.)
Essay on Norwich Castle.—*See* Gurdon (T.)
Essay on Poetry.—*See* Parnell (Dr.)
Essay on the Beautiful.—*See* Taylor (The Platonist)
Essay on Toleration of Papists.—*See* Lloyd (T.)
Essay on Wit, etc.— *See* Morris (C.)
Essay towards Hist. of Bideford.—*See* Watkins (J.)
Essays, etc., by Barry Cornwall.—*See* Procter (B. W.)
Essays, Moral and Political.—*See* Hume (D.)
Essays on Opinions.—*See* Bailey (S.)
Essays on Various Subjects.—*See* More (H.)
Essays.—*See* Montaigne (M. de)
Estienne.—*See also* Blount (T.)
Eton.—*See* Microcosm (The)
Eton.—*See* Miniature (The)
Etonian (The).—*See* Praed (W. M.)
Ettrick Shepherd (The).—*See* Browne (J.)
Eugenio.—*See* Beach (J.)..
Eugenius Philalethes.—*See* Vaughan (T.)
Euphranor, a Dialogue.—*See* Fitzgerald (E.)

Euphrosyne.—*See* Graves (R.)
Europa Speculum.—*See* Sandys (Sir E.)
European Breezes.—*See* Deane (Margery)
Eustace, an Elegy.—*See* Tennyson (C.)
E. V. B.—*See* Boyle (Hon. Mrs.)
Evelina.—*See* D'Arblay (Madame)
Evenings at Haddon Hall.—*See* Calabrella (Baroness de)
E. W.—*See* Williams (E.)
Exercitatio Anatomica, etc.—*See* Harvey (Dr.)
Excerpta Historica.—*See* Bentley (S.)
Excursion to Land's End.—*See* Cook (J.)
Exile of Erin (The).—*See* Deacon (W. F.)
Experience of Life.—*See* Sewell E. M.)
Experienced Hand (An).—*See* Clavel (R.)
Experiment (The).—*See* Defoe (D.)
Explication de Divers Monumens.—*See* Martin (J.)
Exposition of the False Medium, etc.—*See* Horne (R. H.)
Extempore Preaching —*See* Glazebrook (Mr.)
Eye-Witness (An).—*See* Sancroft (W.)

F. (L. De).—*See* Fontenelle
Fabiola —*See* Wiseman (Card.)
Fable of the Bees (The).—*See* Mandeville (Bernard)
Faces in the Fire —*See* Pardon (G. F.)
Faction Displayed.—*See* Defoe (D.)
Facts and Figures from Italy —*See* Mahony (F. S.)
Facts are stubborn things.—*See* Jeffreys (N.)
Factum of the E. of Arran —*See* Turnbull (W. B.)
Fag (Frederick).—*See* Johnson (James, *M.D.*)
Faggot (A) of French Sticks.—*See* Head (Sir F.)
Fair Quaker of Deal.—*See* Shadwell
Fair Vertue.—*See* Wither (G.)
Fair Warning to take heed, etc.—*See* Bromwell (J.)
Fairy Legends of Ireland.—*See* Croker (T. Crofton)
Fairy Prince (The), a Masque.—*See* Colman (G.)
Fairy Tales and Ballads.—*See* Cole (Sir H.)
Fall of Prince Florestan.—*See* Dilke
Falls of Clyde (The).—*See* Black (J.)
False Alarm (The).—*See* Johnson (Dr.)
Familiar Studies in Men.—*See* Stevenson (R. L.)
Fanaticism.—*See* Taylor (I.)
Fane (Julian).—*See* Lytton (R.)
Fane (Violet).—*See* Singleton (Mrs.)
Fanny Hill.—*See* Cleland (J.)
Fantosme.—*See* Memoirs of the Nobility, &c.
Farmer's Tour through England.—*See* Young (A.)
Fasisculus Temporum.—*See* Rolewink (W.)
Father Prout.—*See* Mahony (F. S.)
Faustus.—*See* Shelley (P. B.)

F. B.—*See* Burton (R. F.)
Feast of the Poets (The).—*See* Hunt (Leigh)
Feckenham Charity.—*See* Woodroffe (Dr.)
Felix Holt.—*See* Cross (Mrs.)
Female Prelate (The).—*See* Settle (E.)
Female Quixote (The).—*See* Lennox (Mrs. C.)
Festorum Metropolis.—*See* Bacon (J.)
Few Words (A) on Canada.—*See* Clark (C.)
Fides Anglicana.—*See* Wither (G.)
Field Book (The).—*See* Maxwell (W. H.)
Field and Hedgerow.—*See* Jefferies (R.)
Fifty-one Original Fables.—*See* Crithannah (J.)
Figaro's Hist. of England.—*See* Dowty (A. A)
Finish to Life in London.—*See* Egan (P.)
Firmillien.—*See* Aytoun (Prof.)
First Book of Tullie's Offices —*See* Brinsley (J.)
First part of the Life of Henry III.—*See* Hayward (Sir J.)
First Settlers of New England (The).—*See* Child (Mrs. D. L.)
Fish and Fishing in the U.S.A.—*See* Herbert (H. W.)
Fisher Boy (The) —*See* Ireland (W. H)
Fitzalleyne of Berkeley.—*See* Westmacott (C.)
Fitzvictor (J.).—*See* Shelley (P. B)
Five Letters on the Scriptures —*See* Locke (J.)
Five Pieces of Runic Poetry.—*See* Percy (Bp.)
Five Years in Kaffir Land.—*See* Ward (Harriet)
Flagellum.—*See* Heath (Jas.)
Flag of Truce (The).—*See* Fuller (Hiram)
Flemish Interiors.—*See* Byrne (Mrs. W. P.)
Flights in Paradise.—*See* Pearson (G. C.)
Flim-Flams.—*See* D'Israeli (I.)
Flood of Thessaly.—*See* Procter (B. W.)
Florentine Tales.—*See* Hunt (Leigh) and Powell (T.)
Florio (J.).—*See* Montaigne
Flotsam and Jetsam.—*See* Wigram (S. R.)
Fo'c'stle Yarns.—*See* Brown (T. E.)
Folly in Print.—*See* Raymund
Foreign Bishop (A).—*See* Legh (G.)
Foreigner (A).—*See* Moll (Prof.)
Forest and the Field (The).—*See* Levison
Forest of Fancy.—*See* Constable (H.)
Forester (Frank).—*See* Herbert (H W.)
Forester (The).—*See* Roberts (Sir R.)
Form of Dedication, etc.—*See* Tisdale (R.)
Foster (Frank).—*See* Puseley (D)
Fotheringay and Mary Queen of Scots.—*See* Bradley (Rev.)
Four New Dialogues, etc.—*See* Lyttleton (Lord)
Four Years in France —*See* Best (Mr.)
Four Years in the W. Indies.—*See* Bayley (F. W. N.)
F. R.—*See* Raoul (Mademoiselle)

Fragments in Manner of Sterne.—*See* Brandon (I.)
Fragments of Ancient Poetry.—*See* Macpherson (J.)
Frankenstein.—*See* Shelley (Mrs.)
Fraxi (Pisanus).—*See* Ashbee (H. S.)
Free Thoughts on many Subjects.—*See* Lamb (Rev. R.)
Frere (J.).—*See* Microcosm (The)
Friends in Council.—*See* Helps (Sir A.)
Friendship's Offering.—*See* Ruskin (J.)
From Dawn to Noon.—*See* Singleton (Mrs.)
From Matter to Spirit.—*See* De Morgan
Frost and Fire.—*See* Campbell (J. F.)
Fundamental Charter of Presbytery.—*See* Sage (J.)

G. A.—*See* Gilby (A.)
Gaberlunzie's Wallet (The).—*See* Ballantyne (J.)
Gaelic Songs.—*See* M'Intyre (D)
Gale Middleton —*See* Smith (Horace)
Gambado (Geoffrey).—*See* Cobbold (Rev. R.)
Game of Logic (The).—*See* Dodgson (Rev. C. L.)
Gamekeeper at Home.—*See* Jefferies (R.)
Gardens and Menagerie, etc.—*See* Yarrell
General Hist. of the Christian Church.— *See* Walmsley (Bp.)
General View of Agriculture in Essex.—*See* Young (A.)
Generall Junto (The).—*See* Parker (Henry)
Gentleman (A).— *See* Bedford (H.)
Gentleman (A).—*See* Church (E.)
Gentleman (A).— *See* Copley (L.)
Gentleman (A).—*See* Defoe (D.)
Gentleman (A).—*See* Wallace (J.)
Gentleman (A) of the Univ. of Oxford.—*See* Shelley (P. B.)
Gimcrack (J.).— *See* Gregson (J. S.)
Gimcrackiana.—*See* Gregson (J. S.)
Ginx's Baby.—*See* Jenkins (E.) ..
Giphantia.—*See* De La Roche (C. F. T.)
Glimpse of the World (A).—*See* Sewell (E. M.)
Glory of their Times (The).—*See* Lupton (D.)
Glory and Shame of Britain.—*See* Dunkley (H.)
Glossary of Provincial Words.—*See* Dinsdale (Dr.)
Godartius (Johannes).—*See* Lister (M.)
God's Love to Mankind.—*See* Hourd
Godwin (William).—*See* Baldwin (E.)
Gold, a Legendary Rhyme.—*See* Forrester (A. H.)
Gold.—*See* Ruskin (J.)
Golden Violet (The).—*See* Landon (L. E.)
Good Old Times.—*See* Sewell (E. M.)
G. R —*See* Greene (Robt.)
Grand Impostor Discovered (The).—*See* Keach (B.)
Grand Imposture of the New Church, etc.—*See* Morton (T.)
Grasshopper (The.—*See* Martin (J. B.)

Great Advantage of Eating Pure Bread.—*See* Pownall (I.)
Great Unwashed (The).—*See* Wright (T.)
Greatest Light in the World.—*See* Wallis (J.)
Greek and Roman Hist.—*See* Walker (O.)
Green Bays, etc.—*See* Couch (Q.)
Green House Companion —*See* Loudon (J. C.)
Grey Friar (The .—*See* Thackeray (W. M.)
Greyhound (The).—*See* Walsh
Griffin (Gregory).—*See* Canning (G.)
Grildrig (Sol.).—*See* Miniatures
Grounds and Occasions, etc.—*See* Eachard (J.)
Grove Hill.— *See* Maurice (T.)
G. S.—*See* Sandys (G.)
Guardian's Instruction. - *See* Penton (S.)
Guesses at Truth. - *See* Hare (Bros.)
Guide to the Historian, etc. - *See* Turner (Dawson)
Guide to the Lakes.—*See* West (T.)
Guide to Watering Places.—*See* Forrester (A. H.)
Guillim (J.).—*See* Barkham (J.)
Gulliver's Travels.—*See* Swift (Dean)
Guy Livingstone.—*See* Lawrence (J.)
G. W.—*See* Whitehead (G.)

H.—*See* Halpin (C. G.)
Hajji Baba in England.—*See* Morier (J.)
Half-Hours with Free-Thinkers.—*See* Bradlaugh (C.)
Hamlet, etc.—*See* Caldecott
Hampden in the XIXth Cent.—*See* Morgan (J. M.)
Hamst (Olphar).—*See* Thomas (R.)
Handbook of Fictitious Names.—*See* Thomas (R.)
Happy Hours, etc.—*See* Bradley
Hardcastle (Ephraim).— *See* Pyne (W. H.)
Harold, a Tragedy. - *See* Hopkins (T.)
Harold the Dauntless.—*See* Scott (Sir W.)
Harvest of a Quiet Eye.—*See* Vernon (J. R.)
H. B.—*See* Doyle (John)
H. C.—*See* Ireland (W. H.)
H. E.—*See* Hawarden (Dr.)
"He."—*See* Lang (A.)
Headlong Hall.—*See* Peacock (T. L.)
Heir of Redcliffe.—*See* Yonge (C. M.)
Helen Davenant.—*See* Singleton (Mrs.)
Helen and Olga.—*See* Manning (A.)
Heliodorus, etc.—*See* Gildon (C.)
Hemans (Mrs.).—*See* Browne (F. D.)
Heraldic Anomalies.—*See* Nares (Dr. E.)
Hereditary Right of the Crown.—*See* Bedford (H.)
Hereditary Right of the Crown, etc.—*See* Harbin (Geo.)
Hermippus Redivivus.—*See* Campbell (Dr. J.)

Hermit of Marlow.—*See* Shelley (P. B.)
Heron (R.).—*See* Pinkerton (J.)
H. I.—*See* Hayward (I.)
Hidden Works of Darkness, etc.—*See* Prynne (W.)
Hicover (Harry).—*See* Brendley (C.)
Hierophilos.—*See* McHale (Dr.)
High Elms.—*See* Darwin (Capt.)
Higher Law.—*See* Maitland
High Life and Towers of Silence.—*See* Burnaby (Mrs. F.)
Highways and Byways.—*See* Grattan (T. C.)
Hilda among the Broken Gods.—*See* Smith (W. C.)
Hind Let Loose (A).—*See* Shiells (Alex.)
Hind and the Panther.—*See* Prior (M.)
Hippocrate Dépaysé.—*See* Fontenelle
His Majesty's Propriety, etc.—*See* Clavel (R.)
Histoire des Voyages, etc —*See* Wilton (C.)
Histoire du Ministere d'Armand J. du Plessis.—*See* Vialart (Ch.)
Historia del Fray Gerundio. - *See* Isla (J. F. de)
Historical Essay, etc., on Presbyterians.—*See* Kirkpatrick (J.)
Hist. Memoir of Sherley Bros.—*See* Shirley (E. P.)
Historical Memoranda, etc. (Cooper's Company).—*See* Firth (J. F.)
Hist. Narrative of the Plague.—*See* Defoe (D.)
Historical Parallels.—*See* Malkin (A. T.)
Historical and Poetical Medley.—*See* Cooper (E.)
Historical Tales, etc.—*See* Lawson (J. P.)
Historical Vindication, etc.—*See* Twysden (Sir R.)
Historic of the late Revolution.—*See* Howell (J.)
Historie, etc., of Mary Stuart.—*See* Stranguage (W.)
History of Arbaces.- *See* Johnston (Mr.)
Hist. of Napoleon Buonaparte.—*See* Lockhart (J.)
Hist. of Civil Wars in Germany.—*See* Defoe (D.)
Hist. etc., of Colchester.—*See* Strutt (Mr.)
History of Craven —*See* Carr (Rev. W.)
Hist. of Wars of Charles XII.—*See* Defoe (D.)
Hist. of Cathedral at Durham.—*See* Wassington
Hist. of Art of Engraving, etc.—*See* Chelsum (Dr.)
History of Epsom.—*See* Pownall (H.)
History of Friar Gerund. - *See* Isla (J. F.)
Hist. of the Hoggarty Diamond.—*See* Thackeray
Hist. and Antiquities of Horsham.—*See* Dudley (H.)
History of Huntingdon.—*See* Carruthers (R.)
History of the Jews.—*See* Milman (Dean)
History of Tom Jones —*See* Fielding (H.)
History of Keighley.—*See* Holmes (R.)
History of King's Lynn.- *See* Badeslade (T.)
History of Lady Mandeville.—*See* Brooke (F.)
Hist. of Mary Prince. - *See* Pringle (G.)
History of Noble and Polite Persons.—*See* "Amours"
History of Parisinus.—*See* Ford (E.)

History of the Picts.—*See* Balfour (Sir J.)
History of Pompey the Little.—*See* Coventry (Francis)
History of Eng. and Scotch Presbytery.—*See* Basire (Dr. I.)
History of Religion.—*See* Murray (Rev. J.)
History of the Royal Family.—*See* Salmon (N.)
History of the Sevarites.—*See* Vairasse (D.)
History of Signboards.—*See* Sadler and Hotten
Hist. of Spanish America.—*See* Campbell (Dr. J)
Hist. and Antiq. of Tewkesbury.—*See* Dyde (W.)
Hist. of Sir T. Thumb.—*See* Yonge (C. M.)
Hist. of Westminster Abbey.—*See* Combe (W.)
History of William III.—*See* Bankes (J.)
History of J. Winchcomb.—*See* Deloney (T.)
Hist. of St. Peter's, York.—*See* Gent (T.)
H. J.—*See* Hall (John)
H. J.—*See* Howell (James)
H. N.—*See* Hookes (N.)
Hodge and his Masters.—*See* Jefferies (R.)
Hogg (Cervantes).—*See* Barrett (E. S.)
Hogg (J.).—*See* Browne (Jas.)
Hoglandiæ Descriptio.—*See* Holdsworth (Dr.)
Holy Bible.—*See* Bible
Holy Ghost on the Bench (The).—*See* Hollinworth (Rev. R.)
Home (Cecil).—*See* Davis (Augusta)
Homer, Enquiry into —*See* Blackwell (T.)
Homunculus.—*See* Thackeray (W. M.)
Hookanit Bee.—*See* Wigram (S. R.)
Horæ Iconæ.—*See* Dillon (Sir J.) ..
Horse (The) in Stable, etc.—*See* Walsh (J. H.)
Horse and Hound.—*See* Apperley (C. J.)
Hosea, transl. from the Hebrew.—*See* Horsley
Houghton (Lord).—*See* Milnes (R. M.)
Hours with the First Falling Leaves.—*See* Digby (Kenelm)
H. T.—*See* Hopkins (T)
Huartes (J.) Exam. of Men's Wits.—*See* Carew (R.)
Hughes, A Week's Tramp, etc.—*See* Dickens (C.)
Human Passions delineated.—*See* Collier (J.)
Humble Motion (An) to Parliament.—*See* Hall (J.)
Humourist Physician (A) —*See* Cobbold (Rev. R.)
Humourous Hist. of Dickey, etc.—*See* Paltock (R.)
Humours of Oxford.—*See* Miller (J.)
Hunting Grounds, etc.—*See* Leveson (H. A.)
Hunting of the Snark.—*See* Dodgson (Rev. C. L.)
Hymen's Præludia.—*See* Calprenede
Hymns and Songs of the Church.—*See* Wither (G.)

Iconoclast.—*See* Bradlaugh (C.)
Identity of Junius, etc.—*See* Taylor (J.)

Illustrated Monograph, etc., of Princess of Wales.—*See* Jones (Mrs. H.)
Illustrations of Holy Scripture.—*See* Goadby
Il Musannif —*See* Mackenzie (Capt. C. F.)
Il Nipotismo di Roma.—*See* Leti (G.)
Image Unbroken (The).—*See* Jane (John)
Impartial Inquirer after Truth (An).—*See* Casway (R.)
Imirce, ou la Fille, etc.—*See* Dulaurens (M.)
Impartial Inquiry, etc.—*See* Trye (J.)
Improvisatrice (The).—*See* Landon (L. E.)
Independent Whig.—*See* Gordon
Ingoldsby Legends and Lyrics.—*See* Barham (Rev. R. H.)
Inland Voyage (An).—*See* Stevenson (R. L.)
In Memoriam.—*See* Nicholls (J. A.)
Inquiry into Evidence against Q. Mary.—*See* Tytler (W.)
Inquiry into Glass Painting.—*See* Winston (C.)
Inquiry, Historical, etc.—*See* Tytler (W.)
Inside Passenger (An).—*See* Hook (Theo.)
Intellectual Electricity.—*See* Belcher (W.)
Invisible World Discovered.—*See* Hull (J. H.)
Ionica.—*See* Cory (W.)
I. R.—*See* Rhodes (John)
Irishman (A Bashful).—*See* Deacon (W. F.)
Irish Rebellion.—*See* Brooke (H.)
Irish Sketch Book.—*See* Thackeray (W. M.)
Iron (Ralph).—*See* Schreiner (Olive)
Isabel.—*See* Walpole (Robt.)
Isabella, or the Morning.—*See* Williams (C. Hanbury)
Isaac Commenus.—*See* Taylor (Sir H.)
I Says, Says I.—*See* Nares (Dr.)
Isle of Man.—*See* Britton
It Matters Not Who.—*See* Nares (Dr. E.)
Ivy Leaves.—*See* Varley (Isabella)
I. W.—*See* Watts (Isaac)

J. A.—*See* Astruc (Jean)
Janus.—*See* Dollinger (Dr.)
J. D.—*See* Dennys (J.)
J. D.—*See* Donne (Dr. J.)
Jem Bunt.—*See* Barker (M. H.)
Jesuits.—*See* Evelyn (J.)
Jesuite's Catechisme.—*See* Pasquier (E.)
J. H.—*See* Healey (J.)
J. H.—*See* Howell (James)
J. H.—*See* Hull (J.)
J. M.—*See* Milton (John)
Jockey Club (The).—*See* Piggott (Charles)
Jokeby.—*See* Roby (J.)
John Bull.—*See* Hook (Theodore)

John Bull and His Lamp.—*See* Thackeray (W. M.)
John Buncle Junior.—*See* Cogan (T.)
Johnny Robinson.—*See* Wright (T.)
John Halifax, Gent.—*See* Muloch (Miss)
John Inglesant.—*See* Shorthouse (J. H.)
Johnson (W.).—*See* Cory (W.)
Jones (T. Percy).—*See* Aytoun (Prof.)
Jonsonus Virbius.—*See* Duppa (B.)
Jottings of an Invalid.—*See* Walker (W.)
Journal of a Tour, etc.—*See* Rutland (D. of)
Journal of Adv. in Switzerland.—*See* Longman (W.)
Journal of Llewellyn Penrose.—*See* Eagles (Rev. J.)
Journal of the Heart.—*See* Bury (Lady C.)
Journée de l'Amour—*See* Erotica
Journey to the W. I. of Scotland.—*See* Johnson (Dr. S.)
Journey through England.—*See* Defoe (D.)
Journeyman Engineer (A).—*See* Wright (T.)
Journeyman Mason (A).—*See* Miller (Hugh)
J. R.—*See* Ruskin (J.)
J. S.—*See* Sanford (James)
J. T.—*See* Toland (J.)
J. T.—*See* Torbuck (J.)
Jura Populi Anglicani.—*See* Defoe (D)
Jure Divino.—*See* Defoe (D.)
Justification by Faith.—*See* Berridge (Rev. J.)
Juvenile Researches.—*See* Dudley (Howard)
J. W.—*See* White (J.)
J. W.—*See* Worledge (J.)

Kama Sutra.—*See* Arbuthnot (F. F.)
Kasidah (The).—*See* Burton (R. F.)
Katzleben (Baroness de).—*See* Bowles (Caroline)
Keepsake (The).—*See* Browning (R.)
Keepsake (The).—*See* Dickens (C.)
Keepsake (The).—*See* Thackeray (W. M.)
Kendall (May).—*See* Lang (Mrs. Andrew)
Kerography.—*See* Thackeray (W. M.)
Key to H. B's Caricatures.—*See* Doyle (J.)
K. H.—*See* Keepe (H.)
Khata Phusin.—*See* Ruskin (J.)
Kick from Yarmouth, etc.—*See* Daniel (G.)
Kickleburys on the Rhine.—*See* Thackeray (W. M.)
Kingdom of Christ.—*See* Maurice (F. D.)
King Solomon's Wives.—*See* Lang (Andrew)
Kit Bam's Adventures.—*See* Clarke (Mary Cowden)
K. J.—*See* Keyns (John)
Klosterheim.—*See* De Quincey (T.)
K. McK.—*See* Jerome (J. K.)
Knatchbull-Hugessen.—*See* Brabourne (Lord)

Knickerbocker (Diedrich).—*See* Irving (W.)
Knight (Chas.).—*See* Miniature (The)
Knight Errant (A).—*See* Du Bois
Knighthood, Orders of.—*See* Hanson (Sir L.)
Koran (The).—*See* Skine (L.)
Kyd.—*See* Clark (J. C.) under heading Dickens

L'Aciadiade.—*See* Chevrier (A.)
Lacu (J. de).—*See* Gringore (P.)
Ladies' Calling (The).—*See* Willis (Browne)
Lady (A).—*See* Glasse (Mrs.)
Lady (A).—*See* Godwin (Mrs.)
Lady (A).—*See* M'Taggart (Mrs)
Lady Alimony.—*See* Green (R.)
Lady of Massachussets (A).—*See* Child (Mrs.)
Laich (W.).—*See* Ridpath (G.)
Lamb (C.).—*See* Annual Anthology
Lamb (Charles), a Memoir —*See* Procter (B. W.)
Lamplighter (The).—*See* Dickens (C.)
L'An Deux Mille quatre cent quarante.—*See* Mercier (M.)
Landmarks of a Literary Life. *See* Crosland (Mrs. N.)
Land and Sea Tales.—*See* Barker (M. H.)
Land-Tempest (The).—*See* Prynne (W.)
Langstaffe (Launcelot).—*See* Irving (W.)
La Pucelle D'Orleans.—*See* Voltaire
La Perspective Pratique.—*See* Dubreuil (P. J.)
La Quenolle Spirituelle.—*See* Gringore
Larwood (J.).—*See* Sadler (R. L.)
Last Man (The).—*See* Shelley (Mrs)
La Theologie du Cœur.—*See* Guion (Madame)
Laud (Archbp) Trial of.—*See* Prynne (W.)
Law (W., the Nonjuror).—*See* Walton (C.)
Lay of the Scottish Fiddle.—*See* Scott (Sir W.)
Layman (A).—*See* Taylor (Edgar)
Leaves from A. Crowquill's Memorandum Book.—*See* Forrester
Le Canapé, Couleur de Feu.—*See* Montbron (F. de)
Leçons de Morale et Politique.—*See* Moreau
Le Conte du Tonneau.—*See* Van Effen
Lectures on Polarised Light.—*See* Pereira (J)
Le Dance des Aveugles —*See* Michault (P.)
Lee (Vernon).—*See* Paget (Violet)
Legend of Capt. Jones.—*See* Lloyd (Bp. D.)
Legend of Genevieve.—*See* Moir (D. M.)
Legend of Jubal.—*See* Cross (Mrs.)
Legend of the Chapel of St. Thomas of Acon.—*See* Clark (I. G.)
Legends of Lancashire.—*See* Landreth (P.)
Legends of the Library, etc.—*See* Nugent (Lord)
L. E. L.—*See* Landon (L. E.)
Le Livre a la Mode.—*See* Caraccioli (M. de)

Le Maniere de bien Traduire.—*See* Dolet (Estienne)
Leoni.—*See* Ruskin (J.)
Le Second Enfer.—*See* Dolet (Estienne)
Les Fées, Contes.—*See* Force (Mdlle. de la)
Les Joyeuses Aventures, etc.—*See* Des Periers
Les Œuvres de Bruscambille.—*See* Lauriers (Des)
Les Provinciales.—*See* Pascal (Blaise)
Letter Analysis.—*See* Crawley (T.)
Letter in Defence of the Liturgy.—*See* Piers (H.)
Letter on English Bibles.—*See* Brett (T.)
Letter to a Proselyte.—*See* Jones (G.)
Letter to Author of " Divine Legation," etc.—*See* Lowth (Dr. R.)
Letter to Dr. Bennett.—*See* Woolston (Thos)
Letter to Dr. Lowth.—*See* Brown (J.)
Letter to Dr. Mather.—*See* Clarke (Rev. J.)
Letters and Dissertations.—*See* Crawley (T)
Letters of Hierophilos.—*See* McHale (Dr.)
Letters of Jonathan Oldstyle—*See* Irving (W.)
Letters of Literature.—*See* Pinkerton (J.)
Letters from a Blacksmith, etc.—*See* Kames (Lord)
Letters from a Gentleman, etc.—*See* Burt (Capt.)
Letters from a Lady.—*See* Vigor (Mrs.)
Letters from Edinburgh.—*See* Topham (Capt. E.)
Letters from England.—*See* Southey (R.)
Letters from Scandinavia.—*See* Thompson (W)
Letters from Snowdon.—*See* Craddock (J.)
Letters from Spain.—*See* White (J. Blanco)
Letters from Yorick to Eliza.—*See* Sterne (L.)
Letters on Early Rising.—*See* Buckland (A. C.)
Letters on Management of Hounds.—*See* Horlock (J. K.)
Letters on Norman Tiles.—*See* Major (J. H.)
Letters on Patriotism.—*See* Bolingbroke (Lord)
Letters on Socialism.—*See* Morris (W.)
Letters to an Universalist.—*See* Jerram (C.)
Lettres Philosophiques.—*See* Voltaire
Lexiphanes, a Dialogue.—*See* Campbell (A.)
Leycester's Commonwealth.—*See* Parsons
Liaisons Dangereuses.—*See* Laclos (C. de)
Libellus Gebenis.—*See* Brydges (Sir E.)
Liberal (The).—*See* Hunt (Leigh)
Liberal Critique on the Roy. Acad.—*See* Williams (J.)
Liber Amoris.—*See* Hazlitt (W.)
Library of Romance—*See* Dickens (C.)
Life for a Life (A).—*See* Craik (Mrs.)
Life in London.—*See* Egan (Pierce)
Life in the South.—*See* Jones (S. L.)
Life of a Boy.—*See* Sterndale (Mary)
Life of Warren Hastings.—*See* Gleig (Rev. G. R.)
Life of James II.—*See* Jones (D.)

Life of Bp. Ken.—*See* Anderdon (J. L.)
Life of Marianne.—*See* Marivaux (M. de)
Life of Merlin.—*See* Heywood (Thos.)
Life of Hannah More.—*See* Shaw (W.)
Life of John Mytton.—*See* Apperley
Life of Richard Nash.—*See* Goldsmith (O.)
Lives of the Three Normans.—*See* Hayward (I.)
Life of Raffaello.—*See* Duppa (R.)
Life of R. Savage.—*See* Johnson (Dr. S.)
Life of Schiller.—*See* Carlyle (T.)
Life of E. of Stair.—*See* Henderson (A.)
Life in Paris.—*See* Carey (D.)
Life and Adventures of Peter Wilkins.—*See* Paltock (R.)
Life and Death of the Merry Devil of Edmonton.—*See* Brewer (T.)
Light in the Dwelling.—*See* Mortimer (Mrs.)
Light of Britayne (The).—*See* Lite (H.)
Lights and Shadows of London Life.—*See* Grant (J.)
Limner (Luke).—*See* Leighton (John)
Literary Hist. of N. Testament.—*See* Conder (J.)
Literary Museum.—*See* Waldron (F. G.)
Little (T.).—*See* Moore (Tom)
Little Foundling (The).—*See* Miller (Mrs. H.)
Little Mr. Bouncer.—*See* Bradley
Little Tour in Ireland.—*See* Hole (Dean)
Liturgica Antiqua Hispanica.—*See* Pinio (J.)
Lives of Eminent Modern Painters.—*See* Burgess (J.)
Lloyd (C.).—*See* Annual Anthology
Locker (Fredk.).—*See* Locker-Lampson
Lodore.—*See* Shelley (Mrs.)
Logan (J.).—*See* Bruce (M)
London Clerk (A).—*See* Hughes (T.)
London Hermit (The).—*See* Parke (F.)
London Lyrics.—*See* Locker-Lampson (F.)
London's Resurrection.—*See* Ford (C.)
London and Westminster Rev.—*See* Thackeray (W. M.)
London Sparrow (A) at the Colinderies.—*See* Boyle (Hon. Mrs.)
Longus.—*See* Amyot and Gozzi
Loose Hints on Education.—*See* Home (H.)
Lord's Supper (The).—*See* Paley (J.)
London's Architectural Mag.—*See* Ruskin (J.)
Lounger (A).—*See* Porson (Prof.)
Love and Madness.—*See* Croft (Sir H.)
Loveday (R.).—*See* Calprenede
Love Elegies.—*See* Hammond (W.)
Love Epistles of Aristænetus —*See* Halbed (N.)
Lover of the Celestial Muse (A).—*See* Fullarton (J)
Love's Triumph —*See* Frere (Mary)
Lower Canada Watchman.—*See* Chisholme (D.)
Lucianus Redivivus.—*See* Becket (Andrew)

K

Lucien Greville.—*See* Pettigrew (T. L.)
Lucile.—*See* Lytton (Robt., E. of)
Lucius Davoren.—*See* Maxwell (Mrs.)
Lucubrations, Essays, etc.—*See* Graves (Rev. R.)
Lucullus and Palatable Essays.—*See* Hall (Capt. Byng)
Lux Orientalis.—*See* Glanville (J.)
Lux Renata.—*See* Smedley (Rev. E.)
Lyra Elegantiarum.—*See* Locker-Lampson
Lyrics by H.—*See* Halpin (C. G.)

MacSarcasm (Sir Arch.)—*See* Shaw (W.)
Madre Natura.—*See* Leighton (John)
Magazine of the Ants.—*See* Murray
Mag. of Art.—*See* Tennyson
Magopico.—*See* Haliburton (Dr.)
Malagrowther (Malachi).—*See* Scott (Sir W.)
Manchester Man (A).—*See* Lamb (Rev R.)
Manchester Manufacturer (A).—*See* Cobden (R.)
Man in the Moon.—*See* Fox (C. J.)
Man Mouse (The) taken. etc.—*See* Vaughan (T.)
Mansie Waugh.—*See* Moir (D. M.)
Manual of Chemistry.—*See* Aikens (J.)
Maphaens.—*See* Ellis (John)
Ma Philosophie.—*See* Dorat (M.)
Margaret Catchpole.—*See* Cobbold (Rev. R.)
Margaret de Valois.—*See* Singleton (Mrs.)
Margarita Philosophica.—*See* Reisch (G.)
Marjorie Fleming.—*See* Brown (J.)
Marprelate Tract.—*See* Penry (J.)
Marriage Rites, etc.—*See* Hamilton (Lady)
Martingale.—*See* White (J.)
Marvel (Ik.).—*See* Mitchell (D. G.)
Mary Powell.—*See* Manning (A)
Mary Q. of Scots.—*See* Buchanan (G.)
Mary Q. of Scots.—*See* Collections
Mary Q. of Scots.—*See* Tytler (W.)
Master of the Hounds.—*See* Horlock
Master Tyll Owlglass.—*See* Forrester (R. H.)
Matanasius (C.).—*See* Saint Hyacinthe (Père)
Matho, etc.—*See* Baxter (A.)
May Day (Crane's).—*See* Wise (J. R.)
May Queen.—*See* Boyle (Mrs.)
M.B.I.D.P.F.C.—*See* Boulanger (M.)
Meath (Lord).—*See* Brabazon (Lord)
Meiboni (J. H.) De Flagrorum, etc.—*See* Cust (E.)
Melmoth (Courtney).—*See* Pratt (S. J.)
Member (The).—*See* Galt (John)
Member of the Athenian Soc.—*See* Dunton (J.)
Member of Parliament (A).—*See* Johnson (Dr.)

Memoir of the Controversy, etc.—*See* Orme (W.)
Memoir of the Goddards.—*See* Jefferies (R.)
Memoir of Adml. Hargood.—*See* Allen (J.)
Memoir of Nat Hawthorne.—*See* Japp (A. H.)
Memoires du Marquis de B**.—*See* Beaujeu
Mémoires de la D. de Morsheim.—*See* Laclos
Memoires et Instructions, etc —*See* Godfrey (D.)
Memoirs of an Aristocrat.—*See* Buonaparte
Memoirs of Henry the Great.—*See* Ireland (W. H.)
Memoirs of Author of Ind. Antiq.—*See* Maurice
Memoirs of Jeanne d'Arc.—*See* Ireland (W. H.)
Memoirs of Magopico.—*See* Haliburton (Dr)
Memoirs of Peers of England.—*See* Brydges (Sir S. E.)
Memoirs of Revolution in Bengal.—*See* Campbell (Dr. J.)
Memoirs of Capt. Rock.—*See* Moore (Tom)
Memoirs of Mrs. Robinson.—*See* Robinson (Mrs.)
Memoirs of Sir W. Scott.—*See* Lockhart (J. G.)
Memoirs of Secret Service.—*See* Peterborough (E. of)
Memorabilia Curliana.—*See* Brown (R.)
Memorial des quelques Conferences.—*See* Mothe (De La)
Memorials of the Row Family.—*See* Maidment (J.)
Memorials of a Tour on the Continent, and in Greece.—*See* Houghton (Lord)
Men and Manners in America.—*See* Hamilton (Capt. T.)
Men Miracles.—*See* Llewellyn (M.)
Men and Things in America —*See* Bell (Andrew)
Mercurius Rusticus.—*See* Dibdin (T. F.)
Mercury, or Swift Messenger.—*See* Wilkins (J.)
Meredith (Owen).—*See* Lytton (R , Lord)
Merry Muses (The).—*See* Burns (R.)
Mery Play (A), etc.—*See* Heywood (J.)
Metastasio, the Patriot.—*See* Hamilton (C.)
Metronariston—*See* Warner (Dr.)
Microcosm (The).—*See* Canning (G.)
Microcosmus.—*See* Heylyn (P.)
Middlemarch.—*See* Cross (Mrs)
Milnes (R. M.).—*See* Houghton (Lord)
Miner's Guide.—*See* Hardy (W.)
Miniature (The).—*See* Miniature
Minister's Practice.—*See* Railton (J.)
Minutes of Negociations, etc.—*See* Defoe (D.)
Mirabeau.—*See* Smith (J. S.)
Mirror of the Months.—*See* Patmore (P. G.)
Mirrour (The), a Comedy.—*See* Dell (H.)
Miscellanea Sacra.—*See* Shute (J.)
Miscellaneous Metaphysical Essay.—*See* Casway (R.)
Miseries of Human Life, etc.—*See* Beresford
Missing Link (The).—*See* Ranyard (E. N.)
M. L.—*See* Lister (Martin)

Modern Antique (The) — *See* Gompertz (J.)
Modern Christianity.—*See* Pullen (W. H.)
Modern Greek (A).—*See* Mudie (Robert)
Modern Politics, etc.—*See* Sanscroft (W.)
Monastery of St. Werburgh.—*See* Greswell (Rev. W. P.)
Monitor (The).—*See* Pitt (W.)
Monks and the Giants.—*See* Frere (J. Hookham)
Mons. Catharinæ —*See* Lowth (Bp.)
Montanus.—*See* Skinner (V.)
Month before Sebastopol (A).—*See* Kinglake (A. W.)
Montmartre, Un Citoyen De.—*See* Sennemaud
Mont-Sacré.—*See* Montreuix
Monumethan Excantathus.—*See* White (T.)
Monumenta Westmonasteriensia.—*See* Keepe (H.)
Moonshine.—*See* Potts (Mrs. E. M.)
Moore (Tom).—*See* Anthologia Hibernica
Moralities, or Essays.—*See* Spence (Joseph)
Moral Practice of the Jesuites. — *See* Evelyn (J.)
More News from Salisbury.—*See* Sewell (W.)
Morton (Andrew).—*See* Defoe (D.)
Moses and Aaron.—*See* Womock (L.)
Mrs. Leicester's School.—*See* Lamb (C. and M.)
Mrs. Perkins's Ball.—*See* Thackeray (W. M.)
Mountain Sprites.—*See* Brabourne (Lord)
M. T.—*See* Mall (Thos.)
Much Darker Days.—*See* Lang (A.)
Musæ Cantabrigiensis.—*See* Cambridge
Muscipula.—*See* Holdsworth (Dr. E.)
My Cousin Nicholas.—*See* Barham
My Heart's in the Highlands.—*See* Keddie (H.)
My Life, what shall I do with it?—*See* Phillips (Miss)
My Pocket Book, etc.—*See* Du Bois (E.)
Myrtle (Harriet).—*See* Miller (Mrs. H.)
Mysterious Mother (The).—*See* Walpole (H.)
Mystery of the Temple, etc.—*See* Allen (W.)
My Village, etc.—*See* Croker

Narrative of Attempted Escapes of Chas. I.—*See* Hillier (G.)
Natural Hist. of Enthusiasm.—*See* Taylor (J.)
Natural Hist. of the Passions —*See* Charlton (Dr.)
Natural History of Tuft Hunters.—*See* Buckley (T. A.)
Natural Influence of Speech.—*See* Flamank (J.)
Nature and Human Nature.—*See* Haliburton
N. B.—*See* Baxter (Nathaniel)
Needwood Forest.—*See* Munday
Neville Temple, etc.—*See* Lytton (R.)
New Arabian Nights.—*See* Stevenson (R. L.)
New Brighton Guide (The).—*See* Williams (J.)
Newes from Southampton.—*See* Murford (P.)

New Ordeal (The).—*See* Chesney (Sir G.)
New Robinson Crusoe (The).—*See* Bewick
New Spirit of the Age.—*See* Horne (Rev. R. H.)
New Testament.—*See* Darby
New Testament.—*See* Taylor (Edgar)
New View of London.—*See* Hatton (E.)
New World of Words.—*See* Phillips (E.)
Nights at Sea.—*See* Barker
Nimrod's Hunting Tours, and other Works.—*See* Apperley (J. C.)
Nobilitas Politica, etc.—*See* Glover (R.)
Noblesse Oblige.—*See* Evans (Howard)
Non-Combatant (A.). —*See* Kinglake (A. W.)
No Fiction, etc.—*See* Read (Dr. A.)
Norfolk Lists.—*See* Ewing (W. C.)
North Briton (The).—*See* Wilkes (J.)
North Country Angler (A).—*See* Doubleday (T.)
Northern Memoirs.—*See* Scott (Sir W.)
Notes on Geology of Shropshire.—*See* Eyton (C.)
Notes and Materials, etc., *re* W. Law.—*See* Walton (C.)
Nothing to Wear.—*See* Forrester (A. H.)
Notice of W. T. Harris.—*See* Child (F. J.)
Notices of Sir W. Molesworth.—*See* Woolcombe (T.)
Notizia della vera liberta Fiorentina.—*See* Spannaghel (Baron)
Nouveaux Essais pour determiner, etc.—*See* Peremas (Le Père)
Nuremberg Chronicle.—*See* Alt (G.)
Nut Brown Maid.—*See* Keddie (H.).

Observations on the Reign of K. Charles.—*See* Heylyn (P.)
Observations upon Historie.—*See* Howell
Observations on Poetry.—*See* Ritson (Joseph)
Observations on Regiam Majestatem.—*See* Davidson (J.)
Observations on our Saviour.—*See* Bankes (W.)
Oddities of London Life.—*See* Poole (John)
Ode to the Cuckoo.—*See* Bruce (M.)
Œconomy of Human Life.—*See* Dodsley (R.)
Œconomy of Love.—*See* Armstrong (Dr.)
Of Education.—*See* Walker (O.)
Officer (An).—*See* Anburey (T.)
Old Bushman (An).—*See* Wheelwright (H. M.)
Old Chelsea Bun-House.—*See* Manning.
Old and Experienced Trader (An).—*See* Cluny (A.)
Old Humphrey.—*See* Mogridge (Geo.)
Old Judge (The).—*See* Haliburton (Judge)
Old Lieutenant (The).—*See* Macleod (N.)
Old Maid (An).—*See* Phillips (Miss)
Old Nick.—*See* Dubois (E.)
Old Sailor (The).—*See* Barker (M. H.)
Old Shekarry (The).—*See* Leveson (Maj. H. A.)
Old Vicar (An).—*See* Warter (Rev. J. W.)

Olla Podrida.—*See* Munro (Rev. T.)
On the State of Man, etc.—*See* Cornwallis (Mrs.)
On Decline of Science, etc.—*See* Moll (Prof.)
On the Orbits, etc.—*See* Wilkinson (W.)
On Employment of Time.—*See* Bolton (R.)
On Mutual Tolerance.—*See* Dockray (B.)
One of the Last Century.—*See* Rose (W. S.)
One of No Party.—*See* Grant (Jas.)
One of the Old School.—*See* Mackenzie (Colin)
Onesimus.—*See* Courtier (P. L.)
O. P.—*See* Cromwell (Oliver)
Open Air (The).—*See* Jefferies (R.)
Ophiomaches.—*See* Skelton (Rev. P.)
Opinion d'une Femme.—*See* Raoul (Mademoiselle)
Opinions of Duchess of Marlborough.—*See* Dalrymple (Sir D.)
O'Reilly (Miles).—*See* Halpin (C. G.)
Organization in Daily Life.—*See* Helps (Sir A.)
Origin and Progress of Despotism.—*See* Wilkes (J.)
Orwell.—*See* Smith (Walter C.)
Osmia, Tragedia.—*See* Souza (Catherine De)
Osservazioni Istoriche.—*See* Buonarroti (Filippo)
Other Stories.—*See* Brabourne (Lord)
Oughtred's Circles of Proportion.—*See* Foster (W.)
Ouida.—*See* Ramé (Louise de la)
Our Farm of Four Acres.—*See* Coulton (Miss)
Our Old Nobility.—*See* Evans (Howard)
Our own Special Correspondent.—*See* Warneford (R.)
Our Street.—*See* Thackeray (W. M.)
Our Year.—*See* Muloch (Miss)
Ovid's Heroicall Epistles.—*See* Salstonall (W.)
Ovid's Metamorphoses.—*See* Sandys (G.)
Owlet of Owlstone Edge.—*See* Paget (E. G.)
Oxford.—*See* Amherst.
Oxford Prize Poems.—*See* Ruskin (J.)
Oxford Sausage (The).—*See* Warton (T.)
Oxoniana.—*See* Bliss (Dr.)
Oxonian (An).—*See* Hole (Dean)
Ozanam's Mathematics.—*See* Hilman (D.)

P. (De).—*See* Pauw (M. de)
Page (H. A.).—*See* Japp
Palace of Otranto.—*See* Walpole (Horace)
Palæoromaica.—*See* Black (John)
Palm Leaves.—*See* Houghton (Lord)
Pamela.—*See* Richardson (S.)
Papers on the Army.—*See* Corbet (R.)
Pamphlets by Peter Porcupine, various.—*See* Cobbett (W.)
Paragreens (The) at the Exhibition.—*See* Ruffini (G.)
Paris Sketch Book.—*See* Thackeray (W. M.)

Parley (Peter).—*See* Martin (W.)
Parson Lot.—*See* Kingsley (C.)
Parson's Horn Book.—*See* Browne (Thos.)
Parthenissa.—*See* Orrery
Pascal's Provincial Letters.—*See* Pearce (G.)
Pasquin (Anthony).—*See* Williams (John)
Passages in the Life of Margaret Maitland.—*See* Oliphant (Mrs.)
Passion and Discretion.—*See* Calver (E.)
Past and Present Policy.—*See* Greville (C C.)
Past and Future Emigration.—*See* Napier (E.)
Pastorini (Sign.).—*See* Walmsley (Bp.)
Patchwork.—*See* Locker-Lampson
Paul Periwinkle.—*See* Neale (W. J.)
Paul Pry.—*See* Poole (John)
Pausanias.—*See* Taylor (Thos.)
Pensées Philosophiques.—*See* Sennemaud (Père)
Pensées sur la Nature.—*See* Diderot (M.)
People I have Met.—*See* Grenville-Murray (Hon. E. C.)
Perdita (The Fair).—*See* Robinson (Mrs.)
Perils of the Nation.—*See* Elizabeth (C.)
Perfect Ambassador (The).—*See* Thynn (F.)
Perfumed Garden, etc.—*See* Arbuthnot
Peri (A Penitent).—*See* Pearson (G. C.)
Person of Quality (A).—*See* Settle (E.)
Personal and Literary Memorials.—*See* Best (Mr.)
Personal Narrative of a Journey Overland, etc.—*See* Hook (T.)
Perspective of Impudence, etc.—*See* Lane (J)
Peter's Letters to his Kinsfolk.—*See* Lockhart (J. G.)
Peter of Pontefract (The Late).—*See* Graves (Rev. R.)
Peter Priggins. —*See* Hewlett
Peter Wilkins.—*See* Paltock (R.)
Pet Jessie Anne's Exhibition.—*See* Muir (T. S.)
Petticoat Loose.—*See* Rowlandson
P. H.—*See* Heylyn (P.)
Phantasmagoria.—*See* Dodgson (Rev. C. L.)
Philalethes.—*See* Jones (John)
Philanglus.—*See* Howell (J.)
Philobiblos.—*See* Ireland (J.)
Philopatri.—*See* Parsons (Robt.)
Philophilus Parresiastes.—*See* More (H.)
Philo Scotus.—*See* Ainslie (P.)
Philosophical Enquiry, etc.—*See* Collins (Ant.)
Philosophical Essays.—*See* Watts (I.)
Philosophy in Sport.—*See* Paris
Pickwick Papers —*See* Dickens (C.)
Picture of the Town of Herne Bay.—*See* Godwin (Mrs.)
Pictures of Popular People.—*See* Grant (J.)
Pictures from the Battlefield.—*See* Grenville-Murray (Hon. E. C.)
Pictures in the Tyrol —*See* Topffer (R.)

Piers Ploughman.—*See* Langland (R.)
Pilgrim and the Shrine.—*See* Maitland (S. R.)
Pilgrim's Reliquary (A).—*See* White (T. H.)
Pinch of Snuff (A).—*See* Gibson (T.)
Pindar (Peter).—*See* Wolcot (Dr.)
Pindar's Hair Powder.—*See* Wolcot (Dr.)
Piscator.—*See* Lathy (T. P.)
Piscatorial Reminiscences.—*See* Boosey (T.)
Pitman (Marie J.).—*See* Deane (M.)
P. J.—*See* Pereira (J.)
Plain Dealing with Presbyterians.—*See* Skene (J.)
Plain Description of Meteors.—*See* Fulke (W.)
Plato Redivivus.—*See* Melville (H.)
Play of the Sacrament.—*See* Stokes (W.)
Plutarch's Lives.—*See* Goldsmith (O.)
Poems by C. E. and A. Bell.—*See* Brouté (Sisters)
Poems, 1808.—*See* Browne (F. D.)
Poems ascribed to Burns.—*See* Burns (R.)
Poems on Several Occasions —*See* Carter (Eliz)
Poems supposed to have been, etc.—*See* Chatterton
Poems, by author of "Paul Ferroll."—*See* Clive (Mrs. Archer)
Poems by J. D.—*See* Donne (Dr. J.)
Poems by Three Friends.—*See* Poems
Poems on Several Occasions.—*See* Haddington (E. of)
Poems by Josiah Allen's Wife.—*See* Holley (Marietta)
Poems of Many Years, Poetry for the People.—*See* Houghton (Lord)
Poems (Latin).—*See* Vitis Carolinæ
Poems by F. Locker.—*See* Locker-Lampson (F.)
Poems written at Cambridge.—*See* Marriott (J.)
Poems by a Journeyman Mason.—*See* Miller (Hugh)
Poems by Delta.—*See* Moir (D. M.)
Poems by a Painter.—*See* Paton (Sir Noel)
Poems.—*See* Phillips (Mrs. K.)
Poems on Several Occasions.—*See* Prior (M.)
Poemata Sacra. - *See* Saltmarsh (Jo.)
Poems upon David.—*See* Saltmarsh (Jo.)
Poems, 1830-33.—*See* Tennyson (Lord)
Poésies Helvetiennes.—*See* Bridel (M.)
Poetica Stromata.—*See* Corbet (R.)
Poetical Magazine.—*See* Combe
Poetical Register.—*See* Jacob (G.)
Poetical Works by Δ.—*See* Moir (D. M.)
Poetical Works.—*See* Montague (Lady Mary)
Poetical Works of T. Little.—*See* Moore (Tom)
Poetical Works of Peter Pindar.—*See* Wolcot (Dr.)
Politeuphuia. - *See* Bodenham (J.)
Political Catechism (A).—*See* Robinson (R.)
Political Extracts.—*See* Child (D. L.)
Political Merriment.—*See* Brinsden and Collier

Political Quixote (The) —*See* Buston (G.)
Political Tracts.—*See* Swift (Dean)
Politics for the People.—*See* Kingsley (C.)
Popular Genealogists.—*See* Burnett (G.)
Popular German Stories.—*See* Grimm (Bros.)
Porcelain Tower (The).—*See* Sealy (T. H.)
Porcupine (Peter).—*See* Cobbett (W.)
Portfolio (The).—*See* Byron (Lord)
Portraicture of his Sacred Majestie, etc.—*See* Gauden
Portraits of Public Characters —*See* Grant (J.)
Portraits of the Spruggins Family.—*See* Morley (Countess of)
Post Chaise Companion.—*See* Wilson (W.)
Posthumous Fragments, etc.—*See* Shelley (P. B.)
Pounce (Peter).—*See* Lewis (R.)
P. P.—*See* Pierrugues (P.)
Practice of Pietie.—*See* Bayley (L.)
Præadamitæ.—*See* Peyrère (I. La)
Preaching of Christ.—*See* Irons (W. J.)
Preciosa.—*See* Fitzgerald (Edward)
Prendergast (Paul).—*See* Lee (P.)
Present Constitution, etc., vindicated.—*See* Willes (J.)
Present State of Politics.—*See* Dilke (Sir C.)
Present State of the Universe.—*See* Beaumont (J.)
President (The).—*See* Turner (Dawson)
Priestley's Funeral Speech.— *See* Christie (W.)
Primitiæ et Reliquiæ.—*See* Wellesley (Lord)
Principles of Protestantism.—*See* Appleyard (E. S.)
Print Collector (The).—*See* Maberley (J.)
Prison Thoughts.—*See* Thomas (W.)
Priviledges, etc., of Parliaments.—*See* Priviledges
Privy Councillors, etc.—*See* Young (Sir G. C.)
Prize Essay on Education.—*See* Greenwood (A. B.)
Probationary Odes.—*See* Hawkins (Sir J.)
Professor (The).—*See* Brontë (C.)
Prolusions.—*See* Capell (Edward)
Prolusiones Academicæ.—*See* Tennyson (F.)
Promenade, ou Itinéraire.— *See* Giraldin (M. de)
Prophecies of J. Usher.—*See* Maxwell (J.)
Propheties d'Isaie.—*See* Liere (M.)
Proposal for Correcting, etc.—*See* Swift (Dr. J.)
Proposals for a Council of Trades.—*See* Law (J.)
Prose by a Poet.—*See* Montgomery (J.)
Prosperity or Pauperism.—*See* Brabazon (Lord)
Provocations of Madame Palissy.—*See* Manning (Anne)
Psalmes of David.—*See* Singer (S. W.)
Publicola.—*See* Fox (W. J.)
Puck —*See* Ramé (Mdlle. de la)
Pulpit (The).—*See* Courtier (P. L.)
Punch and Judy.—*See* Collier (J. P.)

Punster's Pocket Book.—*See* Westmacott (C.)
Pupils of St. John the Divine.—*See* Yonge (C. M.)
Puppet-Show (The).—*See* Facetiæ
Pursuits of Literature.—*See* Mathias (T. J.)

Q.—*See* Couch (Quiller)
Quarterly Review.—*See* Dickens (C.)
Queen of the Fairies.—*See* Singleton (Mrs.)
Queenhoo Hall.—*See* Scott (Sir W.)
Queer Folk.—*See* Brabourne (Lord)
Question Royalle.—*See* De St. Cyrian (L'Abbé)
Quicksilver (J.).—*See* Cobbett (W.)
Quinque Illustrium, etc.—*See* Erotica
Quip Modest (The).—*See* Ritson (J.)

Rab and his Friends.—*See* Brown (J.)
Rachde Felley's Okeawnt, etc.—*See* Ormerod (O.)
Ralph Royster Doyster.—*See* Udall (N.)
Random Recollections of Lords, etc.—*See* Grant (J.)
Ranthorpe.—*See* Lewes (G. H.)
Rational Compendious Way, etc.—*See* Keyns (J.)
Rational Madness.—*See* Dibdin (T. F.)
Rational Mystic (A).—*See* Belcher (W.)
Rationale of Political Sentiments.—*See* Bailey (S.)
Ravillac Redivivus.—*See* Hickes (Rev. G)
R. C.—*See* Carew (R.)
Ready Made Family.—*See* Wicks (F.)
Real (Antony).—*See* Michel (Fernand)
Real Life in London.—*See* Egan (P.)
Realmah.—*See* Helps (Sir A)
Reason and Religion.—*See* Worthington (E.)
Reasons, etc., *re* the Bible.—*See* Burgess (Bp.)
Rebecca and Rowena.—*See* Thackeray (W. M.)
Recess (The)—*See* Johnson (J., M.D.)
Recherches Philosophiques.—*See* Pauw (M. de)
Recherches sur l'origine du Despotisme, etc.—*See* Boulanger (M.)
Reclaimed Papist (The).—*See* Cane (J. V.)
Records of the Chase.—*See* Tongue (C.)
Recreations of a Country Parson.—*See* Boyd (A. K. H.)
Recreations in Shooting.—*See* Carleton (Capt. J. W.)
Rector (The) and his Friends.—*See* Helps (Sir A.)
Redding (Cyrus).—*See* Beckford (W.)
Rede me and be not wrothe.—*See* Roy (W.)
Red Flag (The) in J. Bull's Eyes.—*See* Cobbe (F. P.)
Redgap.—*See* Pardon (G. F.)
Red Spinner.—*See* Senior (W.)
Reflector (The)—*See* Hunt (Leigh)
Reflections and Resolutions.—*See* Madden (Dr. S.)
Reflexions, etc , on the Brit. Nation.—*See* Defoe (D.)

Reflexions upon Ridicule.—*See* Bellegarde (J. B. M. de)
Reformation of Manners.—*See* Defoe (D.)
Reformed Monastery (The).—*See* L. B.
Reformed Wife.—*See* Burnaby (C.)
Rehearsals.—*See* Tabley (Lord de)
Reign of K. Charles (The).—*See* L'Estrange (H.)
Rejected Addresses.—*See* Smith (Horace and James)
Rejoinder to Mrs. Stowe.—*See* Cobbe (F. P.)
Relation of the State of Religion —*See* Sandys (Sir E.)
Relation de l'Inquisitione de Goa.—*See* Dellon (M.)
Religio Laici.—*See* Tempest (S.)
Religion of the Heart.—*See* Hunt (Leigh)
Religion of Nature, etc.—*See* Wollaston (J.)
Religious Courtship.—*See* Defoe (D.)
Reliquiæ Eboracenses.—*See* Dering (H.)
Reliques of English Poetry.—*See* Percy (Bp.)
Remaines concerning Britaine.—*See* Camden (W.)
Remarkable Adventures of J. Selkirk.—*See* James (I.)
Remarks on Disputed Points, etc.—*See* Chipman (Ward.)
Remarks on Italy —*See* Addison (J.)
Remarks on the Life of Milton.—*See* Toland (J.)
Remedies suggested, etc.—*See* Seeley (R. B)
Reminiscences of a Scottish Gentleman.—*See* Ainslie (P.)
Rennell (Thos.).—*See* Cambridge
Reply to Edinb. Rev.—*See* Copleston (J. H.)
Reply to a late Answer, etc.—*See* More (Dr. H.)
Reply to Where is Bilteswell ?—*See* Twining (D.)
Report on Silver Coins.—*See* Lowndes (W.)
Representations of the H. of Assembly.—*See* Chalmers (G.)
Reproof to the Rehearsal.—*See* Hooker (Bp.)
Researches on the Origin of Despotism, etc.—*See* Boulanger (M.)
Resident (A).—*See* Massery (Isabel)
Respublica Anglicana.—*See* Withers (G.)
Reuben.—*See* Hawker (R. S.)
Reverberations (Poems).—*See* Gall (W. M. W.)
Reveries of Affection, etc.—*See* Turnley (J.)
Reveries of a Bachelor.—*See* Mitchell (D. G.)
Revolt of the Bees.—*See* Morgan (J. M.)
Reynard the Fox.—*See* Cole (Sir H.)
Rhododaphne.—*See* Peacock (T. L.)
Richard of Cirencester.—*See* Hatcher (H.)
Rich Cabinet, etc. (A).—*See* White (J.)
Richmond, etc.—*See* Gaspey (T.)
Richmond Hill.—*See* Maurice
Rights of the Christian Church.—*See* Tindal (M.)
Rights, Liberties, Authorities, etc.—*See* Louth (Dr. S.)
Ring of Amasis.—*See* Lytton (Robt., E. of)
Rise and Fall of Heresy.—*See* Manning (R.)
Rising Sun (The).—*See* Barrett (E. S.)

River Legends, etc.—*See* Brabourne (Lord)
Robin Hood.—*See* MacNally (Leonard)
Robin Hood Society (The).—*See* Lewis (Richard)
Robinson Crusoe.—*See* Defoe (D.)
Rodonto.—*See* Dalrymple (H.)
Roll of a Tennis Ball, etc.—*See* Atkinson (A.)
Roman de mon Alcove.—*See* "Erotica"
Roman Antiquities, etc.—*See* Moir (D. M.)
Romance of Chivalric Ages.—*See* Cope (H.)
Romantic Land of Hind (The).—*See* Mackenzie (Capt. C. F.)
Rome in the XIXth Cent.—*See* Waldie (E. A.)
Rose and the Ring.—*See* Thackeray (W. M.)
Round about a Great Estate.—*See* Jefferies (R.)
Roving Englishman (The).—*See* Grenville-Murray (E. C.)
Rowley Poems.—*See* Chatterton (T.)
R——l Brood (The).—*See* Wolcot (Dr. J.)
Royal Sin (The).—*See* Croxall (S.)
Runaway Slave (The).—*See* Browning (E. B.)
R. V.—*See* Verstegan (R.)

Sacerdos Paroecialis Rusticus.—*See* Burton (Dr. J.)
Saddi (Nathan Ben).—*See* Dodsley (R.)
Saddle and Sirloin —*See* Dixon (H. H.)
Saint Mary.—*See* Moultrie (Rev. J.)
Salad for the Solitary.—*See* Saunders (F.)
Salathiel —*See* Croly (Dr. G.)
Salmagundi.—*See* Irving (W.)
Salmonia.—*See* Davy (Sir H.)
Salvator Rosa.—*See* Group (The)
Sandford and Merton.—*See* Day (T.)
Sandringham, Past and Present.—*See* Jones (Mrs. H.)
Sans Merci.—*See* Lawrence (J.)
Sarcelle, of "The Field," was Chas. A. Payton.
S. A. T.—*See* Taylor (S. A.)
Satan in Search of a Wife.—*See* Lamb (C.)
Saunders (Jef.).—*See* Smith (Horace)
Savillon's Elegies.—*See* Wallace (J.)
Scanderbeg.—*See* Mottley (J.)
Scene of Delusions.—*See* Lacy (J.)
Scheeps-togt van Ant. Chester, etc.—*See* Chester (A.)
School Candidates (The).—*See* Clarke (H.)
School Lawes, or Qui Hi in English. *See* Milton (J.)
Scotch Presbyterian Eloquence.—*See* Presbytery
Scotiæ Indiculum.—*See* Mudie (Alex.)
Scotland.—*See* Albania
Scotland.—*See* Basire (Dr. I.)
Scotland, Account of Affairs of.—*See* Balcarres (E. of)
Scots Episcopal Innocence.—*See* Ridpath (G.)
Scots Gent. in Swedish Service.—*See* Defoe (D.)

Scott (Sir W.).—*See* Adolphus (J. L.)
Scott (Sir W.).—*See* Burt
Scott and Sebright.—*See* Dixon (H. H.)
Scottish Surnames.—*See* Innes (Cosmo)
Scouring of the White Horse.—*See* Hughes (T.)
Scrap-Book of Literary Varieties.—*See* Dickens (C.)
Scribbleomania.—*See* Ireland (W. H.)
Scripture Revelations.—*See* Whately (Archbp.)
Scrutator.—*See* Horlock (D. W.)
Scrutator.—*See* Horlock (J. K.)
Sea-Board and Down.—*See* Warter (J. W.)
Sea-Pie (The).—*See* Forrester (A. H.)
Seasonable Recommendation, Defence, etc.—*See* Glanville (J.)
Seasonable Treatise (A), etc.—*See* Cooke (E.)
Secretary to the Bd. of Agriculture.—*See* Young (A.)
Secret History, etc.—*See* Haywood (Eliz.)
Secret Hist. of Arlus, etc.—*See* Defoe (D.)
Secret History of the Calves' Head Club.—*See* Ward (E.)
Secret History of London Clubs.—*See* Ward (Ned)
Secret History of Present Intrigues, etc.—*See* Haywood (Mrs.)
Secret History of Queen Zarah.—*See* Manley (Mrs.)
Secret Policy of Jesuits.—*See* Tootle (Rev. H.)
Secrets of Angling.—*See* Dennys (J.)
Secrets of the Invisible World.—*See* Defoe (D.)
Select Pieces of Poetry.—*See* Utterson (E V.)
Select Tracts (Civil War).—*See* Maseres (Baron)
Senilia, sive Poetica, etc.—*See* Mattaire (M.)
Serbski Pesme —*See* Lytton (R.)
Serious Considerations, etc.—*See* Decker (Sir M.)
Sermon taken from an Oxford Scholar, etc.—*See* Higgins (J.)
Sermons of Yorick.—*See* Sterne (L.)
Setting Sun (The).—*See* Barrett (E. S.)
Seven Days (The).—*See* Williams (I.)
Shade of Alexander Pope.—*See* Mathias (T. J.)
Shakespeare.—*See* Heath (Benj.)
Shakespeare.—*See* Morgann (M.)
Shakespeare.—*See* Whateley (T.)
Shakespeare.—*See* Whiter (W.)
Shakespeare.—*See* Hardinge (G.)
Shakespeare Forgeries, Vortigern and Rowena.—*See* Dudley (Sir B. and Lady)
Shakespeare Illustrated.—*See* Lennox (Mrs. Charlotte)
Shadow and Substance.—*See* Forrester
Shadows of the Clouds —*See* Froude (J. A.)
Shelley Letters.—*See* Browning (R.)
Shepherd of Bethlehem (The).—*See* Tucker (Miss)
Shepherds Hunting.—*See* Wither (G.)
Shooting and Fishing Trips.—*See* Clements (L.)
Short Account of Danegeld.—*See* Webb (P. C.)

Short Account of Lichfield Cathedral.—*See* Woodhouse (J.)
Short Compendium of Persecutions, etc.—*See* Symson (P.)
Short Hist. of Regal Succession.—*See* Lindsay
Short Hist. of Standing Armies.—*See* Defoe (D.)
Short Hist. of Westminster Forum.—*See* Turner (Dawson)
Short View of the Political Life, etc.—*See* Pitt (W.)
Short Vindication of the Relapse.—*See* Vanbrugh (Sir J.)
Short Whist.—*See* Coles (B Coles)
Shrewsbury, Account of.—*See* Owen (Hugh)
Shrubs of Parnassus.—*See* Woty (T.)
Shuffling, Cutting and Dealing, etc.—*See* Cromwell (O.)
Sidebotham (John).—*See* Grindon (L. H.)
Sidney's (Sir P.) Ourania.—*See* Baxter (N.)
Sidonia the Sorceress.—*See* Wilde (Lady)
Sigma.—*See* Shaw (J. B.)
Silk and Scarlet.—*See* Dixon (H. H.)
Silas Marner.—*See* Cross (Mrs.)
Silver Watch Bell (A).—*See* Tymme (T.)
Six Cushions (The).—*See* Yonge (C. M.)
Six Letters on Intolerance.—*See* Colebrooke (Sir G.)
Six Months in W. Indies.—*See* Coleridge (H. N.)
Six Portraits, etc.—*See* Sharpe (C. K.)
Six Weeks' Tour in S. of England.—*ee* Young (A.)
Skedaddle.—*See* Warneford (R.)
Sketches by Boz.—*See* Dickens (C.)
Sketches in Ireland.—*See* Otway (C.)
Sketches of Edinburgh Clergy.—*See* Anderson (J.)
Sketches of Poetical Literature.—*See* Moir (D.)
Sketches of Pumps.—*See* Forrester
Sketches and Characters, etc.—*See* Thicknesse (P.)
Sketchley (A.).—*See* Rose (Rev. G.)
Slick (Sam).—*See* Haliburton (Judge)
Small Farms.—*See* Jefferies (R.)
Small Tableaux.—*See* Tennyson (C)
Smiff (O. P. Q. Philander).—*See* Dowty (A. A.)
Smith (J.).—*See* Microcosm (The)
Smith (M.).—*See* Peterborough (E. of)
Smith (R.).—*See* Microcosm (The)
Snob (The).—*See* Thackeray (W. M.)
Social Duties.—*See* Rathbone (W.)
Social Life in Australia.—*See* Massery (I.)
Society of the Learned (A).—*See* Heathcote (R.)
Solar Creation (The).—*See* Lowe (John)
Solicitudes of Absence.—*See* Renwick (W.)
Solitary Traveller (A).—*See* Atkinson (A.)
Some Sober Inspections, etc. (Long Parliament).—*See* Howell (J.)
Some Account of Mrs. C. Singleheart.—*See* Manning (A.)
Some Fruits of Solitude.—*See* Penn (W.)
Somerset House Gazette.—*See* Pyne (W. H.)

Son of Liberty (A).—*See* Church (Dr. B.)
Songs of the Edinb. Troop and Squadron.—*See* Lockhart
Songs of the Holy Land.—*See* Stirling-Maxwell
Songs of the Press.—*See* Timperley (C. H.)
Songs of Singularity.—*See* Parke (F.)
Songs of Two Worlds.—*See* Morris (Lewis)
Sonnets and other Poems.—*See* Shaw (J. B.)
Sonnets, Lyrics, etc.—*See* Tennyson (C.)
Sophocles Electra.—*See* Wase (C.)
Sophy, Adventures of a Savage.—*See* Singleton (Mrs.)
South Sea Bubbles.—*See* Kingsley (C.)
Spain Revisited.—*See* Mackenzie Capt.)
Specimen of an Etymological Vocabulary.—*See* Cleland
Specimen of a Hist. of Oxfordshire.—*See* Warton (T.)
Specimens of German Romance.—*See* Soane (G.)
Speculatum Speculativum.—*See* Wither (G.)
Speculum Episcopi.—*ee* Roberts (Rev. G.)
Spell Bound.—*See* Eldridge (R.)
Spencer (W. T.).—*See* Cross (Mrs.), Crowquill, Cruikshank, Combe, Egan, Phiz, Ruskin. and Spencer
Speranza (Francesca).—*See* Wilde (Lady)
Spirit of "The Book."—*See* Ashe (T.)
Spirit of the Public Journals.—*See* Westmacott
Spiritual Quixote.—*See* Graves (R.)
Splene (Megathym).—*See* Thomson (C.)
Sponge's Sporting Tour, etc.—*See* Surtees (R. S.)
Sportascrapiana.—*See* Wheeler (C. A.)
Sporting.—*See* Apperley (C. J.)
Sporting Scenes and Country Characters.—*See* White (J.)
Sportsman's Friend, etc.—*See* Brendley (C.)
Spring and Summer in Lapland.—*See* Wheelwright (H. W.)
Stable-Talk, etc.—*See* Brendley (C.)
Stafford (W.).—*See* Shakespeare (W.)
Staffordshire Directory.—*See* Bradshaw
State of the C. of Good Hope.—*See* Bird (W. W.)
State of Protestants in Ireland, etc.—*See* King (Archbp.)
Steam Boat (The).—*See* Galt (John)
Stereometry.—*See* Wood (Basil)
St. Irvyne —*See* Shelley (P. B)
St. Magnus of the Orkneys.—*See* Bute (Marquis of)
Stokers and Pokers.—*See* Head (Sir F.)
Stonehenge on the Shot Gun, and other Works.—*See* Walsh
Stories of Waterloo.—*See* Maxwell (W. H.)
Stories and Rhymes.—*See* Mellor (J. W.)
Story of my Heart.—*See* Jefferies (R.)
Story of the Stick.—*See* Micheel (Fernand)
Strange Gentleman (The).—*See* Dickens (C.)
Strangers and Pilgrims.—*See* Maxwell (Mrs.)
Strayed Reveller (The).—*See* Arnold (M)

Strutt (J.).—*See* Scott (Sir W.)
Stud (The).—*See* Brendley (Chas.)
Studies from Life.—*See* Muloch (Miss)
Stultifera Navis.—*See* Ireland (W. H.)
Subaltern (The).—*See* Gleig (Rev. G. R.)
Suggestive Enquiry into Hermetic Mystery, etc.—*See* Scott (Dr.)
Summerley's (Felix) Pleasure Excursions.—*See* Cole (Sir H.)
Sunday under Three Heads.—*See* Dickens.
Sunday School Memorials.—*See* Braidley (B.)
Suppressed Evidence, &c.—*See* Wolcot (Dr.)
Surprising Adventures of Gooroo, &c —*See* Forrester
Survey of Popery (The).—*See* Bell (Thos.)
Survey of Tuscany.—*See* Darlington (Robert)
Sword and Gown.—*See* Lawrence (J.)
Sylva, or the Wood.—*See* Heathcote (Dr. R.)
Syntax, Three Tours.—*See* Combe (W.)
Syntax (Dr.).—*See* Forrester (A. H.)
Synopsis Papismi.—*See* Willet (A.)
Systema Agriculturæ.—*See* Worledge (J.)

Tale of a Tub.—*See* Swift (Dean)
Tales of College Life.—*See* Bradley
Tales of Irish Life.—*See* Whitty (J.)
Tangled Tale (A).—*See* Dodgson (Rev. C. L.)
Tannhauser.—*See* Lytton (Robt.)
Tarantula (The), or Dance of Fools —*See* Barrett
Tasso and Leonora.—*See* Manning (Anne)
Tavern Anecdotes.—*See* Mackenzie (Colin)
T. B.—*See* Blount (Thos.)
T. B.—*See* Brewer (Thomas)
T. D.—*See* Deloney (T.)
Tears and Smiles.—*See* Wolcot (Dr. J.)
Tendrils.—*See* Hawker (R. S.)
Tentamen —*See* Hook (Theodore)
Teresina in America.—*See* Yelverton (T.)
Terræ Filius.—*See* Amherst
Tewtsch Rational, &c.—*See* Berthold (E. Von C.)
T. F.—*See* Thynn (F.)
Thackeray (W. M.)—*See* Taylor (Tom)
Thackerayana.—*See* Thackeray (W. M.)
Thaumaturgus.—*See* Fitzpatrick (P. V.)
The Cathedral.—*See* Williams (Isaac)
The Indicator.—*See* Hunt (Leigh)
The Pantheon.—*See* Godwin (W.)
The Union (Hymns).—*See* Curtis (J.)
The Vampyre.—*See* Polidori
The Victim.—*See* Tennyson (A.)
The Wits.—*See* "Facetiæ"
Thelyphthora, or Treatise on Female Ruin.—*See* Madan (M.)

Theophrastus Such.—*See* Cross (Mrs.)
Theory of Dreams —*See* Ferrier (Dr. J.)
Thesaurus Numismatum —*See* Patin (Chas.)
Thinks-I-to-Myself.—*See* Nares (Dr.)
Thoughts on Currency.—*See* Scott (Sir W.)
Thoughts on a Regicide Peace.—*See* Burke (E.)
Thoughts on the late Transactions.—*See* Johnson (Dr.)
Thomas of Reading.—*See* Deloney (T.)
Three Courses and a Dessert.—*See* Clarke (C.)
Three Estates (The).—*See* Fox (W. J.)
Three Letters, &c.—*See* Wilbraham (R.)
Three Old Ballads.—*See* Deloney (Thos.)
Three Poems.—*See* Le Gallienne (R.)
Tim Bobbin's Lancs. Dialect.—*See* Collier (J.)
Time's Telescope.—*See* Defoe (D)
Timothy Sparks.—*See* Dickens (C.)
Tin Trumpet (The).—*See* Smith (Horace)
'Tis Merry when Gossips, &c.—*See* Rowlands (Sam.)
Titmarsh (M. A.).—*See* Thackeray (W. M.)
To be Read at Dusk.—*See* Dickens (C.)
Tombo-Chiqui.—*See* Cleland (J.)
Tom Raw the Griffin.—*See* D'Oyley (Sir C.)
Tommiebeg Shootings (The).—*See* Jeans (T.)
Tough Yarns.—*See* Barker (M. H)
Toulmin (Camilla).—*See* Crosland (Mrs. N.)
Tour in Quest of Genealogy.—*See* Jones (H.) and Fenton (R.)
Tour Through the Highlands.—*See* Botfield (B.)
Tour Through I. of Thanet.—*See* Cozens (Z.)
Tourney (Count de).—*See* Brosses
Town (The).—*See* Hunt (Leigh)
T.P.A.P.O.A.B.I.T.C.O.S.—*See* Sykes (A. A.)
Tracts for the Times.—*See* "Tracts"
Traditions of the Jews.—*See* Stehelin (J. P.)
Traddutori Italiani.—*See* Maffei (S.)
Tragedie of Lord Boroscho.—*See* Kellie (R.)
Traité de la Politique de France.—*See* Chastelet (M. de)
Transactions of the Loggerville Lit. Soc.—*See* "Facetiæ"
Traveller (A).—*See* Campbell (J. F.)
Travels of an Irish Gentleman.—*See* Moore (T.)
Travels for the Heart.—*See* Pratt (S. J.)
Travels through America, by an Officer.—*See* Anburey (T.)
Travels with a Donkey.—*See* Stevenson (R. L.)
Travels in Town.—*See* Grant (J)
Tremaine.—*See* Ward (R. Plumer)
Trial of Eugene Aram.—*See* Fryer (M.)
Trinity Man (A).—*See* Wright (Thos.)
Triplicity.—*See* Lance (T.)
Tristram Shandy.—*See* Sterne (L.)
True Born Englishman (The).—*See* Defoe (D)

True Hist. of Joshua Davidson.—*See* Linton (Mrs.)
T T. T.—*See* Sealy (T. H.)
Turkish Spy.—*See* Marana (J. P.)
Turtle Dove (The).—*See* Fullarton (John)
Tutor's Assistant.—*See* Forrester (A. H.)
Twain (Mark).—*See* Clemens (S. L.)
Twenty-ninth of May (The).—*See* Pyne (W. H.)
Two Brothers.—*See* Hare
Two Enquiries on Demoniacks.—*See* Sykes (A. A.)

Ubique.—*See* Gillmore (P.)
Ugo Bassi.—*See* Wilde (Lady)
Uncle Joe's Stories.—*See* Brabourne
Unda's Rubbings, etc.—*See* Muir (T. S.)
Undine, a Romance.—*See* Fouqué (De La M)
Unjust Plea Confuted.—*See* Whitehead (Geo.)
Unpublished Verses.—*See* Swinburne (A C.)
Unsentimental Journey through Cornwall —*See* Muloch (Miss)
Urbino (Marchioness).—*See* Noake (Dorothy)
Use and Abuse of Parliaments.—*See* Ralph (J.)

V. Poems by —*See* Clive (Mrs. Archer)
V***** (M. De).—*See* Voltaire
Vade-Mecum to Hatton —*See* Crossley (J.)
Vagabond (The).—*See* Thomas (Julian)
Valerius.—*See* Lockhart (J. G.)
Vane's Story, etc.—*See* Thomson (J.)
Vathek.—*See* Beckford (W.)
Vauxhall Papers (The).—*See* Forrester (A. H.)
Velasquez and his Works. *See* Stirling-Maxwell
Veneres et Priapi.—*See* D'Hancarville
Venus Physique.—*See* Maupertius
Verses (Anonymous).—*See* Findlay (J R.)
Verses on Various Occasions —*See* Newman (J. H.)
Vestiges of Creation, and Sequel.—*See* Chambers (R.)
Vicar of Wakefield.—*See* Goldsmith (O.)
Victoria Regia (The).—*See* Thackeray (W. M.)
Victorious Reigne of Edward III.—*See* May (T.)
View of Agriculture of Oxfordshire.—*See* Young (A.)
View of Newton's Philosophy.—*See* Pemberton (H.)
Village Curate (The).—*See* Hurdis (Dr)
Vindication of All Souls', Oxford.—*See* Buckler (Dr. Ben.)
Vindication of G. Buchanan —*See* Love (J.)
Vindication of the Defence of Christianity.—*See* Chandler (Bp.)
Vindication of the Present Ministry.—*See* Defoe (D.)
Vindiciæ Biblicæ.—*See* Walther (D.)
Vindiciæ Carolinæ.—*See* Hollingsworth (Rev. R.)
Vindiciæ contra Tyrannus.—*See* Languet (H.)
Vinet (E.).—*See* Peletier (J.)

INDEX TO TITLES.

Virginia.—*See* Williams (E. W.)
Virginis Puerisque.—*See* Stevenson (R. L.)
Vision of Piers Plowman.—*See* Langland (R.)
Visionary (The).—*See* Scott (Sir W.)
Visions of Sir Heister Ryley.—*See* Povey (C.)
Vox Cœli.—*See* Scot (Thos.)
Voyage to Abyssinia (A)—*See* Johnson (Dr. S.)
Voyage and Adventures of Capt. Boyle.—*See* Chetwood (W. R.)
V. R.—*See* Verstegan (R.)
Vulgar Errours.—*See* Walker (O.)
Vulgus Britannicus—*See* Ward (E.)

W. A.—*See* Weldon (Sir A.)
Wagstaff (S.).—*See* Swift (Dean)
Walking Gentleman (A).—*See* Grattan (T. C.)
Walks and Talks of an Amer. Farmer.—*See* Olmsted (F.)
Wanderer (The).—*See* Lytton (Robt.)
Wanderings of a Pen and Pencil.—*See* Forrester
Wanderings of a Pilgrim.—*See* Parks (Fanny)
Warren (J. Leicester).—*See* Tabley (Lord de)
War Correspondence.—*See* Forbes (A.)
Wars of Wellington (The).—*See* Combe (W.)
Watchman (The).—*See* Coleridge (S. T.)
Water Lily (The).—*See* Miller (Mrs. H.)
Waterside Sketches.—*See* Senior (W.)
Waverley Novels.—*See* Adolphus (J. L.)
W. C.—*See* Worthington (E.)
Weeds, a Story, etc.—*See* Jerome (J. K.)
Wegelini Sangallenses.—*See* Gataker (T.)
We Pity the Plumage, etc.—*See* Shelley (P. B.)
Westminster Abbey.—*See* Maurice (T.)
W. F.—*See* Fulke (W.)
W. G.—*See* Withers (G.)
What will he do with it?—*See* Lytton (Bulwer)
Whistlecraft (W. and R.).—*See* Frere (J. H.)
White Republican (A).—*See* Fuller (Hiram)
White Wife (The).—*See* Bradley (Rev.)
Who wrote Cavendish's Life of Wolsey?—*See* Hunter (Rev. J.)
Whole Duty of Prayer.—*See* Paley (J.)
Whychcotte of St. John's.—*See* Neale (Erskine)
Wildfowler.—*See* Clements (L.)
Wildgoose (Geoffry).—*See* Graves (R.)
Wild Life in a Southern Country.—*See* Jefferies (R.)
Wild Sports of the West.—*See* Maxwell (W. H.)
Wild Wreath (The).—*See* Coleridge (S. T.)
Wilkes (J.).—*See* Boulanger (M.)
Will Watch.—*See* Neale (W. J.)
Wills of their own.—*See* Dickens (C.)
Winchester (Poems).—*See* Townsend (C.)

Wine and Walnuts.—*See* Pyne (W. H.)
Wise Saws, etc.—*See* Haliburton (Judge)
Wise Virgin (The).—*See* Fisher (James)
W. J.—*See* Wallis (J.)
W. L.—*See* Longman (W.)
W. O.—*See* Walker (O.)
Wolsey (Cardinal).—*See* Cavendish (Geo.)
Woman's Thoughts about Women.—*See* Muloch (Miss)
Wood Magic.—*See* Jefferies (R.)
World (The) and how to square it.—*See* Brendley (C.)
W. P.—*See* Prynne (W.)
Wright (T.).—*See* Halliwell (J. O.)
Wrinkles, or Hints to Sportsmen.—*See* Leveson (Major)
W. S.—*See* Stokes (W.)

Years after.—*See* Manning (Anne)
Yendys (S.).—*See* Dobell (S.)
York Musical Festival.—*See* Hett (Rev.)
Young Pilgrim (The).—*See* Tucker (Miss)
Youngling Elder (The).—*See* Godwin (J.)
Young Scarron.—*See* Mozeen (Thomas)

Zeta.—*See* Froude (J. A.)
Zillah, a Tale.—*See* Smith (Horace)
Zoë.—*See* Colquhoun (J.)
Zohrab the Hostage.—*See* Morier (J.)

A. MAURICE & CO.

Ancient and Modern Booksellers,

23, BEDFORD ST., COVENT GARDEN,
LONDON, W.C.

Telegraphic Address:—
"MNEMOSYNE, LONDON."

FIRST EDITIONS
AND
SCARCE BOOKS.

Catalogues Free.

GLASGOW.

McCLURE'S
Shorthand for the Many

A Short and Easy Guide to SHORTHAND, based on Taylor's famous "loop" system.
8 pp., price *TWOPENCE*.

ROBERT McCLURE,
"Ye Auld Buik Shop,"
206, BUCHANAN STREET, GLASGOW.

The 'Swan' Press
300, South Lambeth Road, S.W.

High-class Work a Speciality.

AUTHORS desiring to bring themselves before the Public cannot do better than submit their MSS. to above firm. All such MSS. carefully read, and the author advised as to their issue or non-publication; estimates of cost also given.

First Editions of Modern Authors

INCLUDING

DICKENS, THACKERAY, LEVER, AINSWORTH, BROWNING, RUSKIN, etc., etc.; Books illustrated by G. and R. CRUIKSHANK, PHIZ, ROWLANDSON, LEECH, ALKEN, SEYMOUR, &c.

The Largest and Choicest Collection offered for Sale in the World.
Catalogues issued, and sent post free on application.
BOOKS BOUGHT.

WALTER T. SPENCER,
27, New Oxford Street, London, W.C.

Telegraphic Address:— "PHIZ, LONDON."

ESTABLISHED 1848.

Richard Amer,

NEW AND SECOND-HAND

LAW BOOKSELLER & EXPORTER,

LINCOLN'S INN GATE, CAREY STREET, W.C.,

Has always on hand a large Stock of Reports in the various Courts, including "THE LAW REPORTS," "LAW JOURNAL REPORTS," "THE JURIST," "WEEKLY REPORTER," LAW TIMES REPORTS," "JUSTICE OF THE PEACE," &c.; also TEXT BOOKS, TREATISES, &c., on ADMIRALTY, COLONIAL, FOREIGN, CIVIL AND ECCLESIASTICAL LAW, TRIALS, &c., &c., at the lowest Market prices.

Catalogues of the above Post Free on application.

EARLY BOOKS A SPECIALTY.

Export Orders promptly executed on receipt of Banker's draft.

VALUATIONS MADE FOR PROBATE, PARTNERSHIPS, INSURANCE, &C.

USUAL DISCOUNT TO THE TRADE.

Man schreibt Deutsch.   *On correspond en français.*

REEVES & TURNER, Law Booksellers & Publishers

100, Chancery Lane, and Carey Street, LONDON, W.C.

THE RECORD INTERPRETER. A Collection of Abbreviations, Latin Words, and Names used in English Historical Manuscripts and Records. Compiled by CHARLES TRICE MARTIN, B.A., F.S.A., Assistant Keeper of the Public Records. 8vo, price 12s. 6d.; post free, 10s. 6d.

WRIGHT'S COURT-HAND RESTORED. The Student's Assistant in reading Old Deeds, Charters, Records, &c. Neatly engraved on Twenty-three Copper Plates, describing the Old Law Hands, with their Contractions and Abbreviations. With an Appendix containing the Ancient Names of Places in Great Britain and Ireland; an Alphabetical Table of Ancient Surnames; and a Glossography of Latin Words found in the Works of the most eminent Lawyers and other Ancient Writings, but not in any Modern Dictionaries. By ANDREW WRIGHT. The Ninth Edition, corrected and enlarged, with Seven New Plates, by CHARLES TRICE MARTIN, B.A., F.S.A., of H.M. Public Record Office. 1879. Price 21s.; post free, 17s. 9d.

Just published. Price 8s. 6d.; post free, 7s. 6d.

GAMBLING (THE LAW OF), CIVIL AND CRIMINAL. With Forms. By WARD COLDRIDGE, M.A., and CYRIL HAWKSFORD, B.A., Barristers-at-Law.

Now ready, 8vo, 10s.; post free, 8s. 6d.

THE LICENSING LAWS, so far as they relate to the Sale of Intoxicating Liquors. By R. M. MONTGOMERY, of the Inner Temple, Barrister-at-Law. Contains full information as to licenses (including theatre, music, and dancing, and billiard licenses), discretion of justices in granting them, duties and liabilities of licensed persons, offences against the Licensing Laws.

THE LAW OF CHARITIES AND MORTMAIN: being a Third Edition of TUDOR'S CHARITABLE TRUSTS. By L. S. BRISTOWE, M.A., and W. I. COOK, Barristers-at-Law. Royal 8vo. 1889. Price 38s.; post free, 31s. 6d.

A TREATISE ON THE MORTMAIN AND CHARITABLE USES ACT, 1891. By LEONARD SYER BRISTOWE, M.A., Barrister-at-Law, Draftsman of the Act, and Joint Author of "The Law of Charities and Mortmain" ("Tudor's Charitable Trusts"). 1891. Price 6s.; post free, 5s. 3d.

Curious Old & Rare Books

GEORGE P. JOHNSTON

33 GEORGE STREET

EDINBURGH

INTERESTING CATALOGUES

post free on application

••••

Reports solicited of early printed Scottish books; anything printed by James Watson or Peter Williamson; at the Holyrood Press; or in Provincial Towns of Scotland

---

JAMES DORMAN,

48, SOUTHAMPTON ROW, LONDON, W.C.

Book=Plates Wanted.

Cash by return for Large or Small Parcels, and fine separate specimens of Book-Plates (ex-libris).

DUPLICATES AND WHOLE COLLECTIONS BOUGHT.
HIGH PRICES GIVEN.

Catalogues of Second=hand Books issued periodically, and sent Post Free on application.

Henry Stevens, Son & Stiles,

DEALERS IN

Rare Books

RELATING TO

— North America,

39, GREAT RUSSELL ST., W.C.

(Opposite the British Museum).

Owners of Books relating to North America are invited to offer them to us in the first instance. Having probably the largest stock of "Americana" in existence, we have consequently the best knowledge of the market, and can therefore generally afford to give the very highest price.

All reports promptly answered, and with an order if possible.

Rare Facetiæ.

Secret History of London Clubs, by the author of "The London Spy," (Ned Ward).

A private re-issue (500 copies only, each numbered), on thick paper, with facsimile of the two curious woodcuts, 5/- nett.

Large Paper, (only 100 done NEARLY OUT OF PRINT), 7/6 nett.

Sent Post Free on receipt of amount. Trade Terms on application.

F. Marchmont,

300, SOUTH LAMBETH ROAD S.W.

To the Trade.

MR. F. MARCHMONT,

Professional Cataloguer

TO THE

Second-hand Bookselling, Pawnbroking, and Auctioneering Trades,

of many years' experience, is open to accept ONE more CONTRACT to compile a Second-Hand Book Catalogue regularly.

☞ *Specimens of Work, Terms, and References on application. Punctuality guaranteed.*

300, SOUTH LAMBETH ROAD, LONDON, S.W.

J. BAMBER & CO.,

The Pilgrim's Head,

292, BOROUGH HIGH STREET, S.E.,

LONDON.

Purchasers & Purveyors.

BOOKS, Antiques, Curios, China, Paintings, Engravings, Autographs, Old Deeds, etc., etc.

Cataloguers.

CAREFULLY compiled catalogues of books, etc., for sale are issued at intervals; a postcard with address will insure participation in the issues, which are limited. Catalogues of private libraries prepared and printed.

Graingerizers.

BESIDES prints of value, Messrs. J. BAMBER & CO. have a large mass of engravings collected for the purpose of extra-illustration. They would be glad of instructions to hunt any subject.

Repairers.

MESSRS. J. BAMBER & CO. make a speciality of repairing; enumeration of articles is useless, as the staff is selected to cope with the repair of anything, from a Chelsea vase to a chime clock, a spinning wheel to a spinet. A trial will surprise and please.

Picture Cleaners, Gilders, Frame Makers,

Dealers in Spirit Varnishes of the highest quality in every branch of manufacture.

SALES ATTENDED ON COMMISSION.

J. BAMBER & CO., 292, Borough High Street.

COLLECTORS

Should always employ an up-to-date Bookseller to look after their wants. Such a Bookseller is

FRANK MURRAY,

Of Derby, Leicester, and Nottingham.

If you are a Collector of **any kind of Books,** send a list of your wants to any of the above Shops and you will be **astonished** at the rapidity with which your wants will be supplied.

The secret is that **FRANK MURRAY** has **unrivalled facilities** for procuring out-of-the-way and Rare Literature. He makes no charge for searching, and his prices are strictly moderate.

CONSULT HIM!

Monthly **Catalogues gratis** from any of his Establishments.

Libraries and small parcels of Books **Bought for Cash** and removed free of all expense, and privacy maintained if desired.

FRANK MURRAY

Moray House, DERBY.
Shakespeare's Head, LEICESTER.
Regent House, NOTTINGHAM.

LONDON.

E. MENKEN,
Antiquarian Bookseller,

3 & 5, BURY STREET,
BLOOMSBURY, W.C.,

Is always open to purchase for prompt cash Libraries or small parcels of Books.

SPECIALITIES:

Antiquarian Literature, Books on London, Guilds, and Railways,

EARLY PRINTED BOOKS, FRENCH ILLUSTRATED BOOKS,

FINE BINDINGS,

AND BOOKS WITH PAINTINGS ON FORE EDGES.

36 pp. Catalogue of New Purchases issued monthly, and sent post free on application.

OVER 50,000 VOLUMES OF STANDARD LITERATURE ALWAYS IN STOCK.

Scarce Books sought for and reported on free of charge to customers.

MAKER OF THE FAR-FAMED "MULTUM IN PARVO" BOOKCASES,
WORKMANSHIP AND FINISH GUARANTEED.

Telegraphic Address: "MENKEN, 3, BURY STREET, BLOOMSBURY."

To Private Collectors, Librarians, &c.

Mr. F. Marchmont

WHO has had 15 years' experience as a Professional Trade Cataloguer, is open to accept engagements to catalogue

Private Collections

of Books, Pictures and Engravings, or Curios, by Contract; also, to prepare Catalogues for

Public Institutions, Free Libraries, Clubs,

etc., on most moderate Terms. Punctuality and satisfaction guaranteed.

Gentlemen dispersing or changing the character of their collections are invited to communicate with Mr. M., who can always introduce *bona-fide* purchasers for the same at the full market value, whether the collection consists of Books, Oil Paintings, Prints, Antique China, Musical Instruments, or Curios.

References and Terms on application.

Reports

of Early Facetiæ, Occult Works, Military and Naval Books, Costume, Fencing, etc., desired.

All URGENT enquiries receive immediate personal attention.

Address—

F. MARCHMONT, 300, South Lambeth Road, S.W.

www.ingramcontent.com/pod-product-compliance
Lightning Source LLC
Chambersburg PA
CBHW020256170426
43202CB00008B/401